ELEMENTARY SCHOOL MATHEMATICS

A GUIDE TO CURRENT RESEARCH

Leroy G. Callahan
Associate Professor
Faculty of Educational Studies
State University of New York at Buffalo
Buffalo, New York

Vincent J. Glennon
Professor of Education and
Director, Mathematics Education Center
University of Connecticut
Storrs, Connecticut

4TH EDITION

Association for Supervision
and Curriculum Development
1701 K Street, N.W., Suite 1100
Washington, D. C. 20006

Contents

Foreword viii
    Delmo Della-Dora

Introduction ix
    Leroy G. Callahan, Vincent J. Glennon

Part One: **Studies Concerning the Curriculum** 1

What are the main sources of the mathematics curriculum? 1

Did the "new math" curricula possess curricular (face)
validity? Were they appropriate? 6

What does research that compared students in "new" and
"traditional" programs seem to suggest? 13

What have we learned from the first National Assessment
of Mathematics (NAEP)? 16

Was (Is) Sesame Street successful in teaching mathematics
concepts to young children? 18

What about the IPI Math Program (Individually Prescribed
Instruction)? 19

What is the place of behavioral objectives in determining
the curriculum in elementary school mathematics? 22

What does the work of Piaget suggest about the cognitive
development of the child? 25

What does the work of Piaget suggest for the curriculum
in elementary school mathematics? 26

What does research on the specific relationship between
elementary school mathematics and Piagetian tasks seem
to suggest? 29

What are some implications for teaching from the work
of Piaget? 30

What cautions and concerns have been expressed about
applying Piagetian theory to mathematics education? 31

What is the influence of schooling in different cultures on the ability to conserve and estimate number? 33

What kind of mathematics program for the kindergarten? 36

How soon should we teach "basic concepts" of mathematics in the elementary school? 37

What is the appropriate scope and sequence for the geometry program in the elementary school? 39

What are some of the possible implications for education as the United States moves toward adoption of the metric system of measurement—Système International (S.I.)? 41

What does research suggest about geometry in the elementary school? 42

Can children learn the elements of mathematical logic? 43

Do summer educational programs for the disadvantaged succeed? 44

What was learned about achievement in mathematics from the International Study? 46

How do children in the United States compare with children of other countries on mathematics achievement tests? 48

Part Two: Studies Concerning the Child **50**

What mathematical knowledge do children have on entering school? 50

What are some variables which may affect mathematical performance of children entering kindergarten? 53

What is the sequence of development of early number behaviors? 55

What contributes to readiness in learning mathematics? 58

Does cultural deprivation have a lasting effect on mathematics achievement? 59

Do ethnic groups differ in patterns of mental abilities such as number facility and space conceptualization? 60

Does the age at which a child enters first grade have an effect on subsequent achievement in elementary school mathematics? 63

Are there differences in achievement in elementary school mathematics between boys and girls? 64

What is known about learning disabilities in elementary
mathematics? _____ 65

Is there a relationship between emotional disturbance in
students and arithmetic disability? _____ 66

What does research suggest about mathematics achievement
of the blind? _____ 67

What is known about the performance of deaf students in
elementary mathematics? _____ 68

What are the learning characteristics of the educable
mentally retarded in mathematics? _____ 69

What mathematics should we teach the mentally retarded,
and how should it be taught? _____ 70

What are some characteristics and concomitants of the
mathematically gifted? _____ 72

What mathematics should be provided for the mathematically
gifted child? _____ 75

Do elementary school students have definite and stable
attitudes about school mathematics? _____ 77

Are attitudes toward elementary school mathematics related
to achievement in elementary school mathematics? _____ 79

What factors seem to influence the development of attitudes
about mathematics? _____ 80

Is anxiety associated with mathematical learning? _____ 81

What are some factors associated with anxiety in
mathematics learning? _____ 82

Is reflective and impulsive behavior associated with
learning in mathematics? _____ 84

What are some other personality dimensions that may have
an effect upon learning in mathematics? _____ 85

Part Three: Studies Concerning the Learning Environment

**Part Three: Studies Concerning the Learning
Environment** _____ **87**

What are some considerations in individualizing
mathematics instruction within the classroom? _____ 87

What is the place of the "informal" classroom in teaching
elementary school mathematics? _____ 89

What is the place of the "math lab" in elementary
mathematics instruction? _____ 92

How can we best group children for learning mathematics? 94

How can mathematics class time be used most effectively? 95

Does class size affect student achievement in elementary
school mathematics? 97

What about the readability of arithmetic textbooks? 98

Do children learn more mathematics in good schools than in
poor schools? 99

Is the mathematical training of elementary school teachers
adequate? 100

Is the "professional" preparation of teachers of elementary
school mathematics adequate? 102

How effective is in-service education? 104

"Teaching Centers"—What is the promise and potential? 106

What are some guidelines for determining performance criteria
in the professional preparation of math teachers? 107

Part Four: Studies Concerned with Teaching
Method 109

What are the main sources of the teacher's methods? 109

What does the research on discovery learning suggest? 113

How is mathematics learning motivated? 115

What are some considerations in choosing physical (concrete)
models in elementary mathematics instruction? 118

What has research suggested about the effectiveness of physical
(concrete) models in facilitating math learning? 122

What part does teacher-student verbal interaction play in
classroom instruction? 123

What is the effect of homework? 124

What emphasis on computational proficiency? 124

What is the place of the hand-held calculator in the
elementary, middle, and junior high school? 125

What is the place of practice (drill) in the contemporary
mathematics program? 126

How do we diagnose learning problems in elementary
school mathematics? 128

How should we evaluate learning in elementary school
mathematics? 130

What are meaningful approaches to instruction in the
primary mathematics program? _____ 132

Should children be allowed to count when finding answers
to number facts? _____ 136

What meaning(s), algorism(s), and sequence(s) for the
operation of subtraction? _____ 137

What about the use of open addition and subtraction
sentences in primary arithmetic? _____ 139

What algorism should be used in dividing by a fraction? _____ 140

What method of division should be used with whole numbers?__ 141

What effect does the teaching of non-decimal numeration
systems have on learning of topics in elementary school
mathematics? _____ 144

How can we improve ability to solve verbal problems? _____ 145

What about CAI (Computer Assisted Instruction) in
elementary school mathematics instruction? _____ 149

References _____ **151**

Index _____ **182**

Foreword

One of the ASCD program thrusts for 1975-76 is research and theory in curriculum development. Publication of the present report on recent research in elementary school mathematics gives evidence of the Association's commitment in this area. However, the fact that this is the fourth edition of a popular booklet, first issued in 1952, indicates that ASCD has nurtured such interests for many years.

There continue to be questions about the "new math" all over the country. The authors deal with this lively issue as well as other topics which generate much discussion among curriculum workers. Among the items given attention in this volume are the implications of the work of Piaget, teaching the metric system, schooling in different cultures, mathematics in special education, and "teaching centers," to name just a few.

The general areas of coverage (curriculum, the child, the learning environment, and teaching method) hold particular interest for classroom teachers, curriculum specialists, and principals. It seems to me that the contents will be of practical assistance to parents and other lay citizens as well. Leroy G. Callahan and Vincent J. Glennon have managed to treat a complex subject in a manner that can be understood and appreciated by all these audiences.

DELMO DELLA-DORA, *President 1975-76,*
Association for Supervision and
Curriculum Development

Introduction

THIS IS THE FOURTH EDITION of this research monograph. The prior editions were published by the Association for Supervision and Curriculum Development in 1952, 1958, and 1968, and each went through several printings. The authors feel much satisfaction in knowing that both the content and the method of presenting it to persons interested in mathematics education have continued so well to meet their needs as to warrant this new edition.

In the years since the first printing of the third edition, 1968, the middle school concept of administrative grouping of children has come of age in many school systems. The content of this monograph, therefore, covers the essential aspects of the school mathematics program of the elementary school (K-4 or K-6) and the middle school (grades 5-7). Then too, since large numbers of students in the junior and senior high schools are still experiencing difficulty in mastering the mathematics of the elementary and middle school levels, the content will be found useful by their teachers and supervisory personnel.

The increasing use of the monograph by college and university level professors and students, graduate and undergraduate, seems to be indicative of a much needed redirection of many mathematics courses. Such redirection would be away from a techniques-only orientation toward an approach based more on theory, out of which the techniques logically eventuate and derive meaning.

As with the prior editions, the reader should keep in mind the following points:

1. Although most of the answers to the questions are research-based, there are many questions that have not been researched in an empirical way but are included in the volume because of their importance to school personnel who must make wise decisions involving the school mathematics program. The authors have attempted to present well-balanced summaries of the several facets of each of these questions.

2. It is not possible to summarize the findings of all available research as well as philosophical and psychological discussions in a volume of this size. Choices had to be made using the criterion of the educational significance of the research to the general problems associated with improvement of mathematical instruction. The reader is urged to consult the original sources for more complete discussions of these and other educationally significant questions.

3. Although school personnel can feel secure in teaching along the lines suggested in the monograph, they should recognize that the answer to any question is subject to modification in the light of subsequent research and non-empirical investigations.

4. The authors wish to make it clear that full responsibility for the accuracy of interpretation of the studies cited and for the valid representation thereof in the paragraphs and tables selected rests with themselves.

Appreciation is expressed to Dr. Gerard Thibodeau, formerly graduate assistant in the Mathematics Education Center, The University of Connecticut, for a scholarly library search and summary of the literature concerned with the mathematics learning of children generally classified as requiring special education. Again, the authors express appreciation to Dr. C. W. Hunnicutt who originally suggested the need for the monograph and co-authored the first and second editions. Also our thanks to John S. Close, graduate assistant in the Mathematics Education Center, the University of Connecticut, for preparing the index.

The suggestions of Margaret Callahan and Deanna Korner for copy-editing and for typing the manuscript are sincerely appreciated.

LEROY G. CALLAHAN
VINCENT J. GLENNON

March 1975

Acknowledgments

Final editing of the manuscript and publication of this booklet were the responsibility of Robert R. Leeper, Associate Director and Editor, ASCD publications. Technical production was handled by Lana Pipes.

We are only just realizing that the art and science of education require a genius and a study of their own; and that this genius and this science are more than a bare knowledge of some branch of science or literature.

ALFRED NORTH WHITEHEAD (1929)

. . . it is true of arithmetic as it is of poetry that in some place and at some time it ought to be a good to be appreciated on its own account—just as an enjoyable experience, in short. If it is not, then when the time and place come for it to be used as a means or instrumentality, it will be just in that much handicapped. Never having been realized or appreciated for itself, one will miss something of its capacity as a resource for other ends. . . .

JOHN DEWEY (1930)

Part One

Studies Concerning the Curriculum

What are the main sources of the mathematics curriculum?

The elementary school mathematics curriculum, like all other subject areas that make up general education, as distinguished from specialized or vocation-oriented education (the former concerned with living, the latter with earning a living), is derived from three sources. Like the farmer's three-legged milking stool, the curriculum is a well-balanced, stable instrument if and only if the three sources contribute to it equally, or at least equitably.

The three sources of the elementary school mathematics curriculum may be referred to as the nature of the learner, the nature of his or her adult society, and the nature of the cognitive area—mathematics. The first of these may be referred to as the expressed needs-of-the-child theory of curriculum, or the psychological theory; the second, as the needs of adult society, social utility, instrumentalism, or the sociological theory of curriculum; and the third, as the structural, the pure mathematical, or the logical theory of curriculum.

Each has something to contribute to a well-designed curriculum. Each theory has its strong supporters and its equally strong opponents; and in each group are some people who are quite unaware that there are any other points of view than their own. Any unilateral, authoritarian view of the curricular basis of the program is an extremist view. In order to have a clear perception of a balanced theory of curriculum, one must first have a clear perception of each of these extremist theories. Each is discussed briefly here.

1. *The psychological basis for curriculum theory.* The question of what mathematics is of most worth to elementary school children can

be viewed from two quite different psychological approaches. One approach can be labeled the cognitive-developmental point of view, the other the clinical-personality point of view. Neither point of view is clearly self-contained; each may draw upon the other to varying degrees depending upon the biases in the professional training of the person doing the viewing.

The cognitive-developmental approach to curriculum theory emphasizes the nature of the subject matter being learned and the developmental process in the learning. The exemplars of this point of view in the world today are Jean Piaget in Switzerland and, in this country, William A. Brownell.

The clinical-personality point of view emphasizes the affective aspect of human development. The extremist point of view is best evidenced in the work and the writing of A. S. Neill, particularly in *Summerhill: A Radical Approach to Child Rearing* (1960). In the entire book of almost 400 pages, the arithmetic curriculum and the methods of teaching it are referred to in only six very brief statements. In essence, Neill dismisses as irrelevant or inappropriate any efforts on the part of teachers or parents to preplan a program in elementary school mathematics. In a word, he is of the opinion that the only honest source of the content, of methods, of learning materials, and of the evaluation, too, must and can only eventuate out of the needs of the child as he expresses them.

2. *The sociological basis for curriculum theory.* Those who advocate a sociological approach only to the selection of content for the elementary school mathematics program are of the opinion that the only worthwhile mathematics is that which has previously been judged of great usefulness to the average adult in business situations and in general life situations. Mathematical topics which do not meet a rigorous interpretation of this criterion, they argue, are not a legitimate part of the general education of the child. Such topics, therefore, become a part of the specialized or vocational education of the older child or young adult, to be learned in a vocational program either in the school or on the job.

Over a 50-year span of professional activity beginning about 1911, Guy M. Wilson and his students have done the greatest amount of research on the question, "What mathematics is important enough in business and life as to be the *mastery* program in the elementary school?" (1951). Wilson answers the question succinctly in these words:

This question can be answered quite specifically and authoritatively on the basis of curricular studies as to the usage of arithmetic in business and life.

It is no longer necessary to rely upon guesswork or mere opinion. This question of essential drill (for mastery) will be discussed again and again in connection with topics of arithmetic, but here it may be noted that the drill material for mastery consists of simple addition—100 primary facts, 300 decade facts, carrying and other process difficulties; simple subtraction—100 primary facts, process difficulties; multiplication—100 primary facts, process difficulties; long division—no committed facts, general scheme and process steps; simple fractions in halves, fourths, and thirds, and in special cases, in eighths and twelfths, general acquaintance with other simple fractions; decimals—reading knowledge only.

(1)	(2)	(3)	(4)	(5)	(6)	(7)	(8)	(9)	(10)	(11)	(12)	
Units	Different fractions	Sears-Roebuck Co. study	Boston Transcript study	United Drug Co. study	Jordan Marsh Co. study	Hotels study	S. S. Pierce Co. study	A. Stocks, bonds, etc.	B. Bank rates	C. Foreign exchange	Total	Percentage
Halves	1	9,069	12,751	2,212	259	110	327	6,175	731	242	31,876	31.184
Quarters	2	6,671	12,717	956	177	29	89	2,624	12,911	296	36,470	35.678
Thirds	2	803	....	110	120	15	1	....	....	....	1,049	1.026
Fifths	4	18	....	4	......	......	1	....	....	....	23	.023
Sixths	5	2	....	100	11	8	1	....	....	....	122	.119
Eighths	7	2,555	12,880	267	1,174	......	9	3,665	....	268	20,818	20.368
Ninths	7	1	....	4	1	......	......	....	....	....	6	.006
Tenths	9	23	....	4	......	......	......	....	....	....	27	.026
Twelfths	11	4	....	76	843	46	......	....	....	....	969	.948
Fifteenths	5	....	....	2	......	......	......	....	....	....	2	.002
Sixteenths	14	682	....	154	......	4	2	....	....	101	943	.923
Twentieths	2	4	....	1	......	......	......	....	....	....	5	.005
Twenty-fourths	4	4	....	....	......	......	1	....	....	....	5	.005
Thirtieths	2	....	....	2	......	......	1	....	....	....	3	.003
Thirty-seconds	31	148	255	4	......	......	......	9,260	10	......	9,677	9.467
Thirty-sixths	4	4	....	....	......	......	......	....	....	....	4	.004
Fortieths	1	....	....	....	......	......	1	....	....	....	1	.001
Forty-eighths	1	1	....	....	......	......	......	....	....	....	1	.001
Fiftieths	1	....	....	....	......	......	1	....	....	....	1	.001
Sixtieths	1	....	....	....	......	......	1	....	....	....	1	.001
Sixty-fourths	8	74	....	....	......	......	......	....	....	....	74	.072
Hundredths	27	133	....	....	......	......	......	....	....	....	133	.130
7/144	......	3	....	....	......	......	......	....	....	....	3	.003
925/1000	......	1	....	....	......	......	......	....	....	....	1	.001
3/4	......	6	....	....	......	......	......	....	....	....	6	.006
Totals	149	20,199	38,603	3,896	2,585	212	435	21,724	13,652	907	102,220	100.00

Columns 3 to 11 of Figure 1 show interesting variations in fractions used in different lines of business. The fraction *one-half* occurs with reasonable frequency in all units. The same is true of *fourths*. *Thirds*, on the other hand, do not appear under the *Boston Transcript* unit, which is chiefly a summary of stock-market quotations.

Figure 1. Showing a Summary of All the Functions of the Dalrymple Study in Terms of Denominators

The essential drill phases of arithmetic for perfect mastery are as simple as that. The load is very small . . . (pp. 3, 4).

The reader who is unacquainted with this extremist point of view might well ask how the data were gathered and collated to form the basis for curricular decisions. Figure 1 shows a classification of fractions (rational numbers named by fractions) used in business situations and gathered over a two-year period in the Boston area. (See Wilson, Table 1, p. 201.)

On the basis of this and similar studies, Wilson concludes that fractions "used in business are much simpler than the fractions (taught) in the schools. It may be remarked also . . . that the operations and combinations of fractions in business are very, very simple in comparison with school practices."

He asks, "Is it possible that we have been wasting much school time on useless fractions? And in going beyond usage on a purely manipulative basis, have we not done much to confuse and defeat the child?"

3. *The logical, or pure mathematical, basis for curriculum theory.* The third source of the curriculum, or the third leg of the farmer's milking stool, to continue our simile, is usually named the logical, or structural, or pure mathematical source. Extremists who hold this point of view exclusively are usually trained as mathematicians and have little insight into or concern for the points of view held by the groups representing either a psychological approach or a sociological approach. Their main concern is that of transmitting the mathematics in a form uncontaminated or undefiled by any relating of the pure structure to socially useful situations. By way of illustration, if a fifth grade group of children studying about Mexico and its people were learning or using, or both, the cognitive capability of multiplying a fraction by two in order to double the amount of some ingredient used in tortillas, this experience would be denigrated by referring to it as "some sort of home economics perhaps but certainly not mathematics."

The historical roots of the sociological theory of curriculum are as old as early human attempts at transmitting the customs of the tribe to the young; and the historical roots of the psychological theory can be found in the writings of Pestalozzi, Herbart, Froebel, and more recently Freud, Adler, Jung, and the cognitive-developmental psychologists, G. Stanley Hall, William James, Charles Hubbard Judd, William A. Brownell, and Jean Piaget. But the historical roots of the "pure mathematical" theory of curriculum can be traced back at least 2,500 years to the beginning attempts of the Greek mathematicians to structure the subject. Substantial contributions to the purification process were made in the past few hundred years by DeMorgan, Hamilton, Peano, and others.

As a consequence of the work of these men and of the abstract nature of the subject, no cognitive area has as elegant a structure as mathematics. Whereas in any subject matter area in the social sciences, say geography, we might list an almost endless set of principles, in the real number system there are only 11 "principles" (properties) or axioms, and three equality axioms.

In part, the recent efforts to purify the elementary school math program may be due to the fact that some few mathematicians, enamored with the elegance of the subject, want all others to see the beauty of the abstract structure as they see it and, in so wanting, press vigorously for the widespread adoption of the pure mathematics approach as the only legitimate theory of curriculum.

4. *Balance among the three theories.* The authors have found it useful in attempting to help school personnel "make sense" out of the ebb and flow of curriculum change to use a model of a triangle to picture the extreme points of view.

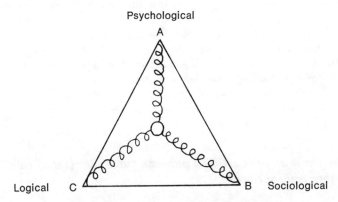

Figure 2. Model of Mathematics Curriculum Theories

Each of the three extremist positions can be viewed as one of the vertices of the triangle. A balance among the three theories can be pictured as a ring held in place by springs each fixed in place at a vertex. The pressures of society on the school curriculum in this century have caused the center of balance to shift often in our century alone. Professional education was interpreted by some child developmentalists as a powerful spring which pulled the center of balance toward point A.

Pragmatism, with its implications for a socially useful curriculum, was viewed by some extremists as sufficient cause to justify pulling the center of balance toward point B, and concern for the logical structure, the purity of the mathematics, caused some extremists to argue for a shift in curriculum toward point C during the 1950's and 1960's. Forces at points A and B are again reasserting themselves during the 1970's.

In each instance, the more extreme the position of a person or the program he advocated, the more it moved from a central position toward one of the three vertices. The curriculum approach implemented by A. S. Neill represents the most radical extremism toward point A, or *at* point A. The curriculum innovations of Guy M. Wilson represent the farthest deviation toward point B. Certain "new math" programs concerned with mathematics for its own sake in the elementary grades represent the greatest distortion of the curriculum in a move toward point C.

The difficulty of obtaining and maintaining balance among the extremes is discussed by Foshay (1961):

A conception of what balance means in the curriculum is a necessity in any time. In these days of upheaval in education, however, such a conception is an urgent necessity. It is possible that the new curriculum patterns, when they have emerged, will prove to be in better balance than anything we have known. However, taken as a whole, it could be that the new curriculum will imply a distorted version of our culture, or our ideals as a people, even what we want an American to be. This has happened in the past, at those times when it has become apparent that the existing curriculum no longer fits the times. The changes have not always proved to be improvements; sometimes, despite the best efforts of wise men, the result has been only to substitute one distortion for another (pp. iii-iv).

Did the "new math" curricula possess curricular (face) validity? Were they appropriate?

The "new math" programs of the recent past grew out of a dissatisfaction with performance of children in "traditional" programs. As with many such educational terms, it is difficult to get agreement on what "new" and "traditional" programs are, and usually impossible to observe "pure" cases of each functioning in the schools. A gross characterization of intent of the "new" math programs does, however, seem possible. The "new math" was intended to be more conceptually meaningful to the learners; rote, meaningless learning was to be deemphasized. Essential mathematical structures, "big ideas," were to be given early emphasis. In turn, these structures would form a conceptual anchorage for specific learnings. The relationships among the essential structures that form the essence of mathematics as a logical-deductive system were also to be exposed to learners, with an expected change in attitude in a positive direction.

Few would question the intent of the function the new programs were to perform. What form did the "new math" take? Was it valid for the children for whom it was intended?

As noted in the previous question—"What are the main sources of the curriculum?"—the new math programs eventuated out of the extremist position held by those who had greatest influence on the "revolution." By and large, these people were originally trained in mathematics as a pure deductive science. Usually unable to see or accept any other curriculum theory, they proceeded to make much needed improvements in the contemporary programs in the only way they could—by making the mathematics more correct, more rigorous, and more deductive, but not necessarily more personally meaningful to the child or more socially relevant.

Receiving a kind of moral support from some cognitive psychologists, notably Jerome S. Bruner, the leaders of the new math revolution also caused some topics traditionally taught on a given grade level to be taught on a lower grade level. This made for a heavy curriculum load on the lower grade levels.

Much of this psychological support for increased emphasis on mathematics structure came from the book, *The Process of Education*, which was Bruner's (1960) summary of discussions held in 1959, seeking ways to improve the school science program. Following a chapter in which he discussed "The Importance of Structure" in learning any subject, Bruner offered the hypothesis that ". . . any subject can be taught effectively in some intellectually honest form to any child at any stage of development" (p. 33). This statement, though a hypothesis, had a strong influence on the content of contemporary math programs and on proposed directions of programs for the future.

Most notable of the latter groups was the futuristic-oriented Cambridge Conference on School Mathematics, sponsored by Educational Services, Inc. (now Education Development Center, Inc.). This conference published three reports. One was *Goals for School Mathematics* (1963), which was a summary of the thoughts of a group of 29 mathematicians and national scientists who were strongly influenced by Bruner's hypothesis.

A valid math curriculum for grades 3-6, according to this extremist point of view, and one which "the schools should be aiming to achieve in ten years, or twenty or thirty" would include these topics:

Grades 3 Through 6

In these four grades we should continue pursuit of the main objective, familiarity with the real number system and geometry. At the same time we must start pre-mathematical experiences aiming towards the more sophisticated work in high school.

The Real Number System

1. Commutative, associative, and distributive laws. The multiplicative property of 1. The additive and multiplicative properties of 0

2. Arithmetic of signed numbers

3. For comparison purposes
   a. Modular arithmetic, based on primes and on non-primes
   b. Finite fields
   c. Study of 2 x 2 matrices; comparison with real numbers; isomorphism of a subset of 2 x 2 matrices with real numbers; divisors of zero; identities for matrices; simple matrix inverses (particularly in relation to the idea of inverse operations and the nonexistence of a multiplicative inverse for zero). Possible use of matrices to introduce complex numbers

4. Prime numbers and factoring. Euclidean algorithm, greatest common divisor

5. Elementary Diophantine problems

6. Integral exponents, both positive and negative

7. The arithmetic of inequalities

8. Absolute value

9. Explicit study of the decimal system of notation including comparison with other bases and mixed bases (e.g., miles, yards, feet, inches)

10. Study of algorithms for adding, subtracting, multiplying, and dividing both integers and rational numbers, including "original" algorithms made up by the children themselves

11. Methods for checking and verifying correctness of answers without recourse to the teacher

12. Familiarity with certain "short cut" calculations that serve to illustrate basic properties of numbers or of numerals

13. The use of desk calculators, slide rules, and tables

14. Interpolation

15. Considerable experience in approximations, estimates, "scientific notation," and orders of magnitude

16. Effect of "round-off" and significant figures

17. Knowledge of the distinction between rational and irrational numbers

18. Study of decimals, for rational and irrational numbers

19. Square roots, inequalities such as $1.41 < \sqrt{2} < 1.42$

20. The Archimedean property and the density of the rational numbers including terminating decimals

21. Nested intervals

22. Computation with numbers given approximately (e.g., find π^2 given π)

23. Simple algebraic equations and inequalities.

Perhaps no area of discussion brought out more viewpoints than the question of how the multiplication of signed numbers should be introduced. The simple route via the distributive law was considered, but a closely related approach was more popular. One observes that the definition of multiplication is ours to make but only one definition will have desirable properties. Others favored an experimental approach involving negative weights on balance boards, etc. Still others favored the "negative debt" approach. Even the immediate introduction of signed area was proposed. It seems quite likely that all approaches should be tried, since there will probably be much variation from student to student concerning what is convincing. The question is evidently not mathematical; it is purely pedagogic. The problem is to convey the "inner reasonableness" of $(-1) \times (-1) = +1$.

Geometry

In the later grades of elementary school, relatively little pure geometry would be introduced, but more experience with the topics from K-2 would be built up. The pictorial representation of sets with Venn diagrams and the graphing of elementary functions using Cartesian coordinates would be continued. In addition, there is much of value in the suggestions put forward by educators in Holland, and described by Freudenthal in an article in the *Mathematics Student* (1956, pp. 82-97), in which many geometrical questions are motivated by problems concerning solid bodies and the ways they fit together. New topics might include:

1. Mensuration formulas for familiar figures

2. Approximate determination of π by measuring circles

3. Conic sections

4. Equation determining a straight line

5. Cartesian coordinates in 3 dimensions

6. Polar coordinates

7. Latitude and longitude

8. Symmetry of more sophisticated figures (e.g., wallpaper)

9. Similar figures interpreted as scale models and problems of indirect measurements

10. Vectors, possibly including some statics and linear kinematics

11. Symmetry argument for the congruence of the base angles of an isosceles triangle.

Logic and Foundations

1. The vocabulary of elementary logic: true, false, implication, double implication, contradiction

2. Truth tables for simplest connectives

3. The common schemes of inference:

$$\frac{P \to Q \text{ and } P}{Q} \qquad\qquad \frac{P \to Q \text{ and } \sim Q}{\sim P}$$

4. Simple uses of mathematical induction

5. Preliminary recognition of the roles of axioms and theorems in relation to the real number system

6. Simple uses of logical implication or "derivations" in studying algorithms, more complicated identities, etc.

7. Elements of flow charting

8. Simple uses of indirect proof, in studying inequalities, proving $\sqrt{2}$ irrational, and so on

9. Study of sets, relations, and functions. Graphs of relations and functions, both discrete and continuous. Graphs of empirically determined functions

10. Explicit study of the relation of open sentences and their truth sets

11. The concepts of isomorphism and transformation (pp. 36-39).

The reader will find it interesting to contrast the curricular "validity" of this proposed curriculum with that of the strict social utility point of view suggested by the example from Wilson's textbook in Figure 1 of this chapter.

Assuming the *Goals for School Mathematics* curriculum to be implemented in 20 years from its publication date 1963, as of this writing (1975) we are well beyond the half way point timewise but not any nearer goalwise than the day it was published. Could the biased enthusiasm of the members of the Goals Committee have caused them to misjudge the appropriateness (validity) of their proposals?

Evidence is increasing that this could be so. There is overwhelming agreement among teachers and professional mathematics educators that most current modern mathematics textbook programs fit reasonably well only the top third of the elementary and middle school children.

Among mathematicians, Newsom (1972) expressed the thoughts of many when he recently stated, "I must confess an early satisfaction (with the new elementary mathematics curricula). Now, however, we are learning that good mathematicians had too free a hand in the development of the programs" (p. 880).

And Henry Van Engen (1972) recently wrote: "Most certainly there is reason to question the degree of formalism that is creeping into the elementary school. Furthermore, the rapid pace of the more usual programs is questionable" (p. 615).

An early and outspoken critic of "new math" was Professor Morris Kline (1966, 1973). A few of his criticisms that bear on the validity question are summarized here.

1. Advocates of the "new math" assumed that when the deductive logic of mathematics was revealed to young students, the students would understand it. The logically sound was assumed to be the pedagogically sound approach to teaching mathematics. Kline suggests that an ordered logical presentation of mathematics may have aesthetic appeal to the mathematician but serves as an anaesthetic to the student. A caution would perhaps seem in order in light of the "bandwagon" type reactions that often characterize educational policy and practices. One should not conclude from Kline's criticism that mathematics should therefore be presented in disordered, illogical manner. Order and logic do have a place in curriculum considerations.

2. Many "new math" programs not only used a rather exclusive deductive approach to mathematics, but also required a rigorous deductive development. Reference was being made to the incorporation into school programs of additional axioms and theorems that introduced a mathematical rigor to explicate ideas that had been implicitly used for years. Kline contends that to ask students to recognize the need for these missing axioms and theorems is to ask for a critical attitude and maturity of mind that is entirely beyond young people.

3. "New math" programs strove to increase the precision of the language used in conveying mathematical ideas. The consequence of that striving was an immense amount of terminology and symbolism. Feynman is quoted by Kline as saying that he sees no need or reason for all this (terminology and symbolism) to be explained or to be taught in school. The real problem in speech is not precise language. The problem is clear language.

4. Many "new math" programs tended to present mathematics for mathematics' sake. Much of the development was divorced from significant real world applications. The assumption was made that the significance would follow from the study of the structure of mathematics. Kline's contention is that mathematical structure cannot be significant for elementary and high school students and it should not be taught at this level.

5. Although most of the material in "new math" programs is the traditional material, it does include some new content such as work

with sets, non-decimal bases of numeration, and congruence. The value of these new topics was purported to be that they are more general and can serve as unifying strands. Kline suggests that the more general the mathematical concept, the emptier it is. The familiar argument that it is efficient to teach the abstract concept early because it comprises several concrete cases at once is groundless. So far as efficiency is concerned, the time that is wasted is the time spent teaching the abstract concept.

Those concerned with a more objective analysis of the new math programs may be interested in a report entitled *An Analysis of New Mathematics Programs* prepared by the National Council of Teachers of Mathematics (1963).

Finally, and perhaps most significantly in discussing the question— "Did the 'new math' programs possess curricular validity?"—we now see the emergence of programs aimed at a particular targeted population. Several publishers have produced modern math programs aimed at the "below average" or "slow learner" population—evidence of the lack of appropriateness of the early new math programs for many children.

And now Education Development Center, Inc. (EDC), which formerly held to a rigorous, structured math theory of curriculum in the publications of some of its projects, has recently announced a program with "a new set of objectives for mathematics education that are more in keeping with contemporary needs and interests" (Lazarus, 1974).

Project ONE claims to have identified five topics that "together comprise a basic 'literacy' in mathematics." These five topics are:

1. Counting and ordering; the number system, decimal notation, and powers of 10; very large and very small numbers, such as 6×10^6 and 6×10^{-6}. Arithmetic with small integers, such as 5×6. Approximate arithmetic, such as $31 \times 49 \simeq 1500$. (We do not include, for example, set theory, number systems other than base 10, arithmetic with elaborate fractions such as $\frac{281}{365} + \frac{2}{9}$, or long division.)

2. The concept of measurement; i.e., the description of real objects and situations in numbers. Units of measurement.

3. The ability to make reasonable, off-the-cuff estimates; e.g., of size, place, time, and quantity. (This is important to a casual, intuitive use of mathematics.)

4. The concept of size-scaling and mapping; the underlying concept of ratio.

5. Graphs in one dimension (number lines), and in two dimensions (crossed number lines).

A second aspect of this new mathematical literacy program is a set of cognitive skills aimed at the development of quantitative thinking—"reasoning, problem solving, and analytic thinking and . . . a knack for turning difficult problems into simpler ones."

The answer to the validity question seems to be that the form in which the "new math" emerged was most valid for the intellectually bright and mathematically talented students. It was less valid for the average student, and least valid for the slow and/or mathematically disinterested. Care must be taken, however, in not jumping to the conclusion that because of the extremism that characterized some of the "new math" programs, the critics are arguing for a return to the rote, meaningless learning and drill-teaching that characterized some traditional instruction.

Care must also be taken not to over-react . . . extremely. Curricular accommodations to student needs on such concerns as degree of abstraction, rigor, formalism, precision, and structure seem to be called for. This does not mean ignoring the place of some of these in the development of a balanced curriculum. Likewise, accommodations to societal needs of mathematics, and the significance that such applications can give the student, seem to be needed. Again, care should be taken not to ignore some of the previously mentioned mathematical concerns for the sake of social utility and social reliance.

What does research that compared students in "new" and "traditional" programs seem to suggest?

Before presenting a summary of some of the studies carried out in evaluating innovative programs, a few general observations can be made. It is probably fair to say that a great deal more effort and energy were committed to curriculum development projects over the past few decades than to well-designed research to study the impact on children of the projects. A multitude of factors may have contributed; only a few possibilities are presented.

One realistic factor may have been that funding agencies subordinated evaluation resources to developmental resources. Since evaluation considerations often follow developmental considerations, money and interest may have waned in the evaluation stages of projects. Another factor may have been the lack of valid testing instruments to measure those higher cognitive processes which many of the programs purported to develop. Still another factor may have been that many innovators were caught up in the "spirit of change" of the times and may have felt constrained by, and therefore disdained, traditional concerns for evaluation of project outcomes on school children.

For whatever the reason, there is not a great deal of "hard" evidence on the advantages or disadvantages of "new" programs. However, some tendencies seem to be justified within the limitations of the existing research.

The most comprehensive program of evaluation was that carried out by the SMSG (School Mathematics Study Group) Panel on Tests (1972). Their undertaking was referred to as the National Longitudinal Study of Mathematical Abilities (NLSMA). Their evaluation thrust was much more comprehensive than the question presented in this section, but they did collect evidence that bears on it.

In making some general observations on the NLSMA Textbook Comparison results, Begle and Wilson (1970) report:

The difference between the SMSG textbook group and most conventional textbook groups at any grade level is largely a contrast of computational-level scales on the one hand and understanding of mathematical ideas as indicated by comprehension-, application-, and analysis-level scales on the other. There are exceptions to this of course (p. 400).

At another point they report:

But not all modern textbooks produced the kind of results that were expected for them. Some of them in fact did rather poorly on *all* levels—from computation to analysis. Those textbooks which did not do very well were for the most part considerably more formal and more rigorous than the SMSG books. . . . This remark on the greater formalism is conjectural; it is an opinion as to a possible general explanation of the poor showing of some modern textbooks (p. 401).

Two other studies that compared SMSG and "traditional" programs of school mathematics at the fourth, fifth, and sixth grade levels are mentioned since they examined longitudinal effects (three years) and were quite well designed studies. Hungerman (1967) found in general that the traditional class did better on the traditional achievement test. In examining achievement on various sub-components of the criterion instruments, she concluded that achievement was closely related to the scope and emphasis of the textbook studied.

Grafft and Ruddell (1968) limited their study to the operation of multiplication, but examined it comprehensively. Comparing the three-year impact of the SMSG program and "traditional" programs, they used as the criteria conventional achievement tests, non-computational objective tests, and individual interview protocols to judge knowledge of structure, and a transfer test which purported to measure the ability to learn more advanced mathematics. Results generally favored the SMSG group on all the criteria except computational ability, where there was no difference. They concluded that the students in the SMSG program had greater understanding and greater transfer ability without diminishing computational achievement. However, this was true only for average and above-average students. No differences in any category were obtained for slow learners.

Other studies comparing modern textbook programs with traditional, or examining the cognitive impact of modern programs, were very limited in scope and design.

A great deal of care must be taken in interpreting the findings from the studies comparing "modern" and "traditional" programs. The tacit assumption is that any differences found can be attributed to the curriculum materials. Brownell (1963, 1967, 1968) raised the more fundamental question: perhaps the differences, if any, and in whichever direction, are due to the skill and enthusiasm of the teacher, not to the materials.

To test his hypothesis, Brownell studied two mathematics programs in Scotland and England. One program (A) involved the use of materials (Cuisenaire rods) which were "new" to the teachers, and the other (B) used traditional methods and materials. Program A was new in the cooperating Scottish schools, but in England where the teachers had been exposed to one new system of instruction after another, they tended to view Program A as just another scheme in a long series.

Brownell found that the reason the children in cooperating Scottish schools did better was not due to the materials but to the teacher's enthusiasm for the new. Using the new raised the teacher's "quality of teaching." To add further support to his hypothesis, Brownell found that in the cooperating English schools, where the novelty of the material no longer held, children in the traditional program did better than children in the experimental program.

Brownell concluded that the significant variable was not the two programs but quality of teaching. It bore out the by no means new fact that an instructional program is one thing in the hands of expert, interested teachers, and another thing in the hands of teachers who do not possess these characteristics.

In summary, the research comparing student performance in "new" and "traditional" programs seems to confirm a common sense prediction. Students in textbook programs that emphasized conceptual aspects of school mathematics tended to demonstrate higher performance on tests composed of conceptual tasks; those in programs that emphasized the less conceptual aspects demonstrated higher performance on the less conceptual skill tasks. Some qualifying trends appear from the data, however. The advantage in performance of students in "new" programs over "traditional" on more conceptually oriented test tasks seemed to be primarily true for higher ability students. Also, there is evidence of classes in "new" programs that do very well on less conceptual as well as conceptual tasks, and classes in "traditional" programs that do very well on conceptual as well as less conceptual tasks. This evidence, together with Brownell's, points out the many non-curricular variables that enter into curriculum evaluation and the complexity of curriculum research.

What have we learned from the first National Assessment of Mathematics (NAEP)?

The National Assessment of Educational Progress (NAEP) is an information-gathering project which surveys the educational attainments of 9-year-olds, 13-year-olds, 17-year-olds, and adults (ages 26-35) in 10 learning areas—one of which is mathematics. The recently released *Mathematics Report* (1975) presents the findings in the two areas of math fundamentals—computation and computation with translation (verbal problem solving).

A sample computation item appears in Figure 3, together with the performance of each age group. And one of the "more complex translations" (verbal problems) appears in Figure 4.

The report states that the sample populations were chosen in such

Add the following numbers:
$ 3.09
  10.00
   9.14
   5.10

	Age 9	Age 13	Age 17	Adult
27.33* (with or without $ sign)	40%	84%	92%	86%
Decimal placement errors (correct numbers)	22	8	2	6
One or two regrouping errors (may misplace decimal)	5	2	2	2
Other unacceptable	27	6	4	6
I don't know or no response	6	1†	+ **	+

* Asterisk indicates correct answer.
† Figures may not add to 100% due to rounding errors.
** Plus equals rounded percents less than one.

Figure 3. Exercise RC01

If John drives at an average speed of 50 miles an hour, how many hours will it take him to drive 275 miles?

	Age 9	Age 13	Age 17	Adult
5½, 5 hrs. 30 min., 5½ hrs., 5.5, etc.*	6%	33%	64%	67%
Wrote down problem right, no or incorrect answer	1	15	13	8
Answering 5 and 25, 5 hrs. and 25	1	11	4	3

* Asterisk indicates correct answer.

Figure 4. Exercise RC13

a way that the results of their assessment can be generalized to an entire population. That is, on the basis of the performance of about 2,500 9-year-olds on a given exercise, we can generalize about the probable performance of all 9-year-olds in the nation.

The data were analyzed by sex, by race, by regions of the country, by parental education, and by size and type of community.

Neither sex has a clear advantage in computational ability since results for males and females varied at the different age levels. At all ages, males generally did better than females on the more difficult exercises and on word problems. Females tended to do better on "pure computation" exercises demanding the application of a specific mathematical process.

In regard to race, the data suggested that the performance of Blacks was generally below that of the nation as a whole. White performance was above that of the nation and was virtually constant at all age levels.

Level of parental education had a considerable influence on performance. Those whose parents had no high school education were from 8 to 13 percentage points below the nation as a whole, while those with at least one parent having some past high school education were 6 to 7 percentage points above the national level.

Results for two types of communities—high metro (in or near large cities and most adults in managerial or professional positions) and low metro (in or near large cities and most adults on welfare or not regularly employed)—differed appreciably from national percentages. The high metro group performed consistently well on almost all the exercises at every level. Overall results for the low metro group were 10 to 16 percentage points below the national levels.

Great care must be taken in trying to interpret this type of group data. Classifications by race, parental education, and community type are

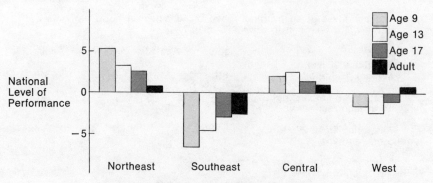

Figure 5. Median Differences from National
Performance Levels by Region

probably not mutually exclusive classifications. Performance differences
attributed to race, for example, may in fact be manifested from a complex
of socioeconomic factors which may include parent education and community type.

The Northeastern region (Figure 5) performed above national levels
at all ages, although this tendency decreased with age. The Southeast was
approximately six percentage points below the nation in overall performance at age 9; however, performance in relation to the nation steadily
improved from ages 13 to adult.

Was (Is) Sesame Street successful in teaching mathematics concepts to young children?

Sesame Street is a series of television programs produced by Children's Television Workshop (CTW) and telecast by more than 200 educational television stations in the United States (and subsequently in
more than 50 nations) beginning November 1969.

End-of-the-year (summative) evaluation was carried out by Educational Testing Service (Bogatz and Ball, 1971) with samples of over
1,000 children, ages three, four, and five, in Boston, suburban Philadelphia, Durham, North Carolina, Phoenix, Arizona, and northeastern
rural California.

A follow-up study from the first year sample was carried out to
assess the continuing effects of viewing over a two-year period on the
at-home, urban, disadvantaged children in Boston, Durham, and Phoenix.

Also, a new study was carried out during the second year of disadvantaged, at-home preschool children in Winston-Salem, North Carolina, and Los Angeles, California, partitioned into experimental (viewing)
and control (non-viewing) groups.

Some general findings reported are:

1. Children who watched the most learned the most. The amount of learning that took place . . . increased in relation to the amount of time the child watched the program. This holds true across age, sex, geographical location, socioeconomic status, mental age, and whether children watched at home or at school.

2. The skills that received the most time and attention on the program were, with rare exceptions, the skills that were best learned.

3. The program did not require adult supervision in order for children to learn. Children viewing at home showed gains as great as, and in some cases greater than, children who watched in school under the supervision of a teacher.

4. The three-year-old children gained the most; five-year-olds the least.

5. Disadvantaged children who watched a great deal surpassed the middle class children who watched only a little.

Some specific findings reported are:

1. Statistically significant results in the second year were found in: function of body parts, naming geometric forms, roles of community members, matching by form, naming letters, letter sounds, sight reading, recognizing numbers, naming numbers, counting, relational terms, classifying using a single criterion, and sorting.

2. Results were not clear in such areas as: naming body parts, recognizing letters, initial sounds, decoding, left-right orientation, counting strategies, number/numeral correspondence, addition and subtraction, double classification, and emotions.

3. The show had no significant impact in: recognizing geometric forms, matching by position, alphabet recitation, enumeration, conservation, and parts of the whole.

4. In no instance did Sesame Street seem to have a negative impact.

The study is summarized this way: "The future will doubtless see more shows on television along the lines of *Sesame Street* addressed to other age groups. We look forward to this future, for the potential value of public television has been demonstrated by *Sesame Street*."

What about the IPI Math Program (Individually Prescribed Instruction)?

The IPI Mathematics Program is a contemporary effort in a long series of efforts extending back almost a century to find ways to adapt the school mathematics program to the varying abilities of children. As with any highly visible program, it has its strong supporters and its equally strong detractors.

One source (Research for Better Schools, 1974) describes the program as an individualized, student-oriented instructional program for grades 1-6. It is constructed around a continuum of over 350 instructional behaviors. The objectives are grouped into 10 learning areas. Components of the system include diagnostic tests, various learning resources, and management aids that facilitate the achievement of the program's objectives. The description further suggests that IPI mathematics can be used in various kinds of school settings and can be used with diverse populations of elementary school children.

The objectives of IPI are seen as: (a) enabling students to progress at their own rate through the learning sequence, (b) developing a demonstrable degree of content mastery in each student, (c) enabling students to acquire self-initiation and self-direction in their learning, (d) fostering the development of problem-solving thought processes, and (e) encouraging self-evaluation and motivation for learning in the children.

The basic assumptions underlying the IPI Mathematics Program have been questioned and are being questioned. Lipson (1974) said,

The program had almost everything going for it—a competent research team, creative instructional designers, cooperating teachers in the field. It had everything except great success. I supervised the development of the first versions of the IPI mathematics modules and can say that the program did *not* produce the dramatic gains that had been hoped for. But why was this true? Were its problems unique? Or were they the same problems that have beset so many innovative programs that promise to revolutionize traditional education? The answer, I feel, is that the program, and many like it, was built on false assumptions (p. 60).

Edgar Dale (1974) discussed one of the assumptions—that of having children work alone.

So we must examine the conventional wisdom about learning and see where it fits and where it doesn't. Conventional wisdom says that we must individualize instruction. Thus, children wind up in a modernized version of a desk, the carrel. But a larger wisdom suggests that our most important learning is social. . . .

Remember that the language laboratory, used to learn a foreign language, did not fulfill its high hopes because the carrel could not seat two or more people. We must both individualize and socialize, having individual and group learning. We need more individualized group instruction (p. 2).

The current IPI program makes some provisions for the social learnings alluded to by Dale. Work on the materials can be carried on in small groups when the teacher sees a need for such grouping.

Erlwanger (1973) studied the mathematical thought processes of a 12-year-old boy, Benny, who was making much better than average progress through the IPI program. It was discovered by Erlwanger that Benny understood incorrectly some aspects of the work. He also had developed learning habits and views about mathematics that would impede his progress in the future.

Erlwanger suggests that Benny's misconceptions "indicate that the weakness of IPI stems from its behaviorist approach to mathematics, its mode of instruction, and its concept of individualization."

Is IPI Mathematics more effective than other contemporary programs? The answer to this question is not easy to find. Well-designed, scientifically rigorous studies are seemingly nonexistent. Findings of research studies that do not meet the canons of scientific research are, of course, many and conflicting.

In the EPIE report *Evaluating Instructional Systems* (1974), we find this summary discussion of summative evaluations:

Students achieve as well or better than non-IPI students on standardized tests, achieve higher than non-IPI students on IPI tests, have a positive attitude towards school and learning, and demonstrate a change in social behavior.

Parent reactions have been highly positive, indicating that their children like school better. Parents also feel that IPI considers individual differences and is a successful experience and that IPI is superior to traditional mathematics programs (p. 58).

While IPI claims the IPI system (math, science, spelling, and reading) has produced effective results with a variety of populations: disadvantaged, rural, and mentally retarded as well as regular populations, EPIE disagrees with this. EPIE states "the data are particularly mixed on the use of IPI with different populations and in different settings. In our estimation, the designs of studies are unable to document whether different findings are a result of the program or of the implementation of the program" (p. 58).

Contrary to the claims made that IPI children achieve as well or better in mathematics than non-IPI children, Suydam and Weaver (undated) reported in a bias-free bulletin that "no substantial evidence to date supports an affirmative answer to this question (Is achievement in mathematics increased by a program of Individually Prescribed Instruction?). When the IPI program . . . is considered, achievement of pupils has generally been found to be approximately equivalent to that of pupils in non-individualized programs."

How does the IPI math program affect a child's self-concept? Myers (1972) reported at a meeting of the American Educational Research Association that "students who have been in IPI programs three years have significantly lower self-concepts than students who have been in IPI programs one or two years . . ." (p. 17).

In the light of these results, the fact that students who had IPI for two or three years had *lower* (italics hers) self-concepts than those who were in their first year of IPI instruction, and the fact that these results were consistent across high achieving and average achieving students, suggest that "the IPI program itself may be causing these decreasing perceptions of self."

In the previously mentioned EPIE report can be found Chart 9 (p. 59), which lists the average cost of IPI math per student as $7.50 for the first year and $7.50 (est.) as the average cost per student over a five-year period. Assuming the cost of a standard textbook as about $4.00 and a life use of four years, the average cost of such a book would be $1.00 per year.

In this "age of accountability" school personnel need to ask whether a seven-fold increase in cost of IPI basic materials can be justified in the light of presently available evidence of the learning outcomes.

Finally, E. P. Smith (1973), writing in his role as President of the National Council of Teachers of Mathematics, expressed his concern that individualized instruction is being viewed by some as a "panacea to cure all of the mathematical ills of all of our students." He goes on to say:

I have no quarrel with those who individualized instruction experimentally with a limited number of classes to perfect techniques and procedures and to compare its effectiveness with that of group or other modes of instruction. But I do deplore the wholesale imposition of the technique on teachers and students with the tacit assumption that the method is superior to any method they have used before. The evidence does not support the assumption (pp. 507-508).

What is the place of behavioral objectives in determining the curriculum in elementary school mathematics?

The nature of educational objectives has, itself, been an object of inquiry for centuries. The past century has seen the emergence of curriculum as a separate area of study within education, and educational objectives have received ever increasing analytic appraisal within this area. As with most streams of inquiry, diverse viewpoints exist, and appeals to recognized authority and empirical evidence are made in support of these disparate views.

In the first part of the present century, those involved with determining the objectives of mathematics education were often influenced by two fields of force: one generated by the "Associationist" theory of learning and one generated by the "Gestaltist" theory of learning. Extremist advocates of the former view were often preoccupied with partitioning mathematics into minute, discrete elements. Extremist advocates of the latter view were often preoccupied with identifying mathematical structure which was viewed as the dynamic force that, in the contemporary vernacular, "put it all together." For teachers of elementary school mathematics this translated into teaching by focusing on a few essential relationships and understandings embedded in the mathematical content.

The latter half of the century has been marked by further analysis of the components of curriculum. Taxonomies, cognitive (Bloom *et al.*, 1956) and affective (Krathwohl, Bloom, and Masia, 1956), have contributed to specificity of objective statements and measurement of objective accomplishments. Analyses of types of cognitive learnings into hierarchical classifications have also contributed to task-specific curriculum formulations (Gagné, 1970). Influence from the "technological" and "management-systems" sectors of the educational establishment, as well as the demand for "accountability" from sectors of society, have given impetus to a neo-behaviorist influence on the mathematics curriculum. For contemporary teachers of mathematics this often translates into teaching a curriculum prescribed and circumscribed by "measurable-behavior objectives."

One counter force to the behaviorist influence on curriculum is the group that views the goals of mathematics in education from a "humanistic" position. Theoretical support for this movement emerges from a new branch of psychology, neo-humanistic psychology, and has been led by such people as Abraham Maslow (1968) and Carl Rogers (1969).

In mathematics education this position has recently been articulated by Braunfeld, Kaufman, and Haag (1973) and Brown (1973). For teachers of mathematics this often translates into teaching a curriculum that is not prescribed or circumscribed but encourages "deep" probes and "creative" explorations of mathematics content by students.

Forbes (1971) has stated his view of the extreme positions on behavioral objectives. For those favoring the behavioral objective view:

All objectives of instruction can and must be stated in terms of student behaviors that are to be exhibited. Anything not so stated is not an objective but merely a vague hope (p. 744).

For those opposed to the behavioral objective view:

The only objectives of instruction that can be stated in behavioral terms are low-level objectives in the cognitive domain. Higher level objectives in this domain and essentially all objectives in the affective domain cannot be so stated. To limit goals of instruction to behavioral objectives would be to limit instruction to the "mechanics" of mathematics (p. 744).

Walbesser (1972) has recited a few of the most prominent claims for writing instructional purposes in terms of behavioral objectives.

1. Informing the learner about the purposes for instruction aids his learning and recall.

2. Behavioral objectives aid the teacher in planning for effective instruction.

3. Knowing the behavioral objectives facilitates the designing of programs of individualized instruction.

4. Learning needs of individual students can be diagnosed more accurately when the expected learnings are precisely stated.

5. The success or failure of educators can be made accountable to the public in terms of the behaviors acquired by students.

6. Each learner can proceed at his own rate of acquisition when a course is set of behaviors to be acquired (p. 436).

Eisner (1967) has stated some concerns about curricula prescribed by behavioral objectives. In summary they are:

1. The amount, type, and quality of learning that occurs in a classroom, especially when there is interaction among students, are only in a small part predictable. Therefore, the dynamic and complex process of instruction yields outcomes far too numerous to be specified in behavioral and content terms in advance.

2. The behavioral objectivists fail to recognize the constraints various subject-matters place upon objectives. Effective instruction in some areas should yield behaviors and products which are unpredictable. The end achieved ought to be something of a surprise to both student and teacher.

3. The assumption that objectives can be used as standards by which to measure achievement fails to distinguish adequately between the application of standards and making of a judgment.

4. Educational objectives need not precede the selection and organization of content. The means through which imaginative curriculums can be built is as open-ended as the means through which scientific and artistic inventions occur. Curriculum theory needs to allow for a variety of processes to be employed in the construction of curriculums.

Others (Nichols, 1972; Atkin, 1968; Allendoerfer, 1971; D. A. Johnson, 1971) have also presented their views on the place of behavioral objectives in mathematics education or related areas.

The issue of behaviorally-stated objectives is one capable of stirring much emotion. Positions on the issue tend to polarize with opposing beliefs about "What is mathematics?" "How does one come to know and appreciate mathematics?" "What mathematics is most valuable to know?" It is an extremely value-laden issue.

The "mathematics as science" or "mathematics as art" issue has ebbed and flowed within the discipline for centuries. The "mathematics education as a science" or "mathematics education as an art" issue is closely related within the applied field of education.

Certain cautions would seem warranted for the classroom teacher considering the place of behavioral objectives in mathematics education. An extreme adherence to behaviorally prescribed objectives in mathematics may so dilute and mechanize learning that students may be deprived of the opportunity and enjoyment of creating mathematics, or a glimpse of its beauty and structure. An extreme "humanistic" view may benefit the few talented students (with talented teachers) who are capable of creating mathematics and gaining enjoyment and appreciation from romantic excursions into the discipline, while depriving the less talented or the disinterested student of the systematic teaching of mathematical skills necessary for productive living.

What does the work of Piaget suggest about the cognitive development of the child?

Research studies that attempt to verify, deny, elaborate, translate, and illuminate the theoretical and empirical works of the Swiss "Master" continue to abound. It is beyond the scope of this monograph to attempt an analysis of Piaget's work, and the many studies by others bearing on his work, which has evolved over a half-century of time. The reader interested in Piaget's writings would do well to sample his works on intelligence (Inhelder and Piaget, 1958), number (Piaget and Szeminska, 1952), space (Piaget and Inhelder, 1956), and geometry (Piaget et al., 1960). For those interested in delving into others' views on Piaget's works, excellent summaries and collections are now available (Flavell, 1963; Rosskopf, Steffe, and Taback, 1971; Lovell, 1971c; Laurendeau and Pinard, 1970).

The following glimpses of Piaget's theory on the development of logical thought are taken from a recent paper presented at the Second International Congress on Mathematical Education (Howson, 1973).

It would seem . . . psychologically clear that logic does not arise out of language but from a deeper source and this is to be found in the general coordination of actions (p. 79).

. . . before all language, and at a purely sensorimotor level, actions are susceptible to repetition and then to generalization thus building up what could be called assimilation schemes. These schemes organize themselves according to certain laws and it would seem impossible to deny the relationship between these laws and the laws of logic (pp. 79-80).

Briefly, there is a whole logic of the action that leads to the construction of certain identities and these go beyond perception and to the elaboration of certain structures (p. 80).

Thus, this initial role of actions and logico-mathematical experience (Piaget distinguishes between "physical experience" and "logico-mathematical" experience; the former refers to acting on objects in order to discover the properties of the objects themselves, the latter refers to the actions carried out by the child on objects), far from hindering the later development of deductive thought, constitutes, on the contrary, a necessary preparation . . . (p. 81).

. . . mental or intellectual operations, which intervene in the subsequent deductive reasoning processes, themselves stem from actions: they are interiorized actions . . . (p. 81).

Coordinations of actions and logico-mathematical experience, whilst interiorizing themselves, give rise to the creation of a particular variety of abstraction which corresponds precisely to logical and mathematical abstraction: . . . (p. 81).

. . . between the age where material actions and logico-mathematical experience are necessary (before 7/8 years old) and the age where abstract thought begins to be possible (towards 11/12 years old and through successive levels until about 14/15 years) there is an important stage whose characteristics are interesting to the psychologist and useful to know for the teacher. In fact, between the age of 7 and 11/12 years, an important spontaneous development of deductive operations with their characteristics of conservation, reversibility, etc., can be observed. . . . At this level the child cannot as yet reason on pure hypotheses, expressed verbally, and, in order to arrive at a coherent deduction, he needs to apply his reasoning to manipulative objects (real or imagined). For these reasons, at this level we refer to "concrete operations" as distinct from formal operations. These concrete operations are, in fact, intermediaries between actions of the preoperational stage and the stage of abstract thought which comes much later (p. 86).

These glimpses of Piaget's developmental theory of logical processes highlight the essential role that action and experience play in development. Piaget's theory also points out the secondary role of language in logical development, at least at the elementary school years. This point of view offers much food for thought, especially in schools where student progress is judged on the basis of verbal behavior.

What does the work of Piaget suggest for the curriculum in elementary school mathematics?

This extremely complex question can probably best be answered quite simply, "a great deal or very little." It all depends on the view taken on the basic questions: "What mathematical knowledge is of most value?" and "Why?"

It may be useful to try to illustrate this point. Take the case of basic combinations of addition of whole numbers. From one perspective the value of knowing these combinations may be described in quite functional and utilitarian terms. From this perspective the value of these learnings is associated with needs in computing, needs in simple social situations, and communication literacy. Knowledge of the basic combinations of addition is then characterized in terms of immediate recall, speed of response, accuracy of response, maturity of response, amount of retention, amount of specific transfer, and comprehension of numerical symbolism and problem solving ability. Given this perspective of "knowledge of basic addition combinations," then it seems that the work of Piaget has little application to the elementary school mathematics curriculum. The work of the "associationist" theorists or "behaviorist" theorists would probably be more relevant.

In another case, mathematics topics at the elementary school level may be viewed and valued for their logico-mathematical meaningfulness—being homogeneous with other topics forming the deductive science of mathematics. From this perspective the experiences with materials used in exploring the basic combinations of addition are valued for the opportunity they present the child to re-invent and elaborate appropriate logico-mathematical processes. Knowledge of the basic combinations of addition is indicated in terms of appropriate deductive operations with their characteristics of conservation, reversibility, and compensation. Given this perspective of "knowledge of basic addition combinations," then it seems that the theory of intellectual development proposed by Piaget has a great deal to say for the elementary mathematics curriculum.

Another basic curriculum difference in elementary school mathematics instruction between Piagetian and more traditional utilitarian-associationist positions involves the use of manipulative materials and symbolic materials. Because of the nature of the logical structures available to the child during the elementary years, actions on—and experiences with—appropriate manipulative objects are essential for logico-mathematical development. But from a more functional-utilitarian perspective, mathematical needs are much more verbal in character, and instruction would put much emphasis on the verbal (both written and oral) mode. The main mathematics delivery system in the elementary school from the Piagetian perspective would consist of appropriate manipulatives for the student to experience and act on in the development of psycho-mathematical, deductive processes. The main delivery system from the more utilitarian-associationist position would mainly consist of printed or orally presented materials.

Implications for measurement and evaluation of instruction from the two different perspectives are also quite evident. Piaget (1973) has pointed out:

> . . . the pupil will be far more capable of "doing" and "understanding in actions" than of expressing himself verbally. In other words, a large part of the structures the child uses when he sets out actively to solve a problem remain unconscious. In fact, it is a very general psychological law that the child can do something in action long before he really becomes "aware" of what is involved—"awareness" occurs long after the action (p. 86).

From a more functional-utilitarian perspective, since much instruction is characterized as "verbal" the child may be much better prepared to respond to verbal testing and evaluation situations. From the Piagetian perspective a child may meaningfully "know" much more than he can verbalize. From the more functional-utilitarian perspective the child may often verbalize more than he meaningfully "knows."

Discussion of the math curriculum from the two perspectives was done to suggest an important point. Care must be taken in "transplanting" a little bit of Piaget into a dissonant "host." The work of Piaget would seem to have major implications for curriculum in a situation where his epistemological view has been studied and found acceptable; his theory of intellectual stage development studied and found acceptable; his view of stages of logico-mathematical deductive processes studied and found sensible. Then a curriculum that reflects these values and theories could gain much from Piagetian procedures. In commenting on philosophical view and educational policy, Piaget (1973) states:

> If Platonism is right and mathematical entities exist independently of the subject, or if logical positivism is correct in reducing them to a general syntax and semantic, . . . it would be justifiable to put emphasis on simple transmission of the truth from teacher to pupil and to use . . . the axiomatic language (of the teacher), without worrying too much about the spontaneous ideas of the children.

> We believe . . . that there exists . . . a spontaneous and gradual construction of elementary logico-mathematical structures and that these "natural" structures are much closer to those being used in "modern" mathematics than to those being used in traditional mathematics (p. 79).

Without awareness of the full range of educational implications from the work of Piaget, little benefit and much disappointment may accrue. Sinclair (1971) has alluded to this:

> . . . there seems to be a regrettable tendency to take Piaget's problem situations and convert them directly into teaching situations.

> Why I think this is regrettable is probably best explained by a metaphor: Piaget's tasks are like the core samples of a geologist taken from a fertile

area and from which he can infer the general structure of a fertile soil; but it is absurd to hope that transplanting these samples to a field of nonfertile soil will make the whole area fertile (p. 1).

What does research on the specific relationship between elementary school mathematics and Piagetian tasks seem to suggest?

Many researchers have examined the various environmental and organismic variables that influence Piagetian tasks. There are fewer empirical studies that have examined the relationship between these tasks and arithmetic tasks that society expects its schools to teach children.

One set of studies that give some insight into the relationship of school mathematics tasks and Piagetian-type tasks has been "The Wisconsin Studies" (Van Engen, 1971). A few results from one study will be recited here. One hundred first-grade children were randomly selected and given four tasks with candies. A correct response to these tasks involved the ability to conserve an equivalence relationship through a physical transformation without being perceptually "duped." For example, a child was confronted with two sets of candies, a set of two and a set of three candies. The child was asked "If I let you take these candies for your friends, would you take the two piles of candy or the one pile" (Here, the experimenter put the candies into one pile) "after I put them together, or does it make any difference? . . . Why?"

Since the children knew some basic addition facts, they were tested on the combinations they were likely to know, namely $2 + 3$ and $4 + 5$. All but one of the children gave the correct response to $2 + 3$ on a paper and pencil test. All but six knew that $4 + 5 = 9$. Figure 6 indicates the frequencies of correct responses on the candy-equivalence transformation tasks. It can be noted that even though the 100 subjects were near "mastery" on the addition combinations $2 + 3$ and $4 + 5$ in a verbal format, only about 50 percent of them were capable of conserving the equivalence relationship through a physical transformation.

LeBlanc (1968) and Steffe (1966) both found a relationship

	Task				Total Score				
	1	2	3	4	0	1	2	3	4
Frequency	54	45	45	42	26	27	10	9	28

Figure 6. Correct Responses by Task and Total Score, N = 100

between conservation of numerousness and ability to perform subtraction and addition problems, respectively. The outcomes of the studies indicated that children who did well on the conservation test did well on the problem solving test. Children who did poorly on the conservation test did poorly on the problem solving test.

Howlett (1973) found a relationship between Piaget-type class inclusion tasks and ability of first graders to perform missing-addend problems. Using only first-grade students who exhibited perfect scores on a canonical control test, for example, sentences of the type $4 + 5 = \square$, he found that students who performed well on the class inclusion tasks showed correspondingly high performance on missing-addend tasks. Likewise, those who did not do well on class inclusion tasks did not perform well on the missing-addend tasks.

Others (Almy, 1966; Overholt, 1965) have found some relationship between Piagetian stage development and achievement on tests of mathematical ability. It is also quite evident that ability on the various Piagetian tasks is closely related to ability on general IQ tests. On some specific arithmetic tasks, Piagetian tasks may relate better than IQ. For example, success on subtraction problems used by LeBlanc (1968) was more closely related to Piagetian conservation ability than to IQ.

The evidence would suggest to the teacher that data relating Piagetian theory to school mathematics are still quite meager and tentative. The arguments for an isomorphism of mental processes between his genetic developmental theory and the systematic learning of conceptual mathematics by children in schools get their primary strength from *a priori* claims rather than empirical evidence.

What are some implications for teaching from the work of Piaget?

Piaget (1973) has mentioned some very general psycho-pedagogical principles.

1. Real comprehension of a notion or a theory implies the re-invention of this theory by the subject. Once the child is capable of repeating certain notions and using some applications of these in learning situations he often gives the impression of understanding; however, this does not fulfill the condition of re-invention.

2. At all levels, including adolescence and in a systematic manner at the more elementary levels, the pupil will be far more capable of "doing" and "understanding" in actions than of expressing himself verbally.

3. The teacher is often tempted to present far too early notions and operations in a framework that is already very formal. . . . the procedure that would seem indispensable would be to take as the starting point the qualitative

concrete levels: in other words, the representations or models used should correspond to the natural logic of the levels of the pupils in question, and formalization should be kept for a later moment as a type of systematization of the notions already acquired (pp. 85-86).

Lovell (1972) has made the following suggestions for elementary school teachers that he believes would aid transformations based on a Piagetian-developmental model:

1. A move from a formal classroom atmosphere, with much talk by the teacher directed to the whole class, to the position where the pupils work in small groups or individually at tasks that have been provided.

2. The opportunity for pupils to act on physical materials and to use games.

3. Social intercourse using verbal language is an important influence in the development of concrete-operational thought. Through exchanges, discussions, agreements, and oppositions, both between children and between adults and children, the child encounters viewpoints that must be reconciled with those of his own.

4. Since mathematics is a structured and interlocked system of relations expressed in symbols and governed by firm rules, the initiative and direction of the work must be the teacher's responsibility. This was often overlooked in the progressive education movement.

5. Alongside the abstraction of the mathematical idea from the physical situation, there must be the introduction of the relevant symbolization and the working of examples, involving drill and practice and problems on paper.

Sawada (1972) has reviewed Piaget's epistemological and biological orientation, as well as his basic constructs used in describing intellectual development, and has suggested some pedagogical implications from these theories. Others (Sime, 1973; Adler, 1966; Inskeep, 1972) have also discussed the work of Piaget in relation to instructional practices in the classroom.

The knowledgeable teacher will notice that many of the implications mentioned are not new. A comparison with implications from learning theorists (for example, Hilgard and Bowers, 1966) will reveal much similarity to what has been stated in the past as principles of good learning for children.

What cautions and concerns have been expressed about applying Piagetian theory to mathematics education?

Over a quarter-century ago, Brownell (1942) wrote that "Piaget's studies seem to provide the most illuminating single description of the way in which children attain power in problem solving." At the same time he summarized some of the criticisms of Piaget's work as it relates to mathematics:

1. Failure to consider sufficiently the prejudicial character of the problem tasks with which Piaget worked. The issue here is two-fold; it involves (a) a definition of reasoning and (b) the nature of the problem task. What one does in a problem situation is largely a function of the type of problem one faces.

2. The second criticism attaches to Piaget's definition of reasoning . . . the highest type of formal, systematic thinking. The objections to this definition are, first, that this kind of thinking is rare; second, that it overvalues verbal expression as a measure of thinking; and third, that it tends to encourage the notion that young children cannot solve problems of any kind.

3. Some are likely to gain the impression that children at certain rather definite ages achieve equally definite levels of thinking. The fact is that children do not move from level to level in an all-or-none way, but that at any one age they reveal the characteristics of several levels of thinking as they deal with different kinds of problems.

4. Piaget's account makes adult reasoning quite unlike children's problem solving. Adults, however, at times betray in their problem solving the same kinds of logical weakness, the same effects of egocentricity, and the same tendency to overt manipulation and movement that are so prominent in children's problem solving.

More recent researchers have continued to caution about too zealous applications of Piagetian theory to education. Baker and Sullivan (1970) have pointed out that one extrapolation from Piagetian theory is the concept of "number readiness." The assumption is that it would be well to assess the child's stage of intellectual development in Piagetian terms before attempting to demonstrate numerical operations which he might not at this point be capable of grasping. Yet the conclusion that such assessments can be made presupposes a well-delineated dichotomy between non-conservation and conservation. Such a supposition is called into question by the fact that their study, and others, suggest that such task variables as interest in the task object (candies or gray checkers) and size of aggregate (4 or 9 objects) may be important factors in the elicitation of number conservation responses in children.

Duckworth (1972) has stated some observations from her work and Piaget's thoughts that also bear on some of Brownell's points. She indicates that Piaget had speculated that some people may reach the level of formal operations in some specific area which they know well without reaching the formal level in others. She goes on to point out that in an area you know well, you can think of many possibilities, and working them through often makes demands of a formal nature. If there is no area in which you are familiar enough with the phenomena to permit you to make sense of complex relationships, then you are not likely to develop formal operations. Knowing enough about things is one prerequisite for wonderful ideas; intelligence cannot develop without content.

Weaver (1972b) and Glennon (1974) have expressed concern about a repetition of history in elementary school mathematics curriculum as a result of overzealous adherence to Piaget's work. This could correspond to the events that grew out of the work of the Committee of Seven (Washburne, 1939) early in this century, and that resulted in an unfortunate push upward in the grade placement of many topics and an unnecessary delay in the introduction of much mathematical work.

Beilin (1971) also has summarized some of the limitations in applying Piagetian theory and practices to mathematics education.

There are few who would deny the enormous contributions that Piaget's work has made to understanding the development of logical reasoning in the child. The cautions and concerns cited in this section in no way deny or question these contributions. They do, however, caution and remind the teacher that learning mathematics in school is an extremely complex and idiosyncratic enterprise.

There is little question that knowledge of the internal, autoregulatory stage development of reasoning described by Piaget can enhance the effectiveness of mathematics instruction in the school. However, there is equally strong evidence of the effect of variables such as experience, motivation, and cultural background on the idiosyncratic nature of learning. Piaget does not deny these forces, but generally subordinates them to development. As Beilin points out, "Piaget has contributed enormously to understanding these relationships, but the story is not yet told."

What is the influence of schooling in different cultures on the ability to conserve and estimate number?

Greenfield (1966) studied conservation of liquids in Senegal, the westernmost tip of former French West Africa, where the subjects were children of the Wolof ethnic group. The subjects were divided into nine groups, according to degrees of urbanization, schooling, and age level.

In the separation by schooling, the first group included 49 rural unschooled children; the second, 67 rural children who attended small French-style village schools; and the third, 65 urban school children from Dakar, the cosmopolitan capital of Senegal. Each of these groups was comprised of three age groups: 6-7 years, 8-9 years, and 11-13 years.

Due to the central control of the Ministry of Education, children attending school received nearly identical educations. Test differences were attributed to differences in urban and rural background.

The experimental situation consisted of a personal interview in the Wolof language with each subject, during which questions concerning conservation were asked. The first part consisted of asking each subject to equalize the water levels in two identical partly-filled beakers; then the experimenter poured the contents of one beaker into a second taller, thinner beaker. The child was asked if the taller beaker contained an amount of water equal to the first or more than the first. In the second part, the experimenter poured the contents of the beaker into six shorter, thinner beakers, and the child compared the amount of water in the original beaker with the total contents of the six small ones. The achievement of conservation was said to be present when a child gave equality responses to both quantity comparisons. The data are presented graphically in Figure 7. (See Greenfield, Chart I, p. 233.)

There was a wider gap between unschooled and schooled Wolof children than between rural and urban children. By the eleventh or twelfth year virtually all the school children had achieved conservation, but only about half of those not in school had done so.

In addition to compiling these data, Greenfield studied the justifications the children gave for their answers. These fitted three main classi-

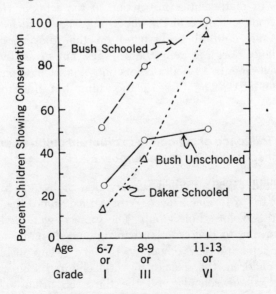

Figure 7. Percent of Different Backgrounds and Ages Exhibiting
Conservation of Continuous Quantity

fications: perceptual (features of the display), direct-action (actual pouring), and transformational (internal reasoning). This last class was subdivided again as indirect-action (imagined pouring) and identity (nothing changed). The school children showed early reliance on perceptual reasons followed by a later decline. In contrast, unschooled children showed a gradual rise with age in perceptual reasons.

In most cases Wolof children used transformational or direct-action reasons as a basis for justifying conservation, just as American children do. However, direct-action assumed greater importance for Wolof children. Those giving a transformational reason were generally thinking of identity. Those children demonstrating lack of conservation followed a pattern similar to American children as the majority gave perceptual reasons. In an attempt to hasten conservation, the pouring was performed behind a screen, a technique found successful on American children. This had little effect on Wolof children. The 20 percent minority of Wolof children (primarily unschooled) who gave direct-action reasons seemed to indicate "magical" thinking, attributing special powers to the experimenter who did the pouring. In an attempt to overcome this, another experiment was performed in which the children actually did the pouring. Conservation increased markedly except among the city school children who originally did not have the "magical" thinking.

Lloyd (1971) worked with elite and poor (Oje) children from Nigeria on conservation tasks. It was found that tasks involving conservation improved with age, and children from elite homes performed at a higher level. Elite Yoruba and American subjects performed in a similar fashion, but the Oje subjects displayed a completely different pattern of success. In general the Yoruba subjects relied on direct-action to support conservation and gave fewer perceptual explanations.

Gay and Cole (1967) studied learning among the Kpelle of Liberia. The result of part of one of their simple experiments with number estimation is presented. American school children, ages seven and nine, and Kpelle illiterate children were compared on estimation of number of dots in random visual displays. The range of numbers was three to ten and each subject viewed the stimulus cards at three different intervals, $1/100$, $1/25$, and $1/10$ second exposure time. The results were plotted in terms of the relative amount of error for the groups. Figure 8 presents the results at $1/100$ and at $1/10$ second exposure time.

Two features seem to be suggested. First, there was less error at the slower speed than the faster speed. Second, there was little or no difference between Kpelle and American children's groups, although Americans had attended school for three or four years and the Kpelle were completely illiterate.

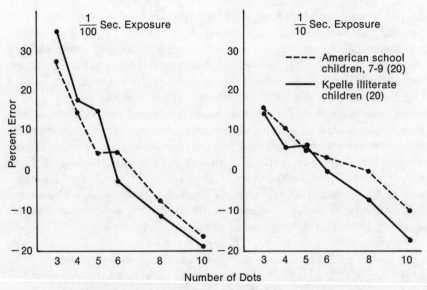

Figure 8. Mean Percent Errors of Kpelle and American Children
in Estimation of Numbers of Dots in Random Visual Displays

Taken collectively these, and other, cross-cultural studies remind the teacher that the growth of some concepts can appear to be quite similar, but the experiential routes to development are obviously, and at times subtly, different.

What kind of mathematics program for the kindergarten?

It is well established both nomothetically and idiographically that children of average ability enter the kindergarten with a substantial amount of mathematical knowledge and hence are ready to learn still more appropriate mathematics when taught by appropriate methods.

But, what mathematics is appropriate and what methods are appropriate? We consider *methods* first. It is generally agreed among cognitive psychologists, most notably Jean Piaget, that knowledge develops best when young children are actively engaged in purposeful behavior. The sensory receptors are the means by which the environment is processed and stored in the brain. Cognitive elements (concepts and understandings) such as "three blocks and two blocks are five blocks," or "four cups of water will fill a quart bottle" are best learned by actively manipulating the materials, then by working with pictures which represent things, and finally with the written symbols.

These modes of learning (learning modalities) are usually named concrete (enactive, hands-on, or manipulative), representational (ikonic, pictorial, or semi-concrete), and symbolic or abstract.

The teacher of kindergarten children can feel very confident that most of them can readily learn much new mathematics easily when learning via the concrete modality.

But what mathematical topics are appropriate? The list, if broken down into elements, would be long indeed. Suffice it to say here that the cognitive material appropriate for many kindergarten children has been identified by experienced teachers, and includes work in the general strands: matching things, classifying things, arranging things in patterns, sets, numeration to 50 or more, finding sums of things to five, concepts of measurement, and a few geometric terms (names of common shapes).

The kindergarten teacher can feel very confident that some systematic teaching of topics such as these is consistent with sound developmental learning.

How soon should we teach "basic concepts" of mathematics in the elementary school?

Imbedded in this question is the prejudgment that basic concepts should be taught. Rationale for this judgment is stated very succinctly by Bruner (1960) when he writes:

The first object of any act of learning, over and beyond the pleasure it may give, is that it should serve us in the future. . . . [A] way in which earlier learning renders later performance more efficient is through what is conveniently called nonspecific transfer or, more accurately, the transfer of principles and attitudes. In essence, it consists of learning initially not a skill but a general idea, which can then be used as a basis for recognizing subsequent problems as special cases of the idea originally mastered (p. 17).

In arithmetic operations such concepts as commutativity, associativity, and distributivity are used over and over again. The use of such concepts as place-value or face-value arises often in arithmetic work. Each new arithmetic process does not consist of an entirely new set of "rules," but makes repeated use of some essential basic concepts. If introduced formally at too early an age, however, this formalistic-axiomatic study becomes a meaningless and useless endeavor for the child. Some of the disillusionment with "new math" may have been overconcern for the formal teaching of conceptual mathematics, with a subordinate concern for the conceptual learning ability of the child. As stated by Whitney (1973): "In brief, our focus has been too much on the subject matter, not enough on the child himself." He illustrates the effect on a child of learning $8 + 4$ from a mathematically insecure teacher following the textbook manual. The presentation is:

$$8 + 4 = 8 + (2 + 2)$$
$$(8 + 2) + 2 \quad \text{by the associative law}$$
$$10 + 2 = 12$$

Here (he suggests) is the effect on the children:

1. The expression $8 + (2 + 2)$ is confusing. Why put in the curly signs? Writing $8 + 2 + 2$ is simpler. Perhaps $2 + 2 = 4$ is recognized, but why choose $2 + 2$?

2. Now the curly signs are moved around. What is a "law"? Does this mean that I am told to do something, and therefore do it? I have really stopped trying to see what this is about, anyway.

3. I feel uncomfortable, especially since the teacher does too. If she is expressing what school is supposed to be like, I do not want to go to school.

4. There is 12 at the end. Why not just count four more than eight, and get twelve?

5. I am told that the 1 in 12 means ten. But I know that you write 10 for ten, not 1. I hope this will stop soon (p. 285).

He proceeds to suggest a way of teaching the task in a manner that is both child-concerned and concept-concerned.

Baumann's study (1966) dealt with the performance that could be expected from second and fourth grade children on the attainment and use of the concepts "commutativity," "closure," and "identity." Evidence from the study suggested that the attainment of these concepts was quite difficult for students. Lovell (1971b) cites Brown's (1969) conclusions that understanding of some of these concepts is reached at about the following ages: closure at seven, identity at seven to eight, commutativity at eight to nine, associativity at eight to nine, and distributivity at ten to eleven years. It is pointed out, however, that children's performance can be advanced or retarded up to four years compared with the norm, depending on the child; pupils can be at a pre-operational stage in some tasks and operational in others; also, the child achieves the operational stage with regard to all the properties tested at the earliest at about nine years of age. Moreover, an understanding of the non-examples of the properties may be delayed for one to two years compared with understanding examples—at least for most pupils.

Crawford (1964) investigated the age-grade trends in understanding the field axioms. A test of the field axioms was constructed and administered to students in grades 4, 6, 8, 9, 10, and 12. The results indicated that mean scores increased significantly from one even-numbered grade to the next in a manner which was generally linear. No significant differences were found between the scores of boys and girls. Intelligence had an increasing effect on the scores as the grade level increased. The order of difficulty of the axioms from easiest to most difficult was: commutativity, inverse, closure, identity, associativity, and distributivity.

Though some studies (Gray, 1965; Schell, 1968) suggest that the concept of distributivity can be learned with some meaningfulness at intermediate grade levels, Weaver's (1973a) study of fourth, fifth, sixth, and seventh graders' comprehension of and sensitivity to use of "the distributive idea" indicates it is not independent of factors such as context, form, and example format. He suggests that too often the study of distributivity is characterized by relatively meaningless and inconsistent "symbol pushing."

The various pieces of research evidence cited would seem to suggest that many of the "basic concepts" essential in learning mathematics develop quite slowly in children. The study of such concepts should probably not be formalized and symbolized at early grade levels—perhaps not in the elementary grades. This does not mean purging conceptual content from the program. Informal, but systematic, instruction which focuses on various essential basic concepts may be entirely appropriate at the elementary level. However, as Phillips (1965) pointed out, we must be careful not to hinder rather than help the child by starting with the "sophisticated end-products" of learning.

What is the appropriate scope and sequence for the geometry program in the elementary school?

There has been a dramatic increase in interest regarding geometry in the elementary school program. Many books and articles have been published that focus on teaching geometric concepts at the elementary school level. In general, there seems to be more agreement on *how* geometry is to be taught in the program than *what* and *when* various topics ought to be taught.

Troutman (1973) has suggested three comprehensive characteristics of an elementary geometry program. First, the content should be useful to the child as he develops, organizes, and extends accurate interpretations of the world about him. Second, the content should be developed in terms of ideas reflecting mathematical methods; these include the study of systematic patterns, relationships among mathematical entities, mathematical models and their relationships to reality, and logical systems that bind together a set of mathematical statements. Third, this view must consider only content that can be legitimately represented in the child's physical and psychological environment.

Piaget (1956) has suggested that children's psychological development is inverted in relation to the development of geometries over time. For example, he suggests that children develop an awareness of the topological characteristics of space prior to the development of Euclidian characteristics of space. As stated by Laurendeau and Pinard (1970):

Thus Piaget asserts more than once that the development of child space appears to reproduce the stages necessary for mathematical construction itself, wherein topological relations are the most basic—though the last to be discovered by mathematicians—and precede the projective and Euclidian structures which derive from them (p. 16).

The National Council of Teachers of Mathematics has devoted a significant amount of space in its journals to teaching geometry in the elementary school. Van Engen (1973) summarized one collection of articles on the topic in the following manner:

1. The method of instruction is of paramount importance. . . . one senses that activities, discovery, guessing (hypothesis), and problem solving should be uppermost in the mind of the teacher as a lesson is being planned.

2. The emphasis on precision of statement and symbolism is almost entirely ignored. The emphasis is on the child's ability to operationally perform tasks, solve problems, and make intelligent guesses to show that he is making progress in organizing some geometric ideas.

3. None of the authors suggests that the geometry of the schools (grades one through eight) should conform to any given geometry—transformational, Euclidian, and so on. . . . The authors are not obsessed with the thought that the geometry program should be placed in a straitjacket by adhering to one postulational system (p. 423).

These observations seem to be appropriate for an earlier compilation of articles regarding geometry in the elementary school (Brydegaard and Inskeep, 1970).

Although there is no specific agreement on a prescriptive scope and sequence for geometry in the elementary school, certain characteristics of the program do seem to emerge. There seems to be agreement that the program should be kept informal and allow for much exploration on the part of the student. The content presented informally should possess mathematical integrity; it should be useful to the children in their interactions with the world about them; and it should be teachable, that is within the cognitive and motivational sphere of elementary school children. This seems to be in line with Meserve's (1973) feelings about geometry for prospective elementary teachers when he writes:

I feel very strongly that prospective elementary school teachers have a serious need for experiences involving explorations in geometry in the pedagogical spirit that they should use in their own teaching. This pedagogical need is much greater than their need for a review of the theorems of secondary school geometry (p. 248).

What are some of the possible implications for education as the United States moves toward adoption of the metric system of measurement—Système International (S.I.)?

Hallerberg (1973) has documented the development and increased use of the metric system in the world over a century and a half. Recent study and legislative action suggest that the metric system will become the predominant system of measurement in the United States within the next decade. A comprehensive listing of advantages of the metric system and the customary system can be found in the Report of· the U.S. Metric Study (DeSimone, 1971).

Many new programs in mathematics at the elementary school level are reflecting the increased use of the metric system. Instructional materials for teaching metric measurement are proliferating. What insights and suggestions have been advanced for the elementary school teacher as the metric move accelerates?

Smith (1974) has stated that since sub-units and multiples of the basic units are related by powers of ten, the learner must understand the decimal numeration system, including decimal fractions, if he is to change from one related unit to another. The teacher must not only provide readiness experiences for learning the metric system, but also consider whether children of differing abilities can understand decimal fractions well enough to change from one unit to another. Also, the teacher must help youngsters understand the new vocabulary.

Another more indirect curricular implication of going metric involves its impact on teaching fractions at the elementary level. Smith points out that most of our needs for fractions arise from using the English system of measurement. After the metric system is in widespread use, what need will we have for fractions in daily life? Can all common fractions be eliminated? He believes that this is not likely, for we shall still sometimes need them for describing ratios and parts of a whole. There is also the mathematical need of students who take algebra to consider, and the readiness that work with fractions in pre-algebra courses provides.

Hilgren (1973) has made some suggestions for educators as they go metric. Some of these follow:

1. Teach the metric system by itself so that teachers and pupils learn

to think in this language of measure. Do not try to learn or teach the metric system through conversion problems, and do not try to learn conversion factors.

2. Prepare the teachers, both in-service and preservice, for the change to the new system of measure is not just a mathematics or science project.

3. Select one member of the faculty to be the metric authority for the school. That person can get information and materials necessary for effective teaching of the metric system to students (p. 266).

The metric system of measurement has been gaining increased use and popularity for well over a century and a half until, at the present time, the United States is the only major country not officially using, or committed to using, the system. In 1948, the Twentieth Yearbook of the National Council of Teachers of Mathematics (Committee, 1948) was devoted to documenting the desirability of officially adopting the metric system in this country. Recent developments seem to indicate that we are well under way on the move to adoption. Smith (1974) states:

> There is no longer any doubt *whether* the United States will move to the metric system—the only question is *when*. It is time for us to look, not merely at teaching the metric system, but at the effects this move will have on teaching all mathematics (p. 1).

What does research suggest about geometry in the elementary school?

Williford (1972) has examined much of the recent research on geometry in the elementary school. Some selected summary statements from his work follow, with illustrative research citations.

1. A majority of very young children (ages 3, 4, 5) possess a variety of geometric skills involving the identification and matching of planar and solid figures, the comparison of linear measurements, and the reproduction of parallel and perpendicular segments (Rea and Reys, 1971; Brumbaugh, 1971).

2. Significantly more geometry is taught in contemporary programs than in the programs in the early half of the century at the intermediate and upper elementary levels (Neatrour, 1968). The opportunity to learn seems to provide an advantage on selected tests of achievement for students in contemporary programs (Weaver, 1966).

3. Instructional variables such as number of concrete examples of geometric concepts, opportunity for manipulative activity, use of guided discovery procedures, all seem to affect learning of geometric concepts. In general, emphasis on these variables seems to have greater impact at early grade levels than at later grade levels (Frayer, 1969; Johnson and Moser, 1971; Scott, Frayer, and Klausmeier, 1971).

4. There seems to be a significant relationship between success in geometry and general reading and mathematics achievement.

5. Various "feasibility studies" have suggested that a variety of geometric topics can be taught to elementary school children (Walter, 1969; Shah, 1969; Williford, 1970).

The elementary school teacher can be quite confident that young children possess some knowledge of various geometric concepts on entering kindergarten. Contemporary programs offer more opportunities than the traditional programs to shape, sharpen, and extend these geometric concepts. Elementary school students will vary greatly, however, in their knowledge of various geometry topics on leaving sixth grade (Schnur and Callahan, 1973). Although many studies have shed some light on the psychological question, "Can children learn certain geometric topics?" the classroom teacher is still faced with the value questions, "Should this topic be taught?" and "When?"

The problem is one of finding time to provide for geometric activities in an already crowded curriculum (Van Engen, 1973).

Can children learn the elements of mathematical logic?

Suppes and Binford (1965) investigated the teaching of mathematical logic to groups of academically talented fifth and sixth grade children. They also extended the study to include the ability of these children to transfer their learning to the reasoning involved in learning the standard school subjects, such as arithmetic, reading, and English.

For comparative purposes, two control groups of university sophomore and junior students studied the same logic textbook. The university students completed in four weeks the material that the children completed in one school year.

On the basis of performance on tests administered to the experimental and control groups, the authors concluded:

1. The upper quartile of elementary school students can achieve a significant conceptual and technical mastery of elementary mathematical logic. The level of mastery attained by the children was 85 to 90 percent of that attained by the university students.

2. The level of achievement can be acquired in an amount of study time comparable to that needed by college students if the study time for the children is distributed over a longer period of time and if they receive considerably greater amounts of direct teacher supervision.

3. There was anecdotal evidence from teachers which suggested that there was some transfer of the learning in the form of increased critical thinking in such subjects as arithmetic, reading, and English (p. 194).

Smith (1966) reported a critical analysis of the study, and Suppes (1967a) presented a reply to Smith's analysis.

Shapiro and O'Brien (1970) replicated parts of, and extended, an earlier study by Hill (1960) which had used sentential logic, classical syllogism, and logic of quantification. It had been found that children at early grade levels could discriminate between a necessary conclusion and its negation. Shapiro and O'Brien's study generally confirmed Hill's findings when similar tasks were used. However, when they included items which were somewhat "opened up," and another response category of "not enough clues" was included, a quite different growth curve was indicated. Their study suggested that meaningful hypothetical deductive thinking cannot be taken for granted in students of elementary school age. The structural form of the logic questions asked the students seemed to affect responses. This was also pointed out by Lovell (1971a) in his work on the development of mathematical proof.

Snow and Rabinovitch (1969) studied the development of conjunctive and disjunctive thinking in children at the elementary school level. They found that disjunctive tasks (red *or* square) were more difficult for children than conjunctive tasks (red *and* square). King (1966) found that disjunctive rules were harder to learn than conjunctive rules for children as well as adults. There would seem to be some aspect of disjunctive groupings that makes them more complex than conjunctive groupings.

From the selected research findings, and also the work of Piaget cited in other sections of this monograph, it would appear that the growth of formal logical reasoning ability develops quite slowly in children. Stone (1972) has remarked:

As far as the school curriculum is concerned, it is evident that only quite elementary topics of logic can be taken up, but some of these can be taught even in the elementary school . . . while others are thought by many experienced teachers to be unsuitable before grades 10 and 11 at the earliest (p. 223).

He goes on to point out:

The most difficult problems in teaching logic as part of the school curriculum are the pedagogical and psychological ones. This is an area in which we need not only intensified discussion, but also much additional experimentation and theoretical analysis. It is in the early stages of the educational process that we are most seriously hampered by our comparative ignorance of the relevant basic psychological factors (p. 224).

Do summer educational programs for the disadvantaged succeed?

Little "hard" evidence is available regarding this question. Shortly after the beginning of federal support of such programs, a report (Coleman and others, 1966) summarized some qualitative observations of a group of 27 consultants who visited a sample of 86 school districts in 48 states, including almost all the nation's major cities.

The personal observations of the consultants are summarized as follows:

1. The single most widespread achievement of the Title I program is that it is causing teachers and administrators to focus new thinking on ways to overcome educational deprivation. . . . For the most part, however, projects are piecemeal, fragmented efforts at remediation or vaguely directed "enrichment." It is extremely rare to find strategically planned, comprehensive programs for change. . . .

2. In distinguishing those classrooms that favorably impressed consultants from those that appeared poor, the explanatory factor most frequently observed was the difference in the quality of relationship—the rapport—between teacher and child.

3. . . . there was frequent lack of involvement of teachers in the formulation of programs they are expected to carry out.

4. One of the most disappointing findings was the failure of most schools to identify and attract the most seriously disadvantaged children.

5. Frequently, heavy purchases of educational equipment are made without examining the educational practices that underlie their use.

Austin, Rogers, and Walbesser (1972) have more recently attempted to review the evidence that has accumulated from the Summer Compensatory Education Program component of Title I of the Elementary and Secondary Education Act of 1965.

The reviewers reached the following conclusions:

1. Summer Compensatory Education programs in elementary mathematics, reading, and language communication have generally shown modest achievement gains. However, since no randomly formed control groups were used, "maturation" remains the threat to the validity of the studies. Further, no data were found to demonstrate whether these gains persist over time.

2. Students reported an increased desire to attend school and learn the cognitive skills. However, no data were reported to indicate if those behavior changes were observable during the school year.

3. While the average amount of federal money spent per child during the summer is approximately equal to the amount of federal money spent per child during the regular school year, there are, at present, no data to compare the programs in terms of student gains.

4. Few objective measures have been used to measure the possible range of student accomplishment. Even when objective measures were used, the unavailability of a control group jeopardizes the interpretation of the results.

5. Relatively few of the programs had behaviorally stated objectives at the outset of the programs to provide direction for evaluation activities.

6. Many of the projects claimed to have been funded too late to allow the implementation of their proposed evaluation procedures (p. 179).

What was learned about achievement in mathematics from the International Study?

Since the third (1968) edition of this monograph, much has been written about the results of the International Study of Achievement in Mathematics (Husén, 1967). Although the study was never intended to be a contest and was not undertaken as a head-to-head competition on achievement test performance between the participating countries, that was often the form reported in the news media of this country. With the mass of data analyzed, and available for analysis, more questions tend to be generated than answered. How the United States fared, and will fare as analysis continues, is often a matter of subjective interpretation. As Featherstone (1974) has suggested, "It is not the research itself, but the *Zeitgeist* that is mainly responsible for how particular findings get interpreted, emphasized, and acted upon" (p. 450).

The overall aim of the project was to compare, with the aid of psychometric techniques, outcomes in different educational systems. T. N. Postlethwaite (1971), executive director of IEA, has presented a general summary statement of the mathematics study in a special issue of the *Journal for Research in Mathematics Education*. Various critiques, analyses, and statements about implications are also included in the issue. Some "Main Results" cited by Postlethwaite follow:

1. Changing the age of entry to school is likely to make no substantial change in mathematics score. Those countries that had an entry age of 5 produced poorer scores in mathematics at age 13 than did countries with an entrance age of 6. Delaying the age of entry to 7 was associated with even lower scores at 13, but the whole pattern suggested that the important variable was not the age of entry.

2. Class size data were conflicting. At the higher levels, smaller classes were associated with superior attainments. At the lower levels, the trend was reversed. There were so many complicating factors in this study that it was almost impossible to separate out the effect of class size from the others, especially since most of them were not under control. It is, at any rate, apparent that merely reducing the size of classes is not likely to increase mathematical attainment significantly.

3. The main difference among countries taking part in the IEA study was in the use made of specialized schools as contrasted with comprehensive schools. Thirteen-year-old students following academic courses in specialized schools attained a higher level than did students following similar courses in comprehensive schools. On the other hand, 13-year-old students following

general courses did better in comprehensive schools than did students following similar courses in schools not containing academic pupils.

4. Retentivity of the school system generally affected achievement scores. Countries retaining higher proportions of an age group showed lower scores where the pre-university population of students was concerned. This appeared to be due not to a lowering of the standards of the best students, but rather to a dipping into lower levels of ability to provide the additional students. "More means worse" only in the sense that the average score of the expanded group is likely to be lower than that of the original smaller group. From the evidence of this inquiry it does not seem likely that the mathematical attainments of the most able students will be affected; on the contrary, the total yield of advanced students is likely to be increased.

5. The coefficients of correlation between achievement and attitudes were small in general. Achievement in mathematics was positively, but weakly, correlated with student belief about the importance of mathematics to society. Achievement scores tended to correlate negatively with attitude toward mathematics as a process and toward the difficulty of learning mathematics. The negative coefficients between achievement and the belief that mathematics is an "open" system occurred in both the younger and older populations.

6. In general, the data suggested that the more training a teacher has received, the better will be the achievement of his students, but this does not hold in all cases.

7. Student's opportunity to learn and achievement were quite highly correlated. One would expect these correlations to be high because the simplest and most plausible explanation of the wide range between countries is variation in the extent to which national curricula provided the student with opportunities to learn the types of materials covered in the test. The question remains as to why certain countries do not introduce particular topics into the curriculum until, for example, the age of 15, when in other countries 13-year-old students are demonstrating adequate performance on these topics.

8. Socioeconomic variability was studied by grouping schools according to whether they were composed of the whole gamut of socioeconomic groups or only narrow ranges of socioeconomic groups. In general, it would seem that students from every occupational group profit more from being in schools with some variability than from being in schools with little variability in social class.

9. The possible difference in sociocultural forces on sex and their impact on mathematics achievement was explored. In each population boys scored higher than girls even when the factors had been held constant. This was true for verbal and computational problems as well as total score. The pooled data suggested that where the learning conditions are more similar, the differences in mathematics achievement between boys and girls will be markedly reduced. Sex differences in achievement are a within-country phenomenon. That is, although the girls of one country were lower in their mathematics achievement

than the boys of that same country, there were a number of countries where these girls were superior to the males of other countries.

How do children in the United States compare with children of other countries on mathematics achievement tests?

Data that supply evidence on this question must be examined with a great deal of caution. As pointed out by Featherstone (1974), "Mass cross-cultural survey data probably should be taken with a pinch of salt" (p. 449). It is extremely difficult to control the myriad of variables affecting mathematics achievement in order to get valid comparisons between and among different countries.

One of the first attempts to put comparative education on a scientific basis was the use of American achievement tests in Fife, Scotland, in 1934. In modest terms, the Scottish Council for Research in Education (1953) says: "The results were not unfavourable to the primary schools in Scotland." Fife "11-year-olds" were found to be 16 months ahead of American children at the same age. This substantial lead in achievement was also found to be present at 7½ years. Much of the advantage for the Fife children was attributed to admitting them to school a year or 15 months earlier than in America.

A quarter-century later, Buswell (1958) reported the results of the administration of an English-made test to approximately 3,000 children in central California. The test was administered to children in the age range of 10 years, 8 months, to 11 years, 7 months, as of the month in which the test was given. Achievement of the two groups was compared on performance of 70 items judged to be free of cultural bias. The mean scores on the total test were 29.1 for English children and 12.1 for the California children. The difference between the scores is statistically significant at well beyond the one percent level.

In a study comparing arithmetic achievement of American and Dutch children, Kramer (1957) found Dutch children in grades five and six to be significantly superior to American children on tests of arithmetic problem solving and arithmetic concepts.

Pace (1966) administered a modified form of Glennon's *Test of Basic Mathematical Understandings* to 2,692 English pupils in their sixth year of elementary education and 1,616 fifth grade pupils and 1,590 sixth grade pupils in central New York State. When age range was held comparable and both groups had the same number of years of instruction, "there was no statistically significant difference between the two groups" in their knowledge of basic arithmetic understandings.

In other studies by Bogut (1959), Thomason and Perrodin (1964), and Tracey (1959), the general findings were that English children achieve higher scores than sub-populations of U.S. children.

The IED study discussed in the preceding section presented achievement data from 12 countries at two "strategic" school levels—near the end of compulsory schooling and at the end of pre-university schooling. The U.S. 13-year-olds ranked eleventh in mathematics achievement (Husén, 1967). Sato (1968) discussed the comparative achievement of the Japanese 13-year-olds, who ranked first in achievement among the 12 countries in the IED study, and the U.S. 13-year-olds.

Dominy (1963) made an analysis of the content of representative sets of textbooks used in England, France, West Germany, the Soviet Republic, and the United States. Comparing books used up to age 11, and using 13 commonly taught topics, she found that the U.S. textbooks had a lighter content load than those books commonly used in England and France, and a heavier content load than those commonly used in West Germany and the Soviet Republic. Dominy concluded that if any alleged superiority of children in these four European countries does in fact exist, it is not possible to say that it is due mainly to more intensive or rigorous textbook programs. Also, as suggested by Featherstone (1974), "Achievement tests are a limited art form. Each culture has distinct educational aims: all cultures want much more for their children than a narrow range of skills that can be measured by achievement tests" (p. 449).

Part Two

Studies Concerning the Child

What mathematical knowledge do children have on entering school?

Brownell (1941b) compiled and analyzed the early research on this question. It was concerned with six- and seven-year-old children at time of entrance into first grade. He concluded that the following skills and concepts seem to be quite well developed by the time most children started the first grade: rote counting by ones through 20; enumeration through 20; identification of number through 10; with objects, the concepts "longest," "middle," "most," "shortest," "smallest," "tallest," "widest"; exact comparison or matching through 5; number combinations with objects to sums of 10; in verbal problems adding 1 and 2, and probably most facts with sums to 6 or 7; unit fractions through halves and fourths as applied to single objects; ordinals through "sixth"; geometric figures "circle" and "square"; telling time to the hour; recognition of all times to the half hour. Extensions of these skills and concepts as well as others were developed to quite a high degree by significant numbers of students in the various samples. The teacher interested in a further breakdown of these concepts and skills should go directly to Brownell's work.

More recent studies have focused on the skills and concepts possessed by the five-year-old when entering kindergarten. These studies by Sussman (1962), Williams (1965), Bjonerod (1960), and Dutton (1963) present some evidence that kindergartners of that time knew as much about arithmetic at the beginning of kindergarten as first grade children did some decades previously. The teacher interested in a thorough breakdown of these concepts and skills should peruse the sources cited.

The more contemporary work of Rea and Reys (1970, 1971) examined the competencies of 727 entering kindergartners in the areas of number, money, measurement, and geometry. Some selected general findings follow:

NUMBER

Numeral Identification—More than 75 percent could identify one-digit numerals; 10-13 were more difficult; less than 25 percent could identify two-digit numerals 14-21.

Sequences—More than 75 percent were able to continue the count when the cues 1, 2, 3 and 5, 6, 7 were provided. Fewer were able to respond correctly when only one number cue was given, and they were asked what came before or after. Generally, they were more competent in responding to what comes "after" than what comes "before."

Cardinal Number—Skills in counting and recognition of small groups were well developed by over 75 percent of all kindergarten entrants.

Ordinal Number—Ordinal skills seemed less developed. Less than 50 percent responded correctly to tasks requiring concepts of second, third, and fourth.

Comparisons—The majority of entrants were able to make small group comparisons.

MONEY

Identify—Over 75 percent could identify a penny, nickel, and dime. Quarter and half-dollar were more difficult. Over 50 percent identified $1.00, $5.00, and $10.00 bills.

Making Change—This was more difficult, and less than 25 percent were able to respond accurately.

MEASUREMENT

Weight—Over 75 percent were able to discriminate between size and weight.

Time—All were able to identify a clock. About 25 percent could identify 12:00 and 3:00 o'clock settings on a clock. Few could identify half-hour settings. Only about 25 percent knew the name for a calendar, but over 50 percent knew its use. Less than 25 percent knew neither day of the week and month of the year they were being tested, nor their birthday.

Linear—About 50 percent were able to identify a ruler and know its use. About 20 percent were able to use a ruler to measure the side of a card.

Temperature—Less than 25 percent could name a thermometer, but over 25 percent knew what it was used for.

GEOMETRY

Shape Matching—Over 90 percent of the children could match a shape with its illustration on paper.

Vocabulary—Over 50 percent correctly labeled square and circle. Triangle, rectangle, and diamond were less frequently labeled correctly. Correct identification of "sides" and "corners" was made by over 75 percent.

Spatial Relations—Determining number of sides or number of corners was more difficult than just identifying them. Over 75 percent could reproduce various lines in given relationship.

Those teachers interested in more specifics of the tasks and tests used in this study should consult the source (Rea and Reys, 1970). The work of Schwartz (1969) and Heard (1970) may give further insight into math concepts possessed by the five-year-old.

Brace and Nelson (1965) attempted to determine the child's understanding of number concepts as revealed by his manipulations of objects rather than by his verbalizations, since there appeared to be some difference between what the child says he knows and how much he knows about what he says. Using Piagetian-type tasks, the following selected conclusions and implications were suggested:

1. The preschool child's ability to count is not a reliable criterion of the extension to which he has developed the true concept of number.

2. Since four-fifths of the children had no knowledge of the invariance of number and tended to believe that the number of objects in a group changed when the arrangement was disturbed, it seems safe to conclude that preschool children have a very limited knowledge of the nature of cardinal number.

3. Since the concept of ordinal number contributed most to the total common variance within the sample tested and was the biggest contributor to differences, wherever significant differences were found, and further, since the relationship of this concept to counting was found to increase with age while that of cardinal number to counting decreased with age, it seems safe to conclude that the concepts of ordinal number and cardinal number do not develop concurrently as is generally believed.

4. A thorough understanding of cardinal number, ordinal number, and rational counting must be established before children are able to understand the concept of place value.

5. The sex of the child does not appear to be a factor in the early development of the concept of number.

6. Since children from homes of high socioeconomic level were significantly superior to those from homes of lower socioeconomic level in their number knowledge, it would appear that environmental factors are important in the child's development of the concept of number.

Kindergarten teachers can be quite confident that the entering student has accumulated a considerable array of mathematical skills and concepts. Since many of these have developed from their spontaneous activities during their preschool years, it could be expected that there would be a great deal of diversity in mathematical abilities. Evidence suggests that this is true; a great deal of variability exists within a group of typical kindergarten entrants. The kindergarten teacher must also be aware of the distinction between the verbalization of mathematical concepts, and performances which demonstrate the stability of these concepts.

What are some variables which may affect mathematical performance of children entering kindergarten?

Rea and Reys (1970) analyzed various subgroups of entering kindergartners on a comprehensive mathematics inventory (CMI). The variables of age, previous education, siblings, parent education, and father's

Previous Education
>   H   kindergartners who had attended Head Start
>   DC   kindergartners who had attended day care centers
>   NS   kindergartners who had attended nursery school
>   N   kindergartners who reported no formal educational experience

Age
>   Let X be the kindergartner's age in months as of September 1, 1968
>   1 $X \leq 62$
>   2 $62 < X \leq 65$
>   3 $65 < X \leq 68$
>   4 $68 < X$

Siblings
>   1   kindergartner who was only child
>   2   kindergartner who was oldest child
>   3   kindergartner who was youngest child
>   4   kindergartner who was not in one of the above groups

Father's Education
>   Let X be years of formal education reported by kindergartner's father
>   1 $3 < X \leq 8$
>   2 $8 < X < 12$
>   3 $12 \leq X < 16$
>   4 $16 \leq X$

Mother's Education
>   Let X be years of formal education reported by kindergartner's mother
>   1 $3 < X \leq 8$
>   2 $8 < X < 12$
>   3 $12 \leq X < 16$
>   4 $16 \leq X$

Father's Occupation (Modified Warner Scale)
>   1   Classic professions such as physicians, dentists, professors, executives, business owners, etc.
>   2   High skilled workers and professions such as teachers, nurses, managers, etc.
>   3   Low or unskilled workers such as clerks, repairmen, secretaries, etc.
>   4   Unemployed or on relief

The Arithmetic Teacher, January 1970; p. 68.

Figure 1. Student Category Codes

occupation were considered. A table of codes for the various breakdowns of students within each category is shown in Figure 1.

A table summarizing the mean scores for various subgroups of kindergartners assessed by the CMI is presented in Figure 2.

	Money	Number	Vocabulary	Geometry
Previous education	M_H = 8.73	M_H = 16.20	M_H = 20.82	M_H = 24.08
	M_{DC} = 10.14	M_{DC} = 24.71	M_N = 22.91	M_N = 27.40
	M_N = 10.59	M_N = 25.24	M_{DC} = 23.71	M_{DC} = 29.57
	M_{NS} = 11.96	M_{NS} = 32.97	M_{NS} = 24.35	M_{NS} = 30.25
Age	M_1 = 9.53	M_1 = 22.80	M_1 = 22.46	M_1 = 26.63
	M_2 = 10.02	M_2 = 23.95	M_2 = 22.73	M_2 = 27.23
	M_3 = 11.62	M_3 = 28.74	M_3 = 23.77	M_3 = 28.53
	M_4 = 12.00	M_4 = 30.53	M_4 = 23.57	M_4 = 28.80
Father's education	M_2 = 10.02	M_2 = 21.25	M_2 = 21.61	M_2 = 26.69
	M_3 = 10.33	M_1 = 24.92	M_1 = 22.61	M_1 = 27.04
	M_1 = 10.58	M_3 = 25.86	M_3 = 23.24	M_3 = 27.73
	M_4 = 12.54	M_4 = 33.59	M_1 = 24.54	M_4 = 29.80
Mother's education	M_2 = 9.39	M_2 = 19.49	M_2 = 21.14	M_2 = 25.60
	M_1 = 10.76	M_1 = 26.11	M_1 = 22.91	M_1 = 27.56
	M_3 = 10.86	M_3 = 26.95	M_3 = 23.48	M_3 = 28.08
	M_4 = 12.74	M_4 = 36.57	M_4 = 24.66	M_4 = 30.28
Father's occupation	M_4 = 8.79	M_4 = 17.07	M_4 = 20.66	M_4 = 24.17
	M_3 = 10.44	M_3 = 24.89	M_3 = 22.82	M_3 = 27.23
	M_2 = 11.32	M_2 = 29.44	M_2 = 23.88	M_2 = 28.88
	M_1 = 12.10	M_1 = 34.06	M_1 = 24.22	M_1 = 29.85

	P.I.	Measurement	Recall	Total
Previous education	M_H = 2.82	M_H = 11.42	M_H = 10.20	M_H = 93.25
	M_{DC} = 3.00	M_{DC} = 13.00	M_N = 12.79	M_N = 115.59
	M_N = 3.62	M_N = 13.95	M_{DC} = 13.57	M_{DC} = 116.71
	M_{NS} = 4.37	M_{NS} = 17.72	M_{NS} = 14.37	M_{NS} = 134.98
Age	M_1 = 3.31	M_1 = 12.66	M_1 = 12.19	M_1 = 108.46
	M_2 = 3.46	M_2 = 13.90	M_2 = 12.36	M_2 = 112.74
	M_3 = 3.56	M_3 = 15.79	M_3 = 13.54	M_3 = 124.77
	M_4 = 4.26	M_4 = 15.89	M_4 = 13.94	M_4 = 128.09
Father's education	M_1 = 3.35	M_2 = 12.34	M_2 = 11.89	M_2 = 106.35
	M_2 = 3.56	M_1 = 13.88	M_1 = 12.62	M_1 = 114.04
	M_3 = 3.60	M_3 = 13.94	M_3 = 13.01	M_3 = 116.74
	M_4 = 4.38	M_4 = 18.12	M_4 = 14.31	M_4 = 136.49
Mother's education	M_1 = 3.41	M_2 = 11.63	M_2 = 11.56	M_2 = 100.98
	M_2 = 3.45	M_1 = 14.24	M_1 = 12.64	M_1 = 116.78
	M_3 = 3.69	M_3 = 14.71	M_3 = 13.26	M_3 = 120.14
	M_4 = 4.78	M_4 = 19.09	M_4 = 14.98	M_4 = 142.09
Father's occupation	M_4 = 2.45	M_4 = 11.07	M_4 = 11.03	M_4 = 94.24
	M_3 = 3.60	M_3 = 13.67	M_3 = 12.65	M_3 = 114.40
	M_2 = 3.64	M_2 = 15.84	M_2 = 13.77	M_2 = 125.87
	M_1 = 4.66	M_1 = 17.74	M_1 = 14.19	M_1 = 135.75

The Arithmetic Teacher, January 1970; p. 71.

Figure 2. Summary of Means for Entering Kindergartners Assessed by CMI

Some general observations from the data include:

Age: Older kindergarten entrants tend to reflect a higher level of achievement than the younger entrants.

Previous education: Entrants with nursery school experience tend to reflect a higher level of achievement than those with no formal experience, or those with child care or Head Start experience.

Parent education: Kindergartners whose father or mother had 16 or more years of formal education tend to reflect a higher level of achievement than those with parents having less education.

Father's occupation: Entrants having fathers with occupations classified as professional or highly skilled tend to reflect a higher level of achievement than those with fathers with unskilled jobs, or unemployed.

Some other general observations not shown in the summary table suggest that sibling relationships did not significantly affect achievement on the CMI, and that girls may tend to perform better than boys on some, but not all, of the subtest areas.

What is the sequence of development of early number behaviors?

Piaget's theoretical work on the development of logical processes in the child has been discussed in Part One of this monograph. The present question focuses on more specific counting and enumeration behaviors of the young child.

Wohlwill (1960) studied the developmental process of 72 children ranging in age from 4:0 to 7:0. A training series and seven tests were administered as part of the experiment. The hypothesized order of difficulty of the seven test tasks, and a brief description, follow:

A. *Abstraction.* The choice and sample cards varied in number (2-4), form (square, circle, triangle), and color (green, red, blue) in such a way that any given sample card matched each choice card on only one of the three dimensions.

B. *Elimination of perceptual cues.* The choice cards were those of the training series while the sample cards contained rectangles drawn in outline and divided into two, three, or four equal adjacent squares.

C. *Memory.* The subject matched the training stimulus card to the position of the corresponding choice stimulus of the training series when the latter was removed from view.

D. *Extension.* The choice cards, as well as the sample cards, contained six, seven, or eight dots in varying configurations.

E. *Conservation of number.* The child correctly matched the number of buttons with the choice cards of Test D, assisted if necessary by the examiner. The examiner then scrambled the configuration of the sample while the subject watched. The subject was asked to match the rearranged sample with the choice cards.

F. *Addition and subtraction.* Test F differed in that while the child watched, a button was added or subtracted from the collection immediately following the configurational match, and the subject was asked to match the new set with the correct choice card.

G. *Ordinal-cardinal correspondence.* The subject was asked to match a sample card containing eight solid bars of increasing length, one of which was colored red to signify the cue-bar, with the training series choice cards.

The results showed only two discrepancies from the hypothesized order. Test B was passed by slightly more children than Test A, and subjects scored higher on Test F than on Tests D and E. A scalogram analysis—a technique for determining whether a sequence of tasks is such that the mastery of any given item presupposes success on all easier items—was carried out.

Wohlwill felt that the tests did not represent a series of fixed and equally distinctive steps on the developmental scale. Rather, he suggested that the developmental process could be more adequately described in three fairly discrete phases: (a) Number is responded to wholly on a perceptual basis. (b) Perceptual support is reduced as mediating structures, that is, the internalized symbols representing the numbers, are developed. (c) The relationship among the individual numbers is conceptualized, leading to such understandings as conservation and cardinality-ordinality.

Potter and Levy (1968) examined the development of one component of counting, itemizing a group exhaustively without repetition. The two major concerns of the study were to discover the age (between two and five) at which the enumerating skill develops and to determine the effects of some informational variables on attainment. In regard to the latter, spatial arrangements of items to be processed were varied. Some were presented in a single horizontal row; some were regularly spaced in rows and columns; some were randomly arranged. Meaningfulness of items, pictured objects versus geometric shapes, was also varied.

Results suggested that with five, six, or nine items, one-dimensional arrangements are easier than two-dimensional arrangements. Within the two-dimensional arrangements, the random array tended to be easier than the orderly one, although this tended to vary with age—the older children found the orderly two-dimensional arrangement relatively easy. There was no consistent difference between the meaningfulness of the two types of items (pictures versus shapes). It was found that the capacity to hold in mind an array of items that one has enumerated shows a steady and dramatic increase in the age range of 2½ to 4 years.

Wang, Resnick, and Boozer (1971) examined three classes of early mathematical behaviors: (a) counting objects, (b) using numerals, and (c) comparison of set size. These mathematical behaviors were analyzed and ordered into hypothesized hierarchies of successively more complex learning tasks. The validity of the hypothesized hierarchy of tasks composing the behaviors was then empirically tested. The hypothesized hierarchy of tasks was confirmed for only one of the three behaviors, using numerals. The data suggested that command over numerals is acquired in a regular sequence, beginning with perceptual matching of the numerals and concluding with the association of sets and numerals. Regarding relationship among classes of behavior, the data suggested that numerals are learned only after counting operations for sets of the size represented by the numerals are well established. The data were unclear with respect to the relationships among the concepts "same," "more," and "less."

D'Mello and Willemsen (1969) studied the order of acquisition of four number tasks. Their data suggested a sequence of rote counting, matching sets with identical physical arrangements, counting a set of specified size, and matching a numeral with a set.

Uprichard (1970) attempted to determine the most efficient instructional sequence through which preschoolers acquire the set relations "equivalence," "greater than," and "less than." Some selected results from the data suggest: (a) the most efficient instructional sequence appears to be "equivalence," "greater than," "less than"; (b) the "less than" relationship is not difficult for preschoolers to learn after they have acquired "equivalence" and "greater than" relationships; and (c) there appears to be a hierarchical relationship among the three set relations.

The complexity of number behavior makes it very difficult to determine a sequence of early number concept development. Rote counting, the ability to touch each item in a set once and only once, and the ability to coordinate these two behaviors are necessary conditions for rational counting. Proficiency with these behaviors seems to increase quite dramatically with age between two and five years. Perceptual arrangement of the items to be enumerated seems to influence counting ability. It would appear that meaningful use of numerals emerges after facility in counting is established. Data on the development of "equivalent," "greater than," and "less than" relations between sets are not consistent. It was interesting to note from the Wang *et al.* (1971) data that although one-to-one correspondence ability is a logical prerequisite to rational counting behavior, the two may be psychologically independent with respect to sequence of acquisition.

What contributes to readiness in learning mathematics?

Various factors, no doubt, contribute to the readiness of a student to learn. The complex interaction of these factors makes it unrealistic to think in mutually exclusive classes of students who are "ready" and "not ready." Swenson (1951) has suggested that to only the uninitiated could readiness appear to be a simple matter of reaching some mythical magical point before which the learner is clearly not ready, and following which he is clearly ready.

Another false dichotomy in the area of readiness of a student to learn involves those educators who would only allow "nature" to take its course in readying children for optimal learning, and those who would only allow for environmental "nurturing" to contribute to learning readiness. Factors of "nature" and "nurture" interact in contributing to a student's optimal readiness to learn mathematics.

One factor that probably contributes to readiness for optimal meaningful learning is prior related subject matter that has been learned. Gagné (1970) has pointed out the importance of order of acquiring subordinate knowledges in a knowledge hierarchy. Brownell (1951) earlier pointed out the difficulties students experience when they do not possess appropriate skills and facts prerequisite to a process.

Physical and mental maturity may be another factor in readiness to learn. The extensive contributions of Piaget to understanding the various stages in intellectual maturity have been examined in Part One of this monograph. Physical maturity and neurological development which contribute to such senses as sight and hearing, so important to learning mathematics, are also considerations in readiness to learn. The importance of physical and neurological development to readiness has been pointed out by such researchers as Ilg and Ames (1964). Ogletree (1974) has incorporated various indicators of "stages" in physical and mental maturing into a theory of "bioplasmic forces." He argues that premature formal instruction will rob the physical body of the growth forces needed to develop the brain to its fullest potential, and may contribute to later frustration and anxiety in learning.

Affective factors and emotional maturity may also contribute to optimal readiness for learning. Questions dealing with the role of attitudes, anxiety, and emotional disturbance are discussed separately within this section of the monograph.

The elementary school teacher can feel quite confident that an awareness for readiness will facilitate learning at all grade levels, not only the primary grades. This awareness should include students' subject-matter readiness, that is, their prerequisite subordinate knowledge; their physical and mental maturity; their emotional maturity; and also their willingness, or commitment, to learn mathematics.

Does cultural deprivation have a lasting effect on mathematics achievement?

The tendency has been to describe the achievement of culturally deprived children in terms of their deviance from the norms of children from the homes of middle class parents. In general, this deviance from the norms increases as the culturally deprived children progress through the grades. Deutsch (1965) has labeled this the "cumulative deficit phenomenon." In regard to this phenomenon, he indicated that it would appear that when one adds a number of years of school experience to a poor environment, plus minority group status, what emerge are children who are apparently less capable of handling standard intellectual and linguistic tasks.

Various studies (Callahan, 1962; Unkel, 1966; Passy, 1964; Montague, 1964) have suggested that children from deprived socioeconomic backgrounds do not perform as well on various mathematical tasks as do the more advantaged socioeconomic children. There appears to be great variability in performance within each group, however.

Dunkley (1965, 1972) reports results that indicate that pupils from deprived backgrounds are not initially prepared to move at the same pace as middle class children in learning mathematics, and many have not reached the same level of cognitive development. Even if teachers allow extra time for mathematics, the task of overcoming the initial lack of experiences that facilitate learning is still extremely difficult.

Ausubel (1964) in discussing this problem lists some of the effects of a culturally deprived climate. They include: (a) poor perceptual discrimination skills; (b) inability to use adults as sources of information, correction, and reality testing, and as instruments for satisfying curiosity; (c) an impoverished language-symbolic system; (d) a paucity of information, concepts, and related propositions.

The retarded language development of the lower socioeconomic child has been pointed out by Deutsch (1965). An important consequence of this retardation in language development is the student's slower and less complete transition from concrete to abstract modes of thought and understanding. Prehm (1966) found that verbal pretraining on a conceptual learning task significantly affected the performance efficiency of culturally disadvantaged children. He concluded that both attention to the pertinent aspects of a stimulus situation and verbalization have a positive effect on conceptual performance.

Ausubel (1964) stated that effective and appropriate teaching strategies for the culturally deprived child must emphasize these three considerations:

1. The selection of initial learning material geared to the learner's existing state of readiness

2. Mastery and consolidation of all ongoing learning tasks before new tasks are introduced so as to provide the necessary foundation for successful sequential learning and to prevent unreadiness for future learning tasks

3. The use of structural learning materials optimally organized to facilitate efficient sequential learning (p. 27).

Do ethnic groups differ in patterns of mental abilities such as number facility and space conceptualization?

Stodolsky and Lesser (1967) studied this question as part of a larger concern for finding ways to maximize the learning of disadvantaged children. They studied the patterns of four mental abilities (Verbal Ability, Reasoning, Number Facility, and Space Conceptualization) in six- and seven-year-old children from different social-class and ethnic

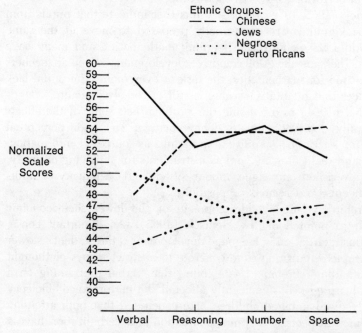

Figure 3. Pattern of Normalized Mental-Ability Scores for Each Ethnic Group

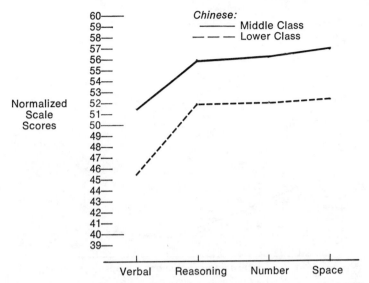

Figure 4. Patterns of Normalized Mental-Ability Scores for Middle- and Lower-Class Chinese Children

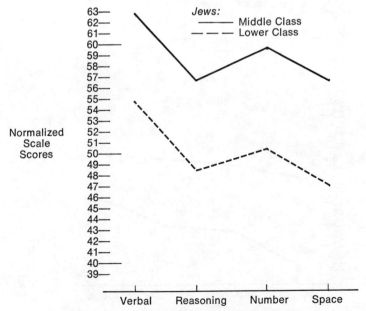

Figure 5. Patterns of Normalized Mental-Ability Scores for Middle- and Lower-Class Jewish Children

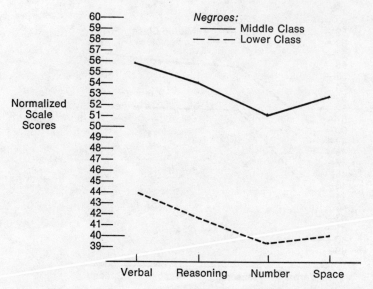

Figure 6. Patterns of Normalized Mental-Ability Scores for Middle- and
Lower-Class Negro Children

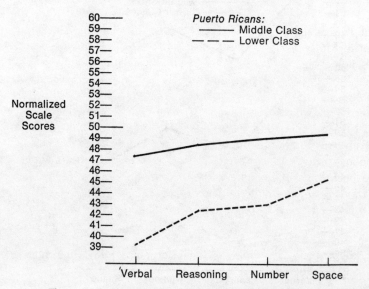

Figure 7. Patterns of Normalized Mental-Ability Scores for Middle- and
Lower-Class Puerto Rican Children

backgrounds—Chinese, Jews, Negroes, and Puerto Ricans. Since the latter two mental abilities are mathematical, their findings are of interest to mathematics education researchers.

. . . the most striking results of this study concern the effects of ethnicity upon the *patterns* among the mental abilities. [Figure 3] shows that these patterns are different for each ethnic group. More important is the finding depicted in [Figures 4-7]. Ethnicity does affect the pattern of mental abilities *and, once the pattern specific to the ethnic group emerges, social-class variations within the ethnic group do not alter this basic organization* (p. 567).

Since it seems to be clearly established that ethnic groups differ in patterns of ability no matter what the social-class level within the ethnic group, providing equal educational opportunity in learning mathematics means teaching to the *strengths* of each ethnic group—"even at the expense of magnifying the differences among the groups" (p. 588).

Perhaps, for the children who are higher in number ability and space conceptualization, the teacher should develop, say, the addition facts through geometric activities; while for the children whose strength is in verbal ability, the teacher might make greater use of verbal learning experiences.

Does the age at which a child enters first grade have an effect on subsequent achievement in elementary school mathematics?

One of the relationships examined in the International Study of Achievement in Mathematics was that between school entrance age and mathematics achievement of 13-year-olds. It was reported that school entrance age bore little relationship to mathematics achievement at age 13, although students entering at six tended to be somewhat superior to those entering at either five or seven (Husén, Volume II, 1967).

Shah (1971) examined the test given to the 13-year-old students in the study and suggested the more restricted conclusion that "entering school at the age of five, six, or seven does not have any significant influence on the performance of the given test at age 13." The point was made that the nature of the test given at age 13 did not necessarily reflect the process-oriented type of math instruction given to children at ages five through seven.

From a cluster of more restricted studies (Baer, 1958; M. L. Carroll, 1963; Carter, 1956; Dickenson and Larson, 1963; Gott, 1963; Ilika, 1963) the data suggested that:

1. The chronologically older child appears to have the advantage

in arithmetic achievement (as measured by standardized tests) over the younger child when given the same school experience.

2. In general, chronological age may have more effect on the academic achievement of boys than on that of girls.

Although the research on this question is not always consistent, the teacher should be aware that chronological age can be a factor in successful, or unsuccessful, achievement. This seems to be especially true if the school makes no accommodation for this age factor. It may be that the chronological age factor is more important for boys than girls. From the evidence it would seem that a child of average or below average intellectual aptitude has an increasingly better chance of achieving satisfactory progress through the grades the older (within the typical range for entrance) he or she is.

Are there differences in achievement in elementary school mathematics between boys and girls?

Fennema (1974) reviewed 36 studies in seeking some clarification on this general question. The previous edition of this monograph, as well as other reviews of research (Garai and Scheinfell, 1968; Suydam and Weaver, 1970), examined some of the data accumulated on the issue and generally reported higher performance by boys than by girls. This difference in the performance data is more apt to appear at the upper elementary level and beyond than at the lower elementary school level. There also may tend to be a differential impact on performance depending on the nature of the mathematical task. The tendency is for girls to do slightly better than the boys on the low level cognitive tasks; the boys tend to do better on the higher cognitive tasks (Carry and Weaver, 1969; Jarvis, 1964).

The gradual emergence of these differences, if they in fact exist, may suggest the impact of an acculturation process. There still may exist many subtle "presses" from the environment that may affect mathematics performance of boys and girls differently. The extent of such impact is suggested from the results of the International Study of Achievement. Husén (1967) reported that the mathematics achievement of males was higher than that of females at the secondary school level in all 12 countries which were studied. He attributed these differences in mathematics achievement to cultural rather than any innate factors.

Fennema is probably quite accurate in concluding that the research on this issue may raise more questions than it answers. Any attempt at unraveling the reason(s) for the possible differential in performance on mathematical tasks between boys and girls is going to require a careful consideration and control of complex environmental variables as well as various personality and organismic variables.

What is known about learning disabilities in elementary mathematics?

The general area of learning disabilities is a difficult one to circumscribe and describe. In a broad sense a person can be classed as learning disabled if a central mental processing disfunction exists which acts as a restriction to attaining full learning potential. Not a great deal is known about the nature and severity of learning disabilities in arithmetic and mathematics. Chalfant and Scheffelin (1969) discuss some reasons for this limited knowledge. Learning disabilities in mathematics may often be associated with difficulties in other areas of the school curriculum. Cohn (1971) indicates that there seem to be quite precise parallels between mathematical achievement and other types of symbol operations.

Following are symptoms and descriptions of disabilities in mathematics taken from some of the literature (Cohn, 1961; Critchley, 1970; Frostig and Maslow, 1973; Johnson and Myklebust, 1967; Kaliski, 1967):

Disturbed horizontal positioning of number sequences

Disarray of the vertical alignment of numbers

Transposition of numbers, 13 for 31

Auditory memory problems—frustration in oral drills

Visual-spatial organization; difficulty in quickly distinguishing difference in shapes, sizes, amounts, or lengths

Difficulty in learning motor patterns for writing numbers

Inability to quickly identify the number of objects in a group

Difficulty in perception of sequences and patterns

Perseveration; practice or drill on one process makes transfer to another process difficult.

Following are some general observations, suggestions, and hints for teaching the learning disabled taken from various sources (Cruickshank, Bentzen, Ratzeburg, and Tannhauser, 1961; Frostig and Maslow, 1973; Johnson and Myklebust, 1967; Kaliski, 1967):

No matter how old the hyperactive child, he should be started at the beginning, both to get a new approach to numbers and to be sure he has a workable number concept.

Mathematics needs to be taught through body movement and manipulation of objects so that it can be understood as denoting change or pertaining to process.

Counting must be mastered because so many math skills are based on counting.

Failure to count properly may result from an inability to establish a one-to-one correspondence; to maintain the auditory series of numerals; or to associate the symbol with the quantity. Instruction should attempt to integrate these facets.

Concrete materials should be used to facilitate numerical thinking.

In contrast to normal children, these students cannot be given manipulative materials and be expected to make generalizations about quantity or size; these relationships must be specifically taught.

The use of fingers for counting and computing should not be discouraged.

The language of arithmetic should be given considerable attention.

Is there a relationship between emotional disturbance in students and arithmetic disability?

Tamkin (1960), using chronological age as the criterion, found arithmetic scores of children receiving residential treatment for emotional disorders were not below expected grade level. Graubard (1964) studied 21 children receiving residential psychiatric treatment. Using mental age as a criterion, none of the subjects was at the expected achievement level in arithmetic computation. Stone and Rowley (1964) used mental age as well as chronological age in their study. The level of achievement in arithmetic was not commensurate with either the mental or chronological age. Feldhusen, Thurston, and Benning (1970) studied achievement of students who exhibited aggressive classroom behavior. Their achievement in mathematics was generally significantly lower than for socially approved groups.

In studies that compared the relative achievement in arithmetic and reading, the results tend to be inconsistent. Glavin and Annesley (1971), using a sample of 130 boys, found significantly higher arithmetic scores than reading scores. Tamkin (1960) and Stone and Rowley (1964) both found arithmetic achievement to be lower than reading achievement.

Schroeder (1965) studied groups of children classified into five categories of emotional disturbance in an attempt to find whether there are differences in school skills among groups. The categories were: (a) psychosomatic problems, (b) aggressive behavior, (c) school difficulties, (d) school phobia, and (e) neurotic-psychotic personalities. Results indicated that children who are emotionally disturbed are not one group who share the same learning characteristics, but are quite different and need various programs for treatment.

Glavin, Quay, and Werry (1971) studied academic gains of conduct-problem children in different classroom settings. Their results, from the relatively small number of pupils in the study, tended to contradict the commonly held notion that a highly structured classroom where there was emphasis on distribution of rewards for academic performance would result in "blowups." The study suggested that attention to academics results in achievement without deterioration of behavior, and, in fact, in some improvement in behavior. Follow-up study of students returned to full-time attendance in regular classes seemed to indicate that, although there had been academic and behavior gains in the structured resource rooms, the gains did not continue upon entry into regular class (Glavin, 1973).

Evidence generally suggests a definite relationship between students with emotional problems and those with arithmetic underachievement. The underachievement is often more marked in arithmetic than it is in reading. The evidence does not shed light, however, on whether arithmetic disabilities are a causal factor in emotional disorder, or vice versa. Classroom settings that are humanely structured and reward academic performance may be beneficial to the academic performance of students with emotional problems. However, the teacher should be aware that students cannot be collected into one "emotionally disturbed" class and be expected to reflect the same disabilities, or growth, under a single treatment.

What does research suggest about mathematics achievement of the blind?

Nolan (1959) administered a Braille adaptation of a standardized arithmetic test to children attending nine residential schools for the blind. Children at the third, fourth, sixth, and eighth grade levels were tested. Results indicated that significant differences in achievement in arithmetic computation existed among the nine schools, and the schools retained the same relative positions for all four grade levels of the test. A wide range of differences in achievement existed between children in the same grade. Areas of low achievement were identified at each of the four grade levels.

Blind students in residential schools seemed to show a consistent retardation in mathematics on standardized achievement tests as reported by Nolan and Ashcroft (1959) and Brothers (1972). Brothers (1973) found somewhat less retardation in mathematics achievement among public school students using Braille or large type materials. Tillman

(1969) found little difference between blind and sighted students on the arithmetic subtest of the WISC when subjects were matched by age and IQ.

As part of a survey carried out by Lewis (1970), teachers of the blind were asked to indicate some of the special problems in learning mathematics faced by visually handicapped students. The most cited problem involved the formation of concepts to permit complete understanding. Nolan (1969) has voiced some concern about the blind child in the more conceptual modern programs in mathematics. Without increased research in means of adapting such programs to the blind, there is the possibility of a decrease in the relative standing of the blind child in mathematics achievement.

What is known about the performance of deaf students in elementary mathematics?

Not a great deal of evidence is available in regard to this question. As reported by Suppes (1974), results on achievement tests tend to indicate that deaf students have a grade-placement deficit on arithmetic achievement scores relative to their chronological age. Hargis (1969) indicates that deaf children achieve close to normal levels when arithmetic skills are measured, but their arithmetic reasoning ability may reflect a deficiency in performance. The suggestion is made that this deficiency in arithmetic reasoning may be caused by a low level of language development. Suppes (1971) has stated that Computer Assisted Instruction (CAI) seems a promising area in the instruction of the deaf, especially when voice-to-voice communication is not possible.

Suppes (1974) has accumulated evidence on equivalence classes of tasks within various mathematical strands, using the CAI mode with 1,500 hearing and 800 deaf students from across the United States. When the mean percentage correct for each of the equivalence classes of tasks of the mathematical strands was plotted for both deaf and normal-hearing students, a relatively close match between curves for deaf and normal-hearing students was found. He was able to conclude that objective features of the curriculum, for example, whether a vertical addition problem has a "carry" or not, dominate the ease or difficulty of exercises in much the same way for both deaf and normal-hearing students.

Another conclusion drawn by Suppes from the data was that the performance of the deaf children is almost always slightly better than that of the normal-hearing children. The data support the thesis that the cognitive performance of deaf children is as good as that of normal-hearing children, when the cognitive task does not directly involve verbal skills in a central way. The suggestion is made that with proper organization of teaching effort, it may be possible to obtain results in arithmetic as good for deaf children as we do for average to slightly below average normal-hearing children.

What are the learning characteristics of the educable mentally retarded in mathematics?

Various researchers have compiled characteristics of mentally retarded students in mathematics (Cruickshank, 1946; Thresher, 1962; Burns, 1962; Noffsinger and Dobbs, 1970). Connally (1973) has recently reviewed much of the research in the area and concluded that it strongly implies that the mentally retarded perform best on computation and functional areas of arithmetic, display definite weakness in those areas of arithmetic requiring verbal mediation, and exhibit weaknesses in work habits typified by careless computational errors, difficulty in following directions, and difficulty in organizing work.

There have been some studies carried out to examine the applicability of the sequence of development postulated by Piaget to mentally handicapped children (McManis, 1969a, 1969b, 1969c, 1970; Lister, 1970; Stephens, Manhaney, and McLaughlin, 1972). In general, it appears to hold true that the developmental sequence postulated by Piaget is also applicable to the mentally handicapped. For the most part, the achievement of mentally handicapped children on Piaget-type tasks is a function of the mental age of the children. One of the findings of Stephens *et al.* (1972) suggested that while retarded subjects do achieve success on measures of concrete thought, they do not perform successfully on tasks involving formal or abstract thought processes.

Connally (1973) pointed out that while research has documented the general mathematics performance pattern of the mentally retarded, it has not determined the extent to which this performance should be attributed to deficiencies associated with mental retardation. Partial responsibility for this performance may rest with curriculum offerings and instructional practices the mentally retarded receive. For example, Cawley (1970) has suggested that one limitation on program development has resulted from the notion that the mentally handicapped are concrete learners. Acceptance of this notion has led to a de-emphasis on development of arithmetical principles and understandings and to a concentration on the development of computational skills. He called for a comprehensive arithmetic program to be developed, tested, and validated for use throughout the school age range of educable mentally retarded students before conceding any permanence to the descriptions of the mentally handicapped in arithmetic that have been drawn from existing research.

What mathematics should we teach the mentally retarded, and how should it be taught?

Connally (1973) has suggested that a common response by teachers to the mentally retarded in the regular classroom is to give more time in working through the regular arithmetic program. He questions this approach since typically the retardate will tend to progress at the rate of approximately one half grade per year. If he is required to work progressively through regular mathematics programs, the content will soon be out of phase with his functional needs. There is a need to ensure that retarded children selectively master the essential elements of the arithmetic program.

Myen and Hieronymous (1970) investigated the importance of various cognitive skills in instructional programs for mentally handicapped children, as perceived by teachers and curriculum experts. A 204-item survey was developed and administered to 20 special class teachers and five curriculum experts for their judgment. The items on the survey were then administered to 1,405 EMH students between the ages of 9 and 18, and also to 2,187 average pupils in grades 3-8. Among the skills rated highest in importance by teachers and curriculum developers were those related to problem solving with money, measurement, and time. Those rated lowest in importance related to skills involving fractions, decimals, and the computation of averages. Of particular interest is the finding that on 162 of the total 204 items of the survey, a developmental lag of five years was observed between the retarded and the representative sample. The investigators suggested that this difference in performance is greater than should be expected in terms of intellectual limitations *per se*, and view this as a consequence of the lateness at which the judge groups recommended the teaching of the 204 items on the survey.

The developmental lag may have explanations other than lateness in curriculum presentation. Cawley and Goodman (1968) suggested that the stress on acquisition of computational facility without emphasis on problem solving, conceptual development, or numerical reasoning may explain the achievement pattern of the EMH children. Cawley and Vitello (1972) have suggested a comprehensive model for arithmetic programming for the EMH child which stresses verbal information processing as well as instructional strategies which promote conceptual development and numerical reasoning.

Armstrong and Senzig (1970) distributed a 70-item questionnaire to 300 randomly selected teachers of the mentally retarded. The questionnaire focused on the opinions of the teachers about the textbook series or curriculum they were utilizing in various areas, including arithmetic. Results pertaining to arithmetic included: (a) 90 percent were currently using their preferred mathematics series; (b) strong points of the preferred series were skill or content orientation, provision for repetition, and provision for remediation or individual differences; (c) main weaknesses were poor pacing, explanations, or transition, and lack of review or practice exercises; (d) major emphasis of texts selected by the teachers was on application skill in the four basic operations achieved through drill and practice; (e) the most important prerequisite for a reading text was that it be interesting and motivating, but few teachers listed this as a consideration for mathematics texts.

For the educable mentally retarded adolescent, much of the work in arithmetic likely should be in connection with the program of occupational education. Kirk and Johnson (1951) state that these students, in general, tend to achieve between the third and fifth grade in their arithmetic abilities. They further state that the context should be carefully chosen on the basis of two principles: (a) the content must include the knowledge, skills, and concepts that will be of most value to them now and in later life; and (b) the methods used should be determined by the special disabilities or abilities of mentally handicapped children.

Several researchers have focused on variables which may improve the verbal problem solving ability of the educable mentally handicapped. Cawley and Goodman (1968) stressed the use of manipulatives and pictorial devices in finding solutions to real problems originating in the classroom. Results of the demonstration program indicated significant improvement on verbal problem solving and on the understanding of principles for the experimental EMH group utilizing the program with trained teachers. Goodstein, Bessant, Thibodeau, Vitello, and Vlahakos (1972) found that the use of pictorial aids resulted in superior performance over the use of no pictures in verbal problem solving ability. The presence of qualitative distractors, that is, a picture not relevant to the solution of the problem, did not seem to affect performance. Some evidence exists (Penner, 1972) that the position of the distractor in the extraneous information sentence of a verbal problem may affect performance. Distractors in the subject noun position appear to be more difficult than distractors in the object noun position.

Several investigations have focused on the use of programmed instruction as a means of instructing EMH children in arithmetic

(Rainey and Kelley, 1967; C. Higgins, 1970; Price, 1963; Smith and Quackenbush, 1960). There generally was no clear and consistent advantage for the programmed approach over other approaches. However, some suggestions of benefits not directly related to final level of achievement were suggested. These benefits included higher rate of retention (C. Higgins, 1970), reduction in time required to attain skills (Price, 1963), and a reduction of negativism and hostility (Smith and Quackenbush, 1960). Bradley and Hundziak (1965) found that the subjects seemed to require additional reinforcement to that given by a teaching machine. The majority of the subjects looked at the teacher for approval after completion of each frame. It appeared as though the teacher was essential to the learning situation for the purpose of encouraging sustained attention to the task.

The teacher faced with instruction of the EMH child in mathematics should be ready to make judgments on what is considered essential to the arithmetic program. Given the essential elements, the program should reflect the appropriate developmental and practice activities that will lead to meaningful understanding. Whenever appropriate, these activities should grow out of real problems originating in the classroom or other significant student experiences. Aside from these concerns, Friedlander (1968) reminds the teacher of the mentally retarded that attention must be paid to: (a) principles of development that govern children's modes of thinking, for example, enactive, pictorial, or symbolic; (b) principles of cognitive adaptation, such as conservation, equivalence, and flexibility; and (c) factors related to visual perception, such as perceptual clarity of instructional materials.

What are some characteristics and concomitants of the mathematically gifted?

Stanley (1974) has sketched the significant systematic studies of intellectual precocity from Galton to the present. The Study of Mathematically and Scientifically Precocious Youth at Johns Hopkins University has gathered a large group of mathematically talented 12- to 14-year-olds for study in attempting to further clarify methods of identification, the nature of their abilities and interests, and the kinds of educational facilitation that may nurture their outstanding talent. The interested teacher should examine the first volume that has been completed on this study, *Mathematical Talent* (Stanley et al., 1974).

Characteristics of mathematically gifted students have been compiled by various writers (Hlavaty, 1959; Junge, 1957; Woolcock, 1961). Weaver and Brawley's (1959) may be considered as typical:

1. Sensitivity to, awareness of, and curiosity regarding quantity and the quantitative aspects of things within the environment

2. Quickness in perceiving, comprehending, understanding, and dealing effectively with quantity and quantitative aspects of things within the environment

3. Ability to think and work abstractly and symbolically when dealing with quantity and quantitative ideas

4. Ability to communicate quantitative ideas effectively to others, both orally and in writing; and to readily receive and assimilate quantitative ideas in the same way

5. Ability to perceive mathematical patterns, structures, relationships, and interrelationships

6. Ability to think and perform in quantitative situations in a flexible rather than in a stereotyped manner

7. Ability to think and reason analytically and deductively; ability to think and reason inductively and to generalize

8. Ability to transfer learning to new or novel "untaught" quantitative situations

9. Ability to apply mathematical learning to social situations, to other curriculum areas, and the like

10. Ability to remember and retain that which has been learned (pp. 6-7).

Keating (1974) has reported on some of the concomitants of mathematical precocity from the Johns Hopkins study cited in the initial paragraph of this section. In regard to liking or disliking school, he reports a general trend that indicates that gifted seventh and eighth grade students who were advanced enough to get the high scores on college-level tests reported less liking for school than gifted who do not do as well on those tests. However, some of the best students did report strong liking for school. This was another expression of the heterogeneousness of this intellectually homogeneous group of students.

He also reported that birth order as a factor in mathematical precocity did not yield significant differences for the group. There may have been some tendency for the second-born in the high group to achieve higher, but the differences did not reach statistical difference. Parents' education level was closely associated with level of achievement on the test scores for the total group. Within the higher group, the pattern was similar, but it was interesting to note that again diversity exists. For example, within the high group, 12 percent of the fathers were reported as not having a high school diploma. Vocationally, there appeared to be overwhelming interest in science-oriented careers.

In this study (Stanley *et al.*, 1974), boys appeared to be superior to the girls. Comparing the individual test scores of boys and girls, it was found that of the 223 boys, 22 percent scored at 600 or more on the SAT-MATA; of the 173 girls, only 2 percent achieved a score of 600. Not only do boys appear to achieve significantly higher scores than girls at both the seventh and eighth grade levels, but the mean discrepancies between boys and girls increase with each higher grade. Astin (1974) comments on these sex differences in mathematical and scientific precocity.

Haggard (1957), in his longitudinal study of 45 highly gifted children, made comparisons among high achievers in reading, spelling, language, and arithmetic. His findings shed light on some non-intellective factors characteristic of gifted achievers in mathematics. He writes:

The high achievers in arithmetic, those who did better on the arithmetic test than would be expected in terms of their overall level of achievement, tended to see their environment as being neither threatening nor overwhelming. Rather, they viewed it with curiosity and felt capable of mastering any problems they might encounter. In viewing their parents and other authority figures, and in their relations with them, they showed less strain than the high general achievers and the high achievers in reading, and greater independence than the high spelling achievers. Furthermore, the arithmetic achievers had by far the best-developed and the healthiest egos, both in relation to their own emotions and mental processes and in their greater maturity in dealing with the outside world of people and things.

The high arithmetic achievers could express their feelings freely and without anxiety or guilt; were emotionally controlled and flexible; and were capable of integrating their emotions, thoughts, and actions. Similarly, their intellectual processes tended to be spontaneous, flexible, assertive, and creative. Of the subgroups studied, the arithmetic achievers showed the most independence of thought, were best at maintaining contact with reality and at avoiding being bound by its constraints, and could function most effectively in the realm of abstract symbols.

In their relations with authority figures and peers, they were more assertive, independent, and self-confident than were the children in the other subgroups. Generally speaking, they related well to others, but if they felt that attempts were being made to impose undue restrictions upon them, they tended to respond with hostility and self-assertion in order to maintain their independence and autonomy of thought and action. . . .

The high achievers in arithmetic showed a cluster of personality and intellectual characteristics which are considered extremely desirable in our society. These include a healthy ego, which is relatively free from conflicts and anxieties; ability to act independently and to get along well with others; and such intellectual qualities as creativity, flexibility, and the ability to deal handily with abstract symbols and relationships (p. 397).

Lovell and Shields (1967) reported on selected aspects of a study of 50 eight- to 12-year-old pupils, all of whom obtained a WISC verbal of 140 or more. They found, as expected, advanced achievement on arithmetic tests. The mean achievement age was 3 years 7 months in advance of chronological age. However, it was interesting to note that these children had great difficulty with problems which required a schema of proportion for solution. Within the context of Piagetian intellectual development, this schema is not available to the child until the stage of formal operations. Few of these gifted students appeared to have attained this operational level, and they had difficulty responding to tasks involving logical thought.

Glennon (1963) gives a warning to teachers in their use of characteristics and factors ascertained from tests for purposes of identifying the gifted students in mathematics when he writes:

Tests . . . tend to be more oriented to the life of the middle and upper class child than to the life of the lower class child. To the degree the tests are thus oriented, they tend to discriminate against the child from the lower socioeconomic class. Hence, the teacher needs to use extra care to make sure that he does not exclude the child who is talented but whose measured intelligence and achievement scores do not clearly indicate his talent (p. 29).

Another reminder regarding the various characteristics and concomitants of the gifted child in mathematics should be underscored; that is the fact that these are not uniformly displayed by every gifted child. No teacher should expect that, because a particular child has been described as "gifted," he will possess, and engage in, all the various attributes ascribed to the gifted child.

What mathematics should be provided for the mathematically gifted child?

Two general approaches are available to the teacher desirous of providing appropriate material for the mathematically gifted student: acceleration and enrichment (Glennon, 1963). Academic acceleration focuses on the characteristic of the gifted student that suggests he can do whatever the average student can do—and do it faster. Thus, acceleration allows the gifted student to travel through the mathematics that has been judged desirable for the average elementary school student at an increased rate.

Enrichment focuses on other characteristics of the gifted student, such as his ability to see relationships, patterns, and structures of mathematical systems. Also, as Gallagher (1960) points out, enrichment would refer to those activities that stimulate productive and evaluative thinking. Thus, enrichment allows the gifted student to broaden and deepen his mathematical insight by introducing new but related topics as well as deepening insights into what is presently taught to the average elementary school student. These two general approaches need not be mutually exclusive, but can be interrelated to facilitate the overall development of the gifted student. Administrative accommodations for handling these approaches are discussed in a separate section of this monograph.

Fox (1974), in commenting on these two general approaches for facilitating educational development of the gifted, states that advocates of the enrichment procedure rarely give concrete suggestions for how this can be accomplished. The classroom teacher is left to devise the enrichment activity. In practice, then, when a student completes the assignment quickly and accurately, more of the same work at the same level is assigned. Gifted students are not challenged by such "busy work." The concept of enrichment for these students should be expanded to include the idea of increasing the depth of coverage and the degree of challenge of the work.

Regarding acceleration in relation to the seventh and eighth grade students in the Johns Hopkins Study, the conclusion was that grade skipping could meet the needs of some of the least advanced of the precocious group, and could be used in conjunction with other alternatives for the more highly advanced students.

Suppes (Suppes and Duncan, 1965; Suppes, 1966; Suppes and Ihrke, 1967, 1970) has reported on the research he is carrying out with gifted elementary school pupils. At this writing, four years of work with this group of children have been reported. Starting with 40 first graders with IQ's greater than 120, the study has continued over the years. By the fourth grade, 30 students still remained in the study. Generally, the students have used the *Sets and Numbers* series as a basic program. Each can proceed through this program at an individual rate. In addition to these activities, each student has short daily paper and pencil drills, or daily work at the remote terminal on appropriate drill and practice programs.

Each year great diversity and variation are reflected in the acquisition and error rates of the participants on the tasks where students are free to proceed at their own rate. It is not unusual for the top student to have completed five or six times more work than the bottom student. Typically, error rates are lower for those students who complete more tasks.

There is some evidence (Sears, Katz, and Soderstrum, 1966) to indicate that the accelerated group did significantly better on standardized achievement tests than a control group. This result would suggest that the accelerated group is not falling behind in the regular mathematics curriculum, even though a good deal of their mathematics curriculum time is spent on the special enrichment topics.

Other studies (Jacobs, Beery, and Lernwohl, 1965; Mullins, 1958) have used enrichment procedures or some combination of enrichment and acceleration, in attempting to provide for the gifted student in mathematics.

The illustrative commentary and citations of research studies suggest that gifted students can handle more complex and abstract mathematics and also can learn much faster than the typical student. Some extremely precocious upper elementary students score as well as bright college freshmen on tests of mathematics and science achievement. This suggests that much independent study has already taken place. As Gallagher (1960) points out, independence appears to be a particularly differentiating feature of gifted children. It would seem imperative that elementary school teachers develop a repertoire of student mathematics experiences that will accommodate the speed, breadth, and depth of ability that are the mark of the mathematically talented. For the very gifted, this may mean providing the time to take on accelerated programs, including courses at the high school or college level.

Do elementary school students have definite and stable attitudes about school mathematics?

Some studies have been carried out which ask children to indicate their likes or dislikes for school subjects. The reactions of the children are usually construed as indications of positive or negative attitudes toward a particular subject in relation to other subjects taught in the elementary schools. These studies have generally indicated that the students will cluster on either end of the "like"-"dislike" dimension in regard to elementary school mathematics, with relatively few having neutral feelings about the subject.

Sister Josephina (1959) asked 900 fifth, sixth, seventh, and eighth graders to select their three best-liked and three least-liked school subjects. When the subjects were ranked as to number of indications by students as "best-liked," arithmetic was ranked in the top three at each grade level. When the school subjects were ranked as to number of indications by students as "least-liked," arithmetic also ranked in the top three. In a similar study of fourth, fifth, and sixth graders in California, Rowland and Inskeep (1963) found arithmetic to be ranked first in indications by students as to the subject liked most; arithmetic ranked fifth (out of 10 subjects) in indications by students as to the subject disliked most. Arithmetic was last in a ranking of school subjects that had not been indicated by students in their indications of "likes" and "dislikes."

Faust (1962), in studying more than 2,500 upper elementary school students from Iowa, found that pupils prefer the "skill subjects" in the following order: arithmetic, reading, spelling, and language. In a more limited study, Fedon (1958) found definite positive attitudes toward elementary school mathematics were being expressed by some students, and definite negative attitudes were being expressed by other students, as early as the third grade. W. J. Callahan (1971) found that when 366 eighth grade students were asked to estimate their general feeling toward mathematics, about 20 percent tended to dislike mathematics and 62 percent tended to like it. About 18 percent were neutral in their feeling.

The work of Anttonen (1969) gives some insight into the stability of student attitudes toward mathematics over a period of time. The period extended from the fifth and sixth grade to the eleventh and twelfth grade. More than 600 students were included in the study. The obtained correlation between early and late mathematics attitude scores was 0.305. Thus, there appeared to be an overall low positive relationship between early and late mathematics attitude scores.

Trends in student attitudes about mathematics do not reflect a particularly optimistic picture. Examination of data from various sources (Anttonen, 1969; Ryan, 1968; Neale and Proshek, 1967; Neale, Gill, and Tismer, 1970) led Neale (1969) to conclude that, although questions may be raised about the generality of these findings and about the interpretation of the declining scores, it is at least fair to hypothesize that current school programs result in a substantial decline in the favorableness of attitudes toward learning mathematics as children progress through school.

Dutton (1956) found that grades five and six were the most crucial in the development of attitudes. W. J. Callahan (1971) found that students felt their attitudes for mathematics developed at each grade level; however, grades six and seven were given as the most important for developing attitudes.

The various studies cited would suggest that elementary school students have quite definite feelings, both positive and negative, about mathematics. These attitudes at early grade levels may not be particularly stable since they do not appear to correlate highly with later attitude scores. The upper elementary and middle school grade levels appear to be an important time in the development of lasting attitudes about mathematics. In general, studies would indicate a decline in favorable attitudes about mathematics as students continue in school.

Are attitudes toward elementary school mathematics related to achievement in elementary school mathematics?

Before discussing this question directly, the problem of measuring this hypothetical construct should be examined. In his comprehensive reviews of research on attitudes toward mathematics, Aiken (1970b, 1972) examined the various tools available for measuring mathematics attitudes of students. In another source (1970a) he points to the problem in relation to the question examined in this section when he states:

A serious problem in drawing conclusions about the interaction between attitudes and achievement concerns the inadequacies of measures of attitudes themselves. The reliability of a Thurstone, Likert, or semantic-differential scale is usually fairly satisfactory at the high school and college levels, but reliable measures of attitudes of elementary school pupils have yet to be devised. In fact, the shortcomings of all self-report inventories at the elementary school level are widely recognized; the limited reading abilities and experiences of pupils with the content of such inventories represent two sources of difficulty (pp. 251, 252).

Neale (1969) cites studies by Anttonen (1969), Ryan (1968), and Husén (1967) in his survey of research on the relationship between attitude and achievement. Aiken (1970b) also examined the various studies carried out during the 1960's which dealt with the relationship of attitude and achievement in elementary school mathematics. Despite the substantial differences in instruments and populations, the correlations between attitude and achievement are generally in the 0.20 to 0.40 range. In other words, there is a modest positive relationship between attitude and achievement in elementary school mathematics. Neale points out that two alternative explanations for such correlations may be given. The first is that favorable attitude causes learning; the second is that learning causes favorable attitude. It is interesting to note from the W. J. Callahan (1971) study that the most frequently cited reason for disliking mathematics was "not good in math, don't learn easily, not sure of myself."

Aiken (1970b) points out that the relationship between attitudes and achievement may vary with the pupil or particular group of pupils. Citing evidence from Cristantiello (1962) he suggests, for example, that correlation between attitude and achievement may vary with ability level. It may be that if attitude is very high or very low, it has a greater influence than ability on achievement, but in the middle range of attitudes ability is the more potent determiner of achievement.

In summary, it can be noted that there is a modest relationship between attitude and achievement in elementary school mathematics. Problems in measurement of the attitude construct with elementary school students, and problems in interpreting the meaning of the correlational studies, make it difficult to present compelling research evidence for the logical argument that positive attitudes toward mathematics play an important role in contributing to mathematical achievement.

What factors seem to influence the development of attitudes about mathematics?

Aiken's (1970b) thorough examination of the research on attitudes led to consideration of various factors, and their relation to mathematical attitude. For a comprehensive consideration of this question, the interested teacher should examine this source. On analyzing various non-intellective factors, social factors, parental factors, curriculum factors, and teacher factors, and their association with attitude toward mathematics, Aiken states that of all the factors affecting student attitudes toward mathematics, teacher attitudes are viewed as being of particular importance.

Studies such as those by Aiken and Dreger (1961), Torrance and Parent (1966), and Peskin (1966) offer some evidence on the importance of the teacher to mathematics attitude development. Eighth graders in the W. J. Callahan (1971) study mentioned, "Good teachers who explain and are sympathetic have helped me like it" as the second most frequent contribution for liking mathematics. Phillips (1973) has recently reported evidence that the teacher's attitude toward arithmetic is significantly related to the student's attitude and achievement. This relation was not evident if the attitude of only the student's most recent teacher was considered. However, when two of the student's teachers of the three previous years had favorable attitudes, student attitude appeared to be related in a positive way.

From their study, Poffenberger and Norton (1956) concluded in regard to early teacher influence that arithmetic and mathematics teachers can have strong positive or negative effects upon students' attitudes and achievement in these areas: (a) they build upon attitudes established by parents; (b) the enthusiastic teacher leads students to like this subject; (c) the teachers who tend to affect students' attitudes and achievement positively have the following characteristics: a good knowledge of the subject matter, strong interest in the subject, the desire to have students understand the material, and good control of the class without being overly strict.

It would seem reasonable that parents may also have an influence on the attitudes of students toward mathematics. Poffenberger and Norton (1959) suggested that parents affect children's attitudes through their expectations, encouragement, and their own attitudes toward mathematics. Alpert *et al.* (1963) found that student attitudes about mathematics were positively related to the amount of mathematics education desired for them by their parents. Attitudes were also positively related to parents' belief that competition was desirable in the modern world. Hill (1967) found that there was more similarity in attitude about mathematics between mother and son than between father and son, but sons appeared to have greater accordance with the expectations of their fathers than with those of their mothers. Levine (1972) reported a rather consistent response between the views of elementary school pupils and their parents regarding the relative importance of mathematics compared to other elementary school subjects.

Aiken (1970c) has also examined the impact of various instructional procedures and curriculum programs on mathematical attitudes of students. Such procedures and programs as rote vs. meaningful teaching, ability grouping, and "modern math" were examined. The general impact on attitudes of these factors appears, at best, to be modest. Haskell (1964) reported that sociometric grouping of students seemed to affect positively attitudes toward a geometric task. J. L. Higgins (1970) studied the effect on attitude of a laboratory, mathematics-through-science, approach to instruction.

The selected studies cited convey an idea of the complexity and idiosyncratic nature of attitude formation. Many factors appear to combine in complex ways in affecting the mathematics attitudes of children. The impacts of teachers and parents, perhaps in that order, appear to make significant contributions, however.

Is anxiety associated with mathematical learning?

Skemp (1971) has described an instructional scenario with which many can easily identify. He writes about a hypothetical lesson where the exposition, though not excellent, is nevertheless not altogether inadequate. Some pupils will understand the point of the expository lesson; some will not. If those who do not understand feel overanxious at their failure, they will no doubt make greater efforts to comprehend. But this over-anxiety can be self-defeating, in that it can actually diminish the effectiveness of their efforts. The more anxious the student becomes, the harder he tries, but the worse he is able to understand, and so the more anxious he becomes. A vicious cycle may be set in motion. For mathematics lessons, at best the anxiety may be aroused in the single situation;

at worst—and this is probably more common—there may be a spread of the anxiety arousal to mathematical tasks in general.

Aiken (1970c) points out that anxiety may have either a negative or positive effect on performance in mathematics, depending on its intensity, the task, and the individual. For instance, Skemp (1971) cites the principle known as the Yerkes-Dodson law, which suggests that the optimal degree of motivation for a given task decreases with the complexity of the task. For a simple task, the stronger the motivation the better the performance; for a more complex task, this is so only up to a point, then further increases in anxiety produce a deteriorating performance on the task.

Studies dealing with mathematics and anxiety fall into two general methodological categories. One set (Hess, 1965; Milliken, 1964) uses somatic (body) expressions which are manifested by individuals when confronted with mathematical tasks; the other uses responses on paper-and-pencil questionnaires as indicators of anxiety (Feldhusen, 1965; McCandless and Castaneda, 1956; McGowan, 1960; Phillips, 1962). The former describes the fluctuations in size of the pupil of the eye, breathing, blood pressure, heart rate, and sweating, when students are faced by mathematical tasks. The latter asks students to respond introspectively to situations stated on the questionnaire. In general, the studies show a significant negative correlation between achievement in mathematics and the various anxiety measures.

Biggs (1965) concluded after examining research on anxiety and learning in mathematics that in arithmetic and mathematics, the inhibition produced by anxiety appears to swamp any motivating effect, particularly where the children concerned are already anxious; or to put it another way, anxiety appears to be more easily aroused in learning mathematics than it is in other subjects.

In answer to the question posed in this section, it appears that anxiety and mathematics are related. In general, high anxiety is associated with lower achievement in mathematics, but this is a complex relationship affected by some of the factors to be discussed in the next section. The work of Natkin (1967) suggests that behavioral therapy techniques may offer some beneficial effect on anxiety arousal in mathematical situations.

What are some factors associated with anxiety in mathematics learning?

The trend in studying anxiety and its effects on learning has been a movement away from the study of "anxiety" toward a study of "anxieties." This approach suggests that an individual could be quite anxious about one part of his school experience and less anxious about other parts.

Dreger and Aiken (1957) carried out a study with college freshmen to see whether a syndrome of emotional reactions to arithmetic and mathematics could be detected that could be labeled "number anxiety." They concluded from their studies that:

1. Number anxiety does appear to be a separate factor from "general anxiety," although the 0.33 correlation indicates some causal relation probably exists.

2. Number anxiety does not seem related to general intelligence.

3. Persons with high "number anxiety" tend to make lower mathematics grades.

In Milliken's (1964) work with college freshmen, he predicted that students who indicated mathematical deficiency would effect greater blood pressure increases under the mathematical stress conditions than those who indicated high proficiency in mathematics with a deficiency in verbal ability. He found that students of both sexes who had exhibited mathematical deficiency did increase in anxiety under stressful mathematics testing, as contrasted with a slight increase during the verbal testing. Yet the mathematically able males also reacted with greater physiological change during mathematical testing than during verbal testing. The females were only slightly more anxious in the mathematical testing.

Another specific anxiety that has been studied is test anxiety (Sarason et al., 1960). Correlational studies carried out between test anxiety and achievement in elementary school mathematics, as shown by standardized test results, indicate a rather consistent tendency for children with high levels of text anxiety to perform more poorly than children with low levels of text anxiety. Frost's (1968) study did not support the contention that test anxiety was more specifically related to educational achievement than general anxiety.

Sarason, Hill, and Zimbardo (1964) reported a stronger negative correlation between level of anxiety and reading test scores than between anxiety and arithmetic test scores for children in grades 2 through 4. Stevenson and Odom's (1965) results in grades 4 and 6 indicated no tendency for the correlations to be higher on any one particular achievement test. Jonsson (1966) found a significant interaction between level of test anxiety and ease or difficulty of a mathematics test. The high-anxious students did not perform well on the more difficult form of the test. Robinson (1973) found a negative correlation between test anxiety and problem solving tasks in mathematics.

It is difficult to make a simple generalization regarding the factors associated with anxiety in mathematics learning. Teachers can be quite confident, however, that high anxiety does have a debilitating effect on achievement in elementary school mathematics. From a selected set of studies, it would seem that association between achievement and anxiety will be affected by such factors in the instructional process as abstractness of the materials to be learned, familiarity with the material to be learned, grade level of the student, sex of the student, socioeconomic status of the student, as well as the type of cognitive processing required in the task.

Is reflective and impulsive behavior associated with learning in mathematics?

It can often be observed that when children are confronted with a problem they may react in very different ways. Some seem to respond immediately with the first thing that comes to mind; others seem to run a series of "validity checks," just to make sure, before responding. Kagan (1971) has suggested that the major cause of a reflective attitude is anxiety over making a mistake. The greater the child's fear of error, the more likely he is to be reflective. If the child is less inhibited and cautious, he may tend to respond to a problem situation in a more impulsive manner.

Cathcart and Liedtke (1969) explored the hypothesis that reflective students achieve higher in mathematics than impulsive students. Using 46 grade 2 students and 12 grade 3 students, and a mathematics achievement test composed of concepts, problems, and basic facts, their data tended to confirm the hypothesis. They concluded that speed of response is not a valid criterion of ability to achieve in mathematics at the primary level. Their data suggested that the students who achieve the best in mathematics are those who are more reflective and take longer to consider their responses. Callahan and Passi (1971) found a tendency for kindergarten children classed as "reflective" to be able to conserve length on a Piagetian-type task more often than those classified as "impulsive," although the relationship did not reach statistical significance.

Schwebel and Schwebel (1974) focused on the effect that differences in conceptual tempo have on the underuse of children's capabilities in problem solving. They hypothesized that impulsive responders would be more likely than reflective responders to "underuse their capabilities." They further hypothesized that if impulsive responders were restrained from answering quickly, they would make better use of their capabilities and perform at a higher level. Forty-nine first and second graders, 30 from lower and 19 from middle socioeconomic class backgrounds, were used in the study. Tasks employed in the study involved two Piagetian class inclusion problems and a number conservation task. One finding was that children from lower socioeconomic class backgrounds who were restrained from impulsive behavior significantly outperformed their unrestrained counterparts. It was also found that, with the control groups, those children responding correctly to the Piagetian tasks were less impulsive in responding than their unsuccessful peers.

Since mathematical tasks may reflect a full range of cognitive processes from high to low, various conceptual tempos may be sought depending on the tasks involved. In dealing with impulsive or reflective children, Kagan (1971) suggests that teachers may have to adopt different strategies for the two groups of children. He writes:

> The teacher should alleviate excessive anxiety in the young child. She should encourage the reflective child to guess when he is not sure and to be less critical of his mistakes. She should encourage the impulsive child to slow down, to think about the accuracy and quality of his answers, and to be concerned with the possibility of error (p. 129).

What are some other personality dimensions that may have an effect upon learning in mathematics?

Self-esteem or self-concept appear to be related to achievement in elementary school mathematics. Peper and Chansky (1970) found relatively high positive correlations between self-esteem and scores on the verbal problem solving section of the Iowa Test of Basic Skills. Gustafson and Owens (1971) found significant positive correlations between self-esteem and mathematics scores on the California Test of Basic Skills. Robinson (1973) found that good problem solvers tended to have higher scores on a test of self-esteem. Other studies (Bodwin, 1957; Fink, 1962) also tend to confirm the relationship between achievement and self-esteem or self-concept.

From a clinical point of view, the relationship between adequacy of self-concept (how a child perceives himself) and achievement in elementary school mathematics is a two-way street. For some children the cause of underachievement may be an inadequate concept of self. ("I never could do anything well.") For others, a history of failure (real or imagined) in mathematics may be the cause which results in an inadequate concept of self.

Hebron (1962) suggested that "extrovert" personality traits may favor the assimilation of the first elementary facts of a novel mathematical task, while the student with more "introverted" traits may be more capable, when this stage is passed, in applying these initial facts in more complex problem situations.

Levy (1943) and Plank (1950) have suggested that the overprotected child will not do as well in arithmetic as in other subjects. Rose and Rose (1961), using larger samples and homogeneous and heterogeneous social groupings, found no support for the overprotection hypothesis as a whole. However, their data suggest that the variable of overprotection is more likely to become operative in the socially homogeneous classroom than in the socially heterogeneous classroom arrangement.

Kemp (1960) studied the achievement of the dogmatic personality. He found that "high dogmatics" had a greater percentage of errors in problems which required the studying of several factors or criteria for decision and the deferring of a conclusion until each factor has been judiciously considered. He suggests that the "high dogmatic" personality has difficulty in tolerating ambiguity and is thus impelled toward a "closure" before full consideration is given to each piece of contributing evidence. This sometimes results in the perceptual distortion of facts and in a conclusion which does not encompass all elements of the problem.

Discussion of these few personality traits, along with previous discussions of attitude and anxiety, underscore the complexity of the teaching/learning act in elementary school mathematics. Skillful teaching of elementary school mathematics must include a sensitive awareness of a student's personality traits. Such sensitivity may improve achievement in school mathematics; this improvement may contribute to a healthier personality.

Part Three

Studies Concerning
the Learning Environment

What are some considerations in individualizing mathematics
instruction within the classroom?

Brownell (1935) pointed out 40 years ago in his research that pupils
do not necessarily learn arithmetic in the manner assumed by the
instructional process. The assumption underlying the drill procedures
used by teachers in his study was that upon seeing or hearing a stimulus
(as $3 + 4$) the student would think the sum (7), and only the sum.
Brownell's interview procedures indicated that this was true of only about
two of every five children in the third grade. The point being made is
that there is a distinction between individualizing instruction and individualizing learning. The locus of control of the former exists in the objective,
educational environment of the student and is difficult to achieve. The
locus of control of the latter exists in the unique personality and experiences of the individual student and is difficult not to achieve.

The question considered in this section is concerned with the educational environment adaptations that may be undertaken to maximize the
learning opportunities for each pupil in mathematics. As Trafton (1972)
has pointed out, individualized instruction essentially implies a point
of view toward pupils and their learning. Success in individualizing
instruction would seem to require study of, and understanding, the
student as an individual; study of, and understanding, the mathematics
from a comprehensive view; and organizing the school and classroom
instruction in order to maximize opportunity for each individual to learn.
The last requirement mentioned is the main focus of this section, but the

reader should not infer that "individualized instruction" is simply associated with a particular classroom management scheme.

Trafton (1972) discussed three levels, or approaches, to individualizing instruction in the mathematics classroom. One was the
"whole-group" approach. He suggests this may be effective for initially
developing ideas and skills. The sensitive teacher may "individualize"
the whole-group lesson by appropriate use of materials, questions, and
written work that may review or extend the idea or skill. Another level
he called the "modified whole-group" approach. This includes such
organization procedures as independent or self-paced progress, ability
grouping, and flexible grouping. Regarding the independent or self-
paced technique, he cautions against the use of this as the sole approach
to instruction, since it may not provide the extended amount of guided
development that most pupils need if they are to learn mathematics as
other than a collection of isolated bits and pieces. He also discussed
modifying the whole-group instruction to include independent, self-
selected activities. Provision for such activities is often incorporated
in the use of mathematics "interest-centers" or mathematics "laboratories"
in the classroom.

Another consideration in individualizing instruction involves the
role of the classroom teacher in making instructional judgments. Henderson (1972) suggests that individualized instruction, in theory, should
provide each individual an opportunity to learn what is appropriate for
him in a mode (or modes), and at a pace, suitable to his abilities and
interests. Judgments on "appropriateness" and "suitability" can be viewed
from two extremes. From one perspective such judgments may be thought
to reside with the teacher; from the other perspective, only the individual
pupil can make judgments regarding "appropriateness" and "suitability."

In attempting to implement the latter point of view some programs
and/or systems have been developed that attempt to be teacher-proof.
The adult in the classroom ("teacher" seems an inappropriate label)
assumes an active managerial role, but a passive instructional role. The
program, or system, provides the means and ways for the individual
student to make the "suitable" and "appropriate" judgments and the
opportunities to learn mathematics without adult interference.

Advocates of the other point of view place the teacher at the center
of a successful individualized program in elementary school mathematics.
Henderson states:

It's the *teacher* that counts in the long run for most students, not
systems of management or types of materials. . . . We can best achieve the
objectives of individualized instruction by humanizing teachers, improving
their expertise, and providing a flexible and reasonable climate in which they

can inspire personal learning in a social context and take into consideration the content, method, and pace appropriate for their individual students (pp. 21-22).

In summary, the classroom teacher who wishes to individualize instruction must be aware that it involves much more than manipulating classroom organization. Essential to success would seem to be an awareness of each child as a unique individual; an awareness of the mathematics curriculum—its logical and cultural composition and contribution; and a repertoire of classroom organizational abilities and techniques. It would also seem useful to clarify the role of the "teacher" vis-à-vis the concept of individualized instruction.

What is the place of the "informal" classroom in teaching elementary school mathematics?

Any contemporary consideration of learning environment must consider the present "informal" classroom movement being experienced in this country. The movement also appears under other names such as "Open Education," "Leicestershire Plan," or the "British Primary Movement." The associated observable classroom characteristics of the movement are the superficial "accidents" of the movement; the "essence" is a cluster of personal beliefs by educators regarding children's learning, development, and the nature of knowledge. These essential beliefs and values have a long tradition among educators. Barth (1971) has developed a collection of assumptions regarding learning and knowledge that may help professional educators come to know the professional-self more clearly and aid in deciding the appropriateness, or inappropriateness, of the movement for them.

Attention was focused on the movement with the report published under the auspices of England's Central Advisory Council on Education, *Children and Their Primary Schools* (1967). The report was prepared by a committee chaired by Lady Plowden, and its general aim was to survey the present state of schools in England and to offer direction for reform. Featherstone (1967a, 1967b, 1967c) popularized the report in this country, and Silberman (1970) encouraged the consideration of the direction of reform as an antidote to some of the "grim" conditions he found existing in the schools of this country.

To underscore the fact that many of the reform directions are far from new, it is enlightening to read some of Rice's (1903) articles that appeared in *The Forum* about the turn of the century. After traveling in Europe, and visiting their schools, he returned to visit schools in this country and prepared a series of articles on his observations. The purpose was to report on the "spirit" of the schools. He found many of the schools "repressive" and gives insight into his desired direction of change when he writes:

I had long believed that elementary education should take into account the normal activities and interests of the child; that the latter should be introduced to the beauties of nature and art; and that he should be as free in his schoolroom as orderly development would permit (p. 451).

Although indefinable, the informal schools do have some broad qualities and concerns that distinguish them from formal or traditional schools, according to Rogers (1972):

1. Informal British schools are distinguished by the degree to which they have become "de-institutionalized." Children move relatively freely about such schools, in classrooms and corridors alive with color and things of all sort. Old chairs, rugs and carpets, ovens and animals, all give a warm, human, non-school atmosphere to the building.

2. Teachers seem to accept a fuller, broader interpretation of the idea of "individualization." Children are seen as unique or different in terms of their total growth patterns as human beings rather than in a narrow, skill development sense.

3. Teachers in informal schools place far more value on detailed observation of a child's work over a long period of time as a primary evaluation source than they do on more formal testing procedures.

4. Teachers (and headmasters or principals) play a far more active role in making day-to-day curricular decisions of all kinds than do their counterparts in more formal schools.

5. Teachers in such schools seem to accept fully the notion that children's learning proceeds from the concrete to the abstract, and that *premature* abstraction is one of the great weaknesses of the traditional school (p. 402).

Again, to underscore the tradition of this line of thought in education, it might be useful to represent a few ideas presented by Johonnot in his 1878 "Methods" book, *Principles and Practice of Teaching*. Of the work of Pestalozzi and Froebel, he writes:

The first and most fundamental principle in all his [Pestalozzi's] work is that the mental powers are unfolded in definite order, and that true instruction must be that which is intelligently adapted to each stage of mental growth, and directly tends to promote the next step of development (p. 124).

The next important principle of Pestalozzi is that the teacher should make the child the subject of profound and careful study. While the general principles of mental philosophy derived from the aggregate study of mind will serve as a guide to general courses of instruction, a special study of the peculiarities of each child is necessary as a guide to the intelligent adaptation of general means to particular cases (p. 126).

. . . all school work should be founded upon the actual experiences of the child. To this end the exercises of the schoolroom should conform as much as possible to matters which interest the child out of school, and all instruction given should start from that which is already possessed (p. 127).

In all the works of the great reformer there is nothing more distinctly shown than that the systematic study of things should precede that of books (p. 127).

The education of children should be based upon self-activity. The needs of every child give rise to desires, and the desires to activities of some kind (p. 136).

The child must be left free to show its activities and express its desires. This freedom is best manifested in play, which is free activity gratifying desires, and, when not perverted, the instinctive and unconscious manner in which well-being is promoted (p. 136).

Whatever gives pleasure to children generally and at all times, always serves to promote their development in some way. . . . the old system of education . . . held that study was valuable in proportion as it was distasteful, and that culture was to be sought in thwarting, rather than in gratifying, natural inclinations (p. 137).

Little empirical evidence exists on the comparison of children's learnings in "formal" and "informal" classroom settings. In a study carried out in British schools Haddon and Lytton (1971) found that students in schools designated as "informal" had significantly higher scores on tests of divergent thinking ability than those students from schools that were "formal." On follow-up studies four years later the results were similar. Scores on objective tests of mathematical achievement appeared to be lower for students from the "informal" classrooms than from the "formal" classrooms.

Though extremely limited, the forementioned study may be a harbinger of consequences of adoption of the "informal" classroom procedure. Recall the general findings comparing children in "new" and "traditional" math classes from an earlier discussion in Part One of this book. In general, students in more conceptually oriented programs did better on tests composed of more conceptual tasks while students in less conceptually oriented programs did better on tests composed of less conceptual, skill, tasks. It well may be that when comparative outcomes of "formal" and "informal" classrooms are made, students in "informal" environments may perform better on "divergent" tasks while those in more "formal" classes may do better on "convergent" tasks. This would again underscore the need by teachers, and others concerned with the education of children, to consider the desired goals of education.

Many educators, during the midst of the "new" math movement, decided that the drop in computational skill scores on objective tests was too much of a price to pay for the limited increase in performance on conceptually-oriented tests. The consequence was often a general disillusionment with all of the "new" math. Without careful thought, a similar disillusionment with the "informal" results could be with us in a few years. It well may be that, again, the drop in performance on convergent-type tests will be viewed as too great a price for the possible limited increase in artistic or creative achievement and some demonstration of divergent-thinking processes. Wallach (1971) has suggested that the implications of "Open Classrooms" may have greater consequences for the children of lower socioeconomic level than for students from more economically affluent homes.

In summary, the informal education movement has its roots in centuries of educational thought. Sensitive observers of the contemporary movement often focus on a "spirit" in describing the "informal" classroom. This spirit seems to be built around such human virtues as trust, faith, respect, and love. Many innovators in this country seem intent on capturing the "spirit" by prescribing buildings without internal walls or by filling classrooms with every possible type of manipulative material, both animate and inanimate. Such preoccupation with the accidental accoutrements of instruction will certainly doom the movement to failure and destine the many beneficial aspects to an undeserved "limbo" . . . until they rise again on the wings of another movement. Barth (1973) has observed:

Open versus "traditional" has become a dangerous, futile ideological battle. We could more profitably direct our energies toward helping each child develop the personal and cognitive skills about which there is widespread agreement among adults (p. 59).

What is the place of the "math lab" in elementary mathematics instruction?

Consonant with the increased interest in "informal" instructional procedures there has been renewed interest in the mathematics laboratory. As with the rationale for the "informal" education movement, the mathematics laboratory approach reflects certain essential beliefs about how students most effectively and meaningfully learn mathematics.

Reys and Post (1973) cite the thoughts and writings of Pestalozzi, Froebel, and Rousseau as giving early impetus to laboratory procedures. Shaaf points out in the introduction to Kidd, Myers, and Cilley (1970) that Perry in England and E. H. Moore in the United States were writing of such procedures around the turn of the present century. Bernard

(1972) traced the mathematics laboratory concept to the work of A. R. Hornbrook in 1895.

Like so many educational procedures in the classroom, the mathematics laboratory defies precise definition. Reys and Post (1973) suggest that it has at least two distinct connotations. One is that of an approach to learning mathematics, while the other is that of a place where students can be involved in learning mathematics. Kidd *et al.* (1970) suggest the following characteristics of the procedure:

1. Relates learning to past experiences and provides new experiences when needed

2. Provides interesting problems for the students to investigate

3. Provides a nonthreatening atmosphere conducive to learning

4. Allows the student to take responsibility for his own learning and to progress at his own rate.

The form and function of any particular laboratory may differ considerably.

As might be expected, research on the achievement results of students who experience mathematics instruction in a laboratory setting are far from consistent or conclusive. Two surveys (Hynes, Hynes, Kysilka, and Brumbaugh, 1973; Vance and Kieren, 1971) of research on mathematics laboratories have been reported recently. Vance and Kieren came to the following conclusions:

1. The research indicates that students can learn mathematical ideas from laboratory settings. However, in maximizing achievement on cognitive variables, other meaningful instruction appears to work as well if not better. This trend carries through for higher-level operations such as transfer and creative use of concrete materials.

2. One generally held feeling about mathematics laboratories is that they promote better attitudes toward mathematics. There is only limited evidence of this in the careful evaluations of activity-oriented mathematics, although some students seem to prefer laboratory approaches to more class-oriented approaches.

3. The "gains" made through a laboratory approach appear to be practical. The research and evaluation reports seem unanimous in concluding that students and teachers can learn to use laboratory approaches easily (pp. 588-89).

The research and evaluation literature suggests that laboratory approaches can be used practically and effectively. However, any effective utilization takes organization. Furthermore, laboratory approaches are not a panacea, but appear to be an effective instructional methodology in a teacher's repertoire.

How can we best group children for learning mathematics?

The question could also be asked: "Does ability grouping increase learning in mathematics?" Or it could be asked: "Does decreasing the range of ability in an instructional group result in increased learning?"

It is a commonly held belief among school personnel that reducing the heterogeneity, or increasing the homogeneity, of a group of children will make it possible for the teacher to bring about a closer fit between the students' ability to learn and the learning experiences. Administrative attempts over the past century have been identified by such expressions as: grade grouping (one-room rural school), X Y Z grouping (by levels of intelligence), "Vestibule" groups, Winnetka Plan, Hosic Cooperative Group Plan (this plan requires teachers to work in small cooperative groups under a group chairman), the Dalton Plan (in which the work was assigned by "contracts"), Platoon grouping, Dual Progress Plan, ungraded primary grouping, ungraded intermediate grouping, departmental grouping, inter-grade ability grouping, and several others.

Far more numerous than the names of the plans are the research studies comparing progress under one plan with progress under some other plan. Shane (1952) summarized the findings of most of the studies this way:

It seems reasonable to conclude that the "best" grouping procedures are likely to differ from one school to another, the most desirable practice often being dependent upon such factors as (a) the competence and maturity of the local staff, (b) the nature of the physical plant, (c) the school size, (d) class size, (e) the local curriculum or design of instruction, and (f) a highly intangible quality—the intensity of the desire of a teacher or a group of teachers to make a particular plan work effectively.

The philosophy and ability of the able teacher are undoubtedly more important than any grouping plan, however ingenious it may be, with respect to creating a good environment for teaching and learning (p. 73).

Perhaps the most substantial and significant study of the effects of ability grouping is that of Goldberg, Passow, and Justman (1966). About 2,200 children in 45 elementary schools in the New York City area were studied over the two school years, grades 5 and 6. In addition to academic achievement measures the researchers gathered data from teachers' ratings of students, from students' ratings of students, and from students' attitudes toward school.

It is commonly believed that narrowing the ability range of a group of children will make it possible for the teacher to make better differentiation of either method or content. Contrary to this belief, this study reports that simply narrowing the ability range does not necessarily result in better adjustment of method or content and does not necessarily result in increased achievement.

When the data were analyzed for the slow children only, it was found that a single teacher who is capable of working with such children could achieve comparable growth in all areas. But, for the gifted children, no single teacher seemed to be able to provide equally challenging learning in all subjects:

The general conclusion (of the study) is that, in predominantly middle-class elementary schools, narrowing the ability range in the classroom on the basis of some measure of general academic aptitude will, by itself, in the absence of carefully planned adaptations of content and method, produce little positive change in the academic achievement of pupils at any ability level. However, the study found no support for the contention that narrow-range classes are associated with negative effects on self-concept, aspirations, interests, attitudes toward school, and other nonintellective factors. Therefore, at least in schools similar to those included in this study, various kinds of grouping and regrouping can probably be used effectively when they are designed to implement planned variations in content and method. The administrative development of students must, therefore, be tailored to the specific demands of the curriculum (p. 167).

In the light of the great amount of research on the effectiveness of various ways of grouping children for instructional purposes, school personnel can feel highly confident that teachers will teach best in that type of grouping of children in which they have the greatest confidence and sense of security. In a word, until some better plan comes along, teachers will tend to teach best when they are teaching the way they like best.

How can mathematics class time be used most effectively?

The ratio of class time spent on developmental activities compared to drill and practice activities has been the focus of a group of investigators over the past few decades (Milgram, 1969; Shipp and Deer, 1960; Shuster and Pigge, 1965; Zahn, 1966). Their accumulated evidence suggests that children learned arithmetic skills better by spending less time on drill and practice and more time on meaningful developmental activities.

There was general agreement among the studies that the classes which devoted 50 percent or more time to developmental activities performed better on achievement tests than those classes devoting 50 percent or more class time to drill and practice work. This was generally true for all ability levels of students, but increased time on developmental activities may be most beneficial for the students who are mathematically talented.

Activities classified as "developmental" in these studies referred to classroom procedures intended to increase understanding of the number system, fundamental operations, and applications of number in everyday experiences. Activities such as teacher demonstrations, teacher explanations, group discussions, work with manipulative materials, and laboratory activities were classified as "developmental." In general, such individual pupil tasks as assigned exercises from textbooks, kits, dittos, and tapes were classified as "drill and practice" activities.

Milgram (1969) attempted to ascertain how elementary school teachers tended to use class time in mathematics. Using a team of observers, the study found the following use of class time in intermediate grade classrooms:

1. Time spent going over previous assignment   25%
2. Time spent on oral or written drill   51%
3. Time spent on introducing new math concepts
   or developmental activities   23%
4. Time of unrelated interruption   1%

This suggests that many teachers spend the major portion of mathematics class time in correcting assignments and drill and practice activities.

The importance of using time wisely in teaching was underscored recently by Conant (1974). The study identified the varied tasks that teachers perform in grades 1 to 4 and the amount of time devoted to each pursuit. Observers followed each of 47 teachers around for a full day, recording in detail the time spent in different kinds of activities. The central finding of the study was that teachers spend only 30 percent of their time in activities that are even remotely related to academic instruction and learning—100 minutes out of the 5½-hour school day. Of the 100 minutes, an average of 75 minutes were devoted to language arts, 18 minutes to numbers/math, and no more than one or two minutes daily to any other curriculum area.

Evidence would suggest that at least 50 to 75 percent of math class time should be devoted to meaningful developmental activities. Drill and practice activities should not be ignored, but 25 to 50 percent of class time appears to be ample. There is evidence that a disproportionate amount of class time is still spent on correcting homework and drill and practice activities. As suggested by Riedesel (1971), "In most cases an increased amount of exploration time results in a better understanding of the topic, better retention, and thus less need for drill" (p. 179).

Does class size affect student achievement in elementary school mathematics?

Using fourth-grade children, Moody, Bausell, and Jenkins (1973) found that manipulation of class size influenced the learning of selected mathematical content when that manipulation took the form of reductions in class size from an average standard. Teacher-pupil ratios of 1/1, 1/2, 1/5, and 1/23 were used in the study. An examination of means of the four groups indicated that although small-group instruction was incremental when compared to large-group instruction, large-group instruction could be considered more efficient in terms of total learning produced per unit of instruction time (and per teacher).

In a study carried out in the San Diego school system ("Report to the Board," 1965), 36 classes at the first, third, and fifth grade levels of three different size categories were compared for achievement. The evidence suggested that small class size favored achievement in arithmetic at the first and third grade levels, but no significant differences were found at the fifth grade level. Size categories used were:

Small classes:	Grade 1	25-28
	Grade 3	26-29
	Grade 5	29-31
Medium classes:	Grade 1	30-32
	Grade 3	32-34
	Grade 5	34-36
Large classes:	Grade 1	36-39
	Grade 3	38-41
	Grade 5	38-41

Menniti (1964), in studying achievement in parochial elementary schools, found some evidence of a significant difference in achievement in mathematics in favor of small classes for the below-average and average pupils. The achievement of the upper IQ groups showed no significant differences between classes of various sizes.

The great amount of variability found in the class size research would seem to indicate that high or low achievement can be observed at all levels of class size, within reason. Small classes do not automatically bring about significant increases in achievement. However, the weight of evidence seems to favor the smaller classes. The knowledgeable and sensitive professional teacher can probably operate more efficiently and effectively, and positively affect mathematics achievement, in a class of small size rather than a large one.

What about the readability of arithmetic textbooks?

Studies that have been concerned with the vocabulary of elementary school textbooks in arithmetic generally have pointed up the great variability in number of new vocabulary words introduced at each grade level as well as the rate or pace at which the new words are introduced. Hunt (cited in Buswell and John, 1931) reported on an analysis of six third-grade books whose aggregate vocabulary was composed of 2,993 different words, of which only 350 occurred in all six books. Similarly, Repp (1960) reported on an analysis of five third-grade books whose aggregate vocabulary was composed of 3,329 different words, of which only 698 occurred in all five books. She also reported that the average number of new words per page ranged from 3.98 to 6.78 in the five texts analyzed. The range of actual number of different new words, page by page, went from 0 to as high as 69 different new words on one page. Regarding the technical vocabulary of arithmetic, Hunt reported a total of 306 words, of which only 34 were used in all six books she examined.

By applying a reading-level formula to five different commercial textbook series, Heddons and Smith (1964) concluded that the readability level of the five selected commercial texts seemed to be generally above the assigned grade level. They also found a great deal of variation of reading level both between and within the various textbooks at a given grade level. Smith (1969) applied a reading formula to 11 seventh- and eighth-grade mathematics series. Again, great variability of levels of reading was found within each series, ranging from the fourth grade to the college level. Generally, the reading material did not progress from the easy to the more difficult. There was, rather, a distribution of very easy and very difficult material throughout the books.

Some studies have attempted to assess the commonality of vocabulary introduced in arithmetic texts and reading texts at the same level. Generally the intersecting set of vocabulary words is quite small. Reed (1965) analyzed two basic reading series, grades one to three, and two basic arithmetic series, grades one to three. The study found 217 different technical vocabulary words in the two arithmetic series. Of these 217 different technical terms, only nine were also introduced in either of the two reading texts. Stauffer (1966), in analyzing seven different basic reading series at the primary level, and three different arithmetic books at the primary level, concluded:

. . . even if a child had mastered all the different words presented in *all* of the seven reading series (at a given grade level), he would still need to learn to read at least one half of the words presented in the arithmetic series in arithmetic class. This means that he would need to be prepared to deal with these words semantically (meaning) and phonetically-structurally (speaking) in order to grasp and deal with arithmetic problems or discussions (p. 144).

The evidence from the various researchers cited would suggest that there is great variation in the vocabulary of various textbooks in elementary school mathematics. Where stress is put on meaningfulness in learning, as well as individual discovery of some of the material to be learned, it seems imperative that the student be able to read the instructional material with a high degree of competence and confidence. With this in mind, the teacher of elementary school children should be quite sure that he must be a teacher of the reading of arithmetic.

Do children learn more mathematics in good schools than in poor schools?

Another way to phrase this question would be: "Will increased educational opportunity improve intellectual achievement?" Contrary to common opinion, little evidence seems to support an affirmative response to this question. That is, it is probably quite true that an increase in educational quality in the form of teachers, books, buildings, and other educational resources will not result in a corresponding increase in educational achievement, desirable attitudes, and aspirations. The Coleman Report (1966), an ambitious study of equality of educational opportunity, presents and discusses data collected in a survey of 600,000 children enrolled in grades 1, 3, 6, 9, and 12 of about 4,000 schools representing a cross-section of all public schools in the United States.

The researchers used tests of verbal ability, reading ability, and mathematical and analytical skills; gathered pertinent sociological information concerning the children and their parents; and assembled information on the attitudes and aspirations of the children.

The highest average scores were attained by white children, followed in order by Oriental Americans, American Indians, Mexican Americans, Puerto Ricans, and Negroes.

Variations in the amount of money used to increase quality in the schools have much less effect on the child's achievement than do his family background and social environment. That is, a direct increase in the amount of educational opportunity built into the school in whatever form(s) will not result in any appreciable increase in educational attainment.

The student's self-concept is a very significant factor in his or her academic achievement. Negro students who have an adequate self-concept, who believe they can control their environment and their future, will score higher on achievement tests than white students who feel inadequate and unable to control themselves, their social and economic milieu, and their future.

The authors (Coleman and others, 1966) conclude:

> The data suggest that variations in school quality are not highly related to variations in achievement of pupils. . . . The school appears unable to exert independent influences to make achievement levels less dependent on the child's background—and this is true within each ethnic group, just as it is between groups (p. 297).

Is the mathematical training of elementary school teachers adequate?

In one of the first direct attacks at pointing up the inadequacy of preparation of elementary school teachers in mathematics, Glennon (1949) found that in-service teachers had mastered an average of 55 percent of the understandings basic to the computational processes taught in grades one through six. Subsequent administrations of the Glennon instrument by other investigators (Weaver, 1956; Bean, 1959; Kenney, 1965) over a period of years generally have produced comparable results. Callahan (1966), using a test sampling more of the "modern" mathematics programs of the day, found that the percentage of mathematics content known by teachers had not increased. Koeckeritz (1970), using the same instrument, found no significant differences between high school sophomores, college seniors, and in-service elementary school teachers. None of these groups achieved greater than 50 percent mastery of the test items. It would seem that whether traditional or modern, mathematics knowledge of elementary school teachers remains a real professional problem.

Certain variables seem to affect performance of elementary school teachers on tests of mathematics achievement. Some studies (Todd, 1966; Callahan, 1966) have indicated significant negative correlation between scores on tests of mathematical knowledge and number of years of teaching experience. Other studies (Gibney, Ginther, and Pigge, 1970a, 1970b) have suggested that grade level taught and preference for teaching certain subject matter in the elementary curriculum also may influence mathematics achievement scores.

Hicks (1968) pointed out the disparity of content between elementary school math programs as reflected in basal series and the content of mathematics texts for teachers. He suggested that there were topics included in the mathematics texts for teachers that had little or no counterpart among currently used children's series. Other writers (Dienes,

1970a; LeBlanc, 1970) have urged a closer relationship between the content of the elementary mathematics programs and the preparation of elementary school teachers in mathematics. This relationship would be not only in content, but also in the instructional processes used in mathematical preparation courses for elementary school teachers.

The Committee on the Undergraduate Program in Mathematics (CUPM) of the Mathematical Association of America conducted a study of requirements and offerings of mathematics in the preservice education programs for teachers in the elementary schools in the late 1950's and early 1960's. The results of the study reflected a need for upgrading mathematics course offerings. The CUPM group made the following recommendations in regard to mathematics courses at the college level for prospective elementary school teachers ("The Training of Elementary School Mathematics Teachers," 1960):

1. A course or a two-course sequence devoted to the structure of the real number system and its subsystems

2. A course devoted to the basic concepts of algebra

3. A course in informal geometry.

Subsequent surveys such as those by Fisher (1967), Foster (1970), and Hunkler (1971a) seem to suggest that the CUPM recommendations were generally not totally implemented in the preparation of elementary school teachers. There did seem to be an increase in courses dealing with the structure of the real number system, but the geometry and algebra recommendations were generally not achieved. That there was improvement in the number of course offerings is indicated by the results of a follow-up study by CUPM in 1966. Two results are shown in Figure 1 (*Recommendations,* 1971, p. 2).

	1962	1966
Percent of colleges requiring no mathematics of prospective elementary school teachers	22.7	8.1
Percent of colleges requiring five or more semester hours of mathematics of these students	31.8	51.1

Figure 1. Mathematics Requirement Changes

As a result of continued study and discussion, as well as the significant changes in school mathematics during the 1960's, and those changes that can be expected to take place in the 1970's, the CUPM published a new set of recommendations in 1971 (*Recommendations,* 1971). The new recommendations attempted to promote integration of course sequences and applications of mathematics. Some flavor of the recommendations may be gained from the following paragraph:

We propose that the traditional subdivisions of courses for prospective elementary school teachers into arithmetic, algebra, and geometry be replaced by an integrated sequence of courses in which the essential inter-relations of mathematics, as well as its interactions with other fields, are emphasized. We recommend for all such students (prospective elementary teachers) a twelve semester-hour sequence that includes development of the following: number systems, algebra, geometry, probability, statistics, functions, mathematical systems, and the role of deductive and inductive reasoning (p. 10).

They recommended two possible sequences of courses, but suggested there were many ways of organizing the content and encouraged experimentation and diversity.

Recommendations for the preparation of elementary school teachers have also been published by the Cambridge Conference group (*Goals for Mathematical Education,* 1967). In the "Caveat" to the report it is stated that it "is hoped that the report will inspire debate, controversy, and experiment, and that from these will eventually emerge guidelines which can actually be used." The report contains two general proposals for elementary teachers. One proposal is quite closely associated with the mathematics required to teach the K-6 math curriculum proposed earlier by the Cambridge group (*Goals for School Mathematics,* 1963). The other proposal is aimed more at including mathematics that may produce more positive teachers' attitudes and promote desirable intellectual characteristics in prospective elementary school teachers.

In summary, it seems that the need to upgrade the mathematical knowledge of elementary school teachers is still present. A few studies (Bassham, 1962; Postlethwaite, 1971) furnish some evidence on the relationship between teacher mathematics knowledge and student achievement. Recommendations for upgrading the preservice mathematics preparation of teachers exist. The challenge is in making the recommendations a reality.

Is the "professional" preparation of teachers of elementary school mathematics adequate?

Whitehead stated in his *Aims of Education* (1929) that, "The art and science of education require a genius and a study of their own; and this genius and this science are more than a bare knowledge of some branch of science or literature" (p. 6). The preceding question was concerned with the mathematical knowledge of elementary school teachers. This question deals with "professional" knowledge of teachers. What is meant by "professional" knowledge?

Anderson (1957a) writes:

It is only as a teacher masters the discipline(s) which bears on his work, as, for example, a physician masters anatomy, that he can be considered to have professional education (p. 365).

In somewhat the same vein, Melton (1959) writes:

. . . education is to psychology and the social sciences as engineering is to the physical sciences and as medical practice—especially preventive medicine—is to the biological sciences (p. 97).

Glennon (1965) illustrates this interpretation of mathematics education and the disciplines from which it draws as shown in Figure 2.

The Art and Science of Teaching Mathematics											
Cultural Foundations				Psychological Foundations				Mathematics			
Philosophy	Sociology	History	Cultural Anthropology	Learning Theory	Personality Theory	Developmental	Clinical	The real number system	Algebra	Geometry	Theory of number

Figure 2.

Glennon goes on to state:

. . . the mathematics teacher is not a psychologist as such; nor is he a philosopher as such, a historian, a sociologist, a cultural anthropologist, a clinical psychologist, a personality theorist, etc., as such. But he should have some general competence in several of these basic disciplines. From these disciplines he must draw the principles which help him find answers to his two constant professional questions: *What* mathematics *should* I teach? and *How should* I teach that mathematics to children of varying capacities and personality traits? (p. 136).

Callahan (1966) attempted to measure the "professional" knowledge and the "mathematical" knowledge of teachers in-training and in-service. At all three levels—in-service teachers, college seniors completing their work in elementary education, and freshmen who had indicated their desire to become elementary school teachers—the achievement was higher on the "mathematical knowledge" instrument than on the "professional knowledge" instrument. Koeckeritz (1970) found there was a significant difference favoring in-service teachers and senior preservice elementary teachers over freshmen on the professional knowledge instrument. The mean achievement on this section of the test did not exceed 35 percent by any of the different levels tested.

Years ago, Robinson (1936) compared teachers' knowledge of the fundamental principles of arithmetic with their knowledge of methods of teaching arithmetic. He concluded that the professional courses in arithmetic in the professional schools for teachers had been no more successful in eliminating methodological difficulties than they had been in eliminating subject matter difficulties. There is some evidence that there may have been more concern and progress on the subject matter than on the professional knowledge in subsequent years.

How effective is in-service education?

Sarason and Sarason (1969) have stated some impressions of the importance of the teacher in any attempt at curriculum change in the schools. In regard to a school system's change to a "modern math" curriculum they observed:

. . . 2. It was clear from the beginning that the first objects of change would concern the classroom teachers who were minimally, if at all, participating in any of the decision-making. There seemed to be no recognition that the teachers would be faced not only with a problem in learning but in unlearning as well, with all its attendant consequences.

3. Perhaps the most distinct impression we received was that the problem of changing the math curriculum was viewed as a relatively simple one in the sense that once the administrative details could be worked through—once the "system" could get the teachers into the learning situation— the process of change would present no particular problem. That some teachers would not look enthusiastically at the new math, that some teachers did not want to devote nonschool time to learning and unlearning, that the amount of time it was expected to take teachers to understand the new math was on the brief side . . . these and other possibilities were not considered in such a way that the complexity of the process would become apparent (p. 92).

They go on to observe:

. . . changing curricula without changing styles of thinking and teaching is the hallmark of the difference between change and innovation (p. 93).

Given the importance of effecting change in teachers, what does research indicate about in-service education of teachers in mathematics? Houston and DeVault (1963) were interested in three questions regarding in-service work in elementary school mathematics:

1. Does the in-service education program increase the teachers' and their pupils' understanding of mathematical concepts?

2. What was the relationship between the teachers' initial level of understanding prior to the in-service education program and the pupils' increase in achievement?

3. What was the relationship between the teachers' increase in achievement and the pupils' increase in achievement?

They concluded from their study that: (a) the in-service education program was effective in increasing mathematics achievement both for pupils and for teachers; (b) there was a negligible relationship between the teachers' initial mathematical achievement prior to the in-service education program and the pupils' growth in mathematical achievement during the program; and (c) growth in understanding of the mathematical concepts of the in-service program was related to pupils' growth in understanding of those mathematical concepts specifically developed in the in-service program.

Ruddell and Brown (1964) evaluated three approaches to in-service work with teachers. One approach was a "one shot" affair in which the consultant spent a full day with teachers before the beginning of classes in September. Another approach spread 10 in-service sessions over the year, each session lasting about half a day. Sessions included a general meeting plus two demonstration classes. Each participant observed about one-half of the demonstration classes. A third procedure made use of "intermediaries." A person from a given school and grade level was chosen to attend the in-service sessions, which included the general session and demonstrations. The participant then reported back to the teachers in their schools.

Student gains on achievement were measured over a year's time. It was found that in grades 3, 4, 5, and 6, significant differences between mean gains were shown at every level, and in each instance it favored the second group (the group of teachers whose in-service sessions were spread over the year—10 half-days). The researchers concluded that some type of direct contact between consultant and teacher is necessary to bring about change in teachers' mathematical knowledge and understanding. Furthermore, teachers' knowledge and understanding can be changed just as much from an intense "one shot" program as from a slowly paced, long-range program, but this change is not reflected in the children's achievement.

Greabell (1969) compared effectiveness of a "systematic modern," a "crash modern," and a "traditional" approach to implementing a mathematics program in elementary school mathematics. He concluded that the "systematic modern" seemed most beneficial for students. This approach was characterized as one in which:

1. The school district systematically studied the various programs (math) and selected one to fit its needs

2. The district has had an in-service program to prepare the teachers, administrators, and parents for transition

3. The district staff is continually evaluating their results with the goal of improving instruction.

Organizationally, Sherrill (1971) found that in a given school system the elementary teachers:

1. Preferred in-service over summer courses

2. Preferred an integration of math content and method, with about a 50-50 distribution of emphasis

3. Preferred joint planning by school personnel and university personnel

4. Preferred organization across schools in the system, but by grade-level groupings.

Other studies (Hand, 1967; Hunkler, 1971b) have suggested that such variables as type of instructor for the in-service course and duration of the participation by teachers may also have an effect on achievement of students and teachers.

In summary, it seems fair to say that mid-career education of teachers is crucial if change in education is to be achieved. Such organizational variables as cooperative planning, grade-level classes for teachers, duration of the program, and type of instructor may affect the results of the program. It would seem important to keep in mind that the complexity of educational change, including teacher change, is often underestimated.

"Teaching Centers"—What is the promise and potential?

Little research is available at this time as evidence on the efficacy of teaching centers in the United States. However, as suggested by Schmieder and Yarger (1974), "The teaching center is one of the hottest educational concepts on the scene today" (p. 5).

Bailey (1971) describes the centers as follows:

Teachers' centers are just what the term implies: local physical facilities and self-improvement programs organized and run by the teachers themselves for purposes of upgrading educational performance. Their primary function is to make possible a review of existing curricula and other educational practices by groups of teachers and to encourage teacher attempts to bring about changes (p. 146).

The appeal of the idea of the teaching center grows out of its attempt to deal with some questions that have confronted teacher educators for years. These questions include:

1. How can service and in-service educational personnel development be successfully linked?

2. How can curriculum development and staff development be effectively integrated?

3. How can generally uncommunicative educational constituencies (students, teachers, administrators, supervisors, college and university staff, community interests) best share experiences and resources?

4. How can educational personnel be continually renewed in their ability and vigors? (Schmieder and Yarger, 1974, p. 5).

The teaching center idea is a relatively recent development in Great Britain. The related growth of the idea in the United States can probably be traced to our general interest in some of the educational movements in Great Britain. Eddy (1974) has indicated that approximately 650 centers are now in existence in Britain. A recent survey suggests that teaching centers are growing rapidly in this country (Joyce and Weil, 1973). Collins (1974) has compiled some interesting case studies of existing teaching centers in the United States.

The professional teacher would do well to study the literature on the emerging concept of "Teaching Centers." An annotated bibliography of some sources is presented by Poliakoff (1974) in a recent publication devoted to the consideration of Teaching Centers. The concept seems to be an exhilarating one for the classroom teacher. But Pilcher (1973) has pointed to some realistic political and educational problems involved in trying to implant the British model into the U.S. educational system. An enlightened awareness of the political dimensions of educational power adjustments inherent in the "center" concept may give this potentially good idea a fighting chance to survive.

What are some guidelines for determining performance criteria in the professional preparation of math teachers?

There has been considerable rethinking going on over the past years in regard to teacher certification. Many states are moving toward some form of competency-based teacher education (CBTE). With such a system, individuals desiring to teach children in the public schools would be judged on the basis of performance, not on degrees held or number of courses taken. It is beyond the scope of this monograph to examine all the facets of CBTE. A perusal of the report of the Committee on National Program Priorities in Teacher Education, chaired by Rosner (1972), would give a good initial insight into the various aspects of CBTE.

The Commission on Preservice Education of Teachers of Mathematics of the National Council of Teachers of Mathematics has recently developed *Guidelines for the Preparation of Teachers of Mathematics* (1973a). *Guidelines* was designed for the use of individuals in planning teacher education programs at the college and university levels and to provide criteria for use by accreditation agencies in evaluating teacher education programs. *Guidelines* is intended to emphasize program design rather than the competencies of specific individuals matriculating through a program. A recent publication ("Guidelines," 1973b) presents an overview of the content of the 32-page *Guidelines* pamphlet.

Guidelines is divided into three subsections corresponding to (a) the academic and professional knowledge a prospective teacher should possess, (b) the professional competencies and attitudes a prospective teacher should exhibit, and (c) the responsibilities of the institution providing the teacher education programs. The first two sections are written in a style consistent with or suggestive of competency-based programs.

The first section, describing the academic and professional knowledge, contains subsections concerning not only mathematics but also the philosophical, historical, psychological, and sociological foundations of education. The competencies advocate that each teacher know more mathematics than he is required to teach and reflect a belief in the significance of the applied and cultural aspects of mathematics.

The second section concerns the knowledge and attitudes a prospective teacher should demonstrate while working with learners under supervision. The section includes guidelines concerning items such as communication in the classroom, curricular and instructional planning, diagnosis, and evaluation.

The final section of the guidelines concerns institutional responsibilities. These are detailed in terms of characteristics of staff, program, and resources which would facilitate students' acquisition of the competencies described in the first two sections.

The movement toward competency-based teacher preparation has not been embraced by all mathematics educators. Rising (1973) has expressed his concern about performance criteria for the preparation, certification, and evaluation of teachers. It would seem that if this movement is to succeed in upgrading the professional preparation of teachers, the key will be in the wisdom educators use in interpreting and implementing criteria judged desirable. If professional preparation becomes a dehumanized enslavement to lists of performance criteria, failure to upgrade professional preparation seems assured.

Part Four

Studies Concerned with Teaching Method

What are the main sources of the teacher's methods?

The mathematics "revolution" of the late 1950's and 1960's is usually perceived as being solely concerned with improving *what* mathematics should be taught. To this end, the writers of the monograph discussed the main sources of the curriculum as the first question in Part One.

At least of equal importance in the "revolution" was and still is the question: "What are the main sources (theories) of the teacher's methods?" Whereas the question of curriculum content is fairly easy to comprehend and debate, the question of method—"*How* should I teach?"— is less well understood, and hence progress is less well recognized and agreed upon.

But the problem of *how* one should teach is not a new one. Plato clearly illustrates the method used by his teacher, Socrates, in the dialogues with his friends. In these teaching situations Socrates uses a form of teaching through telling—in which the telling is done in the form of questions. It was his great skill in this style of teaching which caused Socrates to believe and teach, incorrectly, that people are born with all knowledge. It was the task of the teacher, he reasoned, to cause the child or adult to recall or call forth this knowledge when questioned by the teacher.

In our century, the roots of the question of method in the teaching of elementary and middle school mathematics were clearly and brilliantly identified long before the math revolution, in the now classic treatise by William A. Brownell (1935). He identified and described three theories of arithmetic, each of which involves *both* content and method—*what* to teach and *how* to teach. Brownell named these as the drill theory, the incidental-learning theory, and the meaning theory. This lucid exposition of the rationale for each theory and powerful defense for the meaning theory found a ready audience which changed the teaching of arithmetic during the late 1930's, 1940's, and 1950's and fathered the psychology of the new method of the late 1950's and 1960's to a greater extent than most of the "reformers" may ever know.

But the method of the new math can be studied as methods *per se*. Here we discuss three major sources of the teacher's method. The first of these is identified by such terms as telling, by expository methods, by didactics, by lecturing. The role of the teacher is perceived as a process of pouring (content) into an empty vessel (the learner), somewhat similar to philosopher John Locke's *tabula rasa,* or blank state, concept of the role of the mind in the teaching-learning process.

Research studies of the verbal interaction between teacher and child and among children in the mathematics class clearly indicate that "telling," whether by the spoken word or by the printed word, is by far the dominant method. Despite the fact that most of what teachers themselves know was learned from being told, orally or in printed form, "telling" has received more than a few brickbats during the years of the new math revolution. However, Carroll (1968) has provided us with a strong defense of learning from being told and sums up his position:

> Despite its relative neglect in educational psychology, learning from being told has a glorious past. Its future may be even more glorious if we will take the trouble to examine it with the attention we have paid to other—less interesting—ways of learning (p. 10).

The second major source of the teacher's method is identified by such terms as discovery, guided discovery, heuristics, inquiry, and hypothetico-deductive. This method became associated with the new math as *the* method-arm of the revolution. Presumably, the new math should and could only be taught well through some form of discovery-oriented teaching.

Then, too, it must be kept in mind that the new method of the new math had a double purpose. Obviously, one objective was the cognitive product—that of learning mathematics as mathematics. The other objective was that of having children learn cognitive process—such as that of learning to think the way mathematicians think. There the emphasis is on the strategies of thinking mathematically—the heuristics of discovery.

Bruner (1961) identified four benefits that might be derived from the experience of learning through the discoveries that one makes for oneself: (a) an increase in intellectual potency, (b) a shift from extrinsic to intrinsic rewards, (c) learning the heuristics of discovering, and (d) an aid to conserve memory.

While accepting the ideas and values of a teaching method that is discovery-oriented, Friedlander (1965), correctly, discussed the danger that these very important ideas about teaching and learning "might lose their potency due to oversimplification, misunderstanding, empty ritualistic application, and the frustrated disappointment among both teachers and students that would be sure to follow" (p. 36).

My true conclusion is that the factor of judgment is crucial. When we recognize the complications of the teaching and learning process, with all its delicate balances between freedom and discipline, between imagination and critique, between fact and concept, and between memory and forgetting, it hardly seems likely that any one method or formula can fit all cases. Only the wise intervention of the teacher's judgment can hold these shifting stresses in equilibrium (p. 36).

The third major source of the teacher's method may be identified as psychotherapy. Whereas in the two major methods previously discussed—teaching as telling and teaching as guided discovery—the emphasis is on the mathematics (product and/or process), the emphasis in teaching as psychotherapy is on the phenomenal self. Whereas in the first two major sources of method the emphasis is on cognition, in the third the emphasis is on affect. And whereas the former are teacher centered, the latter is learner centered.

Psychotherapy as a method is not new and, of course, is not a parallel development of the math revolution. Its origins go back in this century to the first decade and the start of the mental hygiene movement with the publication of Clifford Beers' book *The Mind That Found Itself* (1908).

Symonds (1949) discussed the similarities of and differences between education and psychotherapy. Among the similarities he listed:

1. Both teachers and therapists should treat children as individuals with potentialities for progressively taking over direction of themselves.

2. Both teachers and therapists are counseled to accept the child as he is—no matter how stupid, lazy, dirty, resistive, or disorderly.

3. Both teachers and therapists have a responsibility to understand the child (p. 7).

Among the differences, Symonds listed:

1. A teacher is principally concerned with the world of reality and his task is to help children to become effective in the real world. A therapist, on

the other hand, according to Rogers, gives his attention primarily to the feelings expressed by a child.

2. A teacher feels and expresses love, but avoids hate; a therapist does not express either love or hate.

3. The teacher stimulates, encourages, directs, guides. The therapist, on the other hand, consistently avoids using any influence in the form of suggestion, advice, or encouragement (p. 10).

The leading contemporary exponent of the role of therapeutic methods in facilitating learning is the distinguished and many-times-honored psychologist Carl R. Rogers. According to Rogers (1969), the central issue of methods is to set students free for self-initiated, self-reliant learning.

From a lifelong study, he identifies principles which will support this approach to learning. Among these are:

1. Human beings have a natural potentiality for learning.

2. Significant learning takes place when the subject matter is perceived by the student as having relevance for his own purposes.

3. Learning is facilitated when the student participates responsibly in the learning process.

4. Self-initiated learning which involves the whole person of the learner—feelings as well as intellect—is the most lasting and pervasive (p. 157).

While Carl Rogers is the leading theoretician of psychotherapeutic principles, the leading practitioner in applying the theory in school situations is (the late) A. S. Neill. In his major work, *Summerhill: A Radical Approach to Child Rearing* (1960), Neill expresses the belief that whether a school has or has not a special method for teaching long division is of no significance. The child who *wants* to learn long division will learn it no matter *how* it is taught.

Clearly, to Neill and other extremists, method is a function of self-initiated, self-purposing behavior on the part of the learner.

We have summarized here, all too briefly perhaps, the three major sources of the teacher's method: teaching as telling, teaching as some

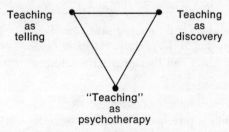

Figure 1. Methods of Teaching

form of discovery, and "teaching" as psychotherapy. We can now represent these three in the triangular-shaped model of Figure 1.

This model represents the metes and bounds of the ball park in which the game of teaching methodology is played—whether the subject matter is mathematics, spelling, social studies, or whatever.

Maintaining a reasonable balance among all three extremist positions by drawing upon each in appropriate amounts for appropriate children and appropriate kinds of learning is the high art and science of the teaching-learning act.

What does the research on discovery learning suggest?

Discovery learning in elementary school mathematics continues as an object of inquiry for educational practitioners and researchers. Experimental research has not made a great contribution to enlightenment regarding the contributions of learning by discovery, but has given additional insight into the complexity of the teaching/learning process. Wittrock (1966) has analyzed the discovery issue and focused on some of the independent, dependent, and intervening variables that must be recognized and accounted for in experimental research on discovery learning. This analysis gives some insight into the complexity of experimental research on discovery learning. Yet the complexity suggested is probably a conservative description, for as suggested by Hawkins (1966), "surely all such systems are gross and stilted when compared to the human child" (p. 12).

What would be desirable for the classroom teacher is some evidence that would suggest conditions under which limited instructional guidance would make the greatest contribution to facilitating student learning, and under what conditions maximum instructional guidance makes the greatest contribution. Cronbach's (1966) statement that there is precious little substantiated knowledge about what advantages discovery procedures offer, and under what conditions these advantages accrue, remains accurate.

One of the most extensive studies of the effects of discovery teaching was carried out by Worthen (1968). A total of 538 fifth and sixth grade students participated in the study. Initial learning, retention, and transfer were measured with tests of conceptual knowledge, heuristic ability, and attitude.

The data suggested that the expository treatment was superior in producing initial achievement. The discovery treatment seemed to be superior in producing results on the retention and transfer tests. This was true on concept tests as well as the heuristic process used in the criterion transfer procedure. There appeared to be no differences in attitudes as a result of the two procedures. A subsequent reanalysis of the data (Worthen and Collins, 1971) using classes as the experimental units rather than individual students resulted in some changes in the initial conclusions.

Olander and Robertson (1973) studied the effect of discovery and expository methods of teaching fourth grade students. The experiment continued for 31 weeks and involved 374 students. Results were judged on the bases of performance on the Stanford Achievement Test and a test of Mathematical Principles and Relationships.

The data suggested that pupils experiencing the expository treatment were better in computation on both the post-test and retention test. Those experiencing the discovery treatment seemed to have better attained the ability to apply mathematical knowledge. Scores on the Principles and Relationships test suggested no difference between the two treatments.

In a further statistical examination of interaction effect, the data suggested the following:

1. Pupils scoring in the lower part of the range on the Computation pretest improved more when taught by the expository procedure; pupils scoring higher improved more under the discovery technique.

2. Pupils scoring lower on the Concepts pretest benefited more from the discovery approach; those scoring higher profited more under the expository approach.

3. Pupils scoring lower on the Applications pretest improved more from the expository technique; those scoring higher profited more when taught by the discovery technique.

4. On the Principles and Relationships test, pupils instructed under discovery techniques started off better than those taught the expository approach, and they continued to improve at a greater ratio (p. 43).

Bassler, Hill, Ingle, and Sparks (1971) used programmed materials in studying the effect of intermediate instructional guidance and maximum instructional guidance in learning mathematical topics at the fourth, sixth, and eighth grade levels. No differences were found between the maximum and intermediate guidance groups. One procedural problem with the study was the apparent lack of interest of participants in using programmed materials after the first few days of the experiment.

Richards and Bolton (1971) studied 265 children in their final year at three junior schools. Subjects were matched on social class, intelligence, and time devoted to mathematics teaching. The major difference between schools was in mathematical instruction procedures; one used discovery methods, one used traditional methods, one used a balanced procedure.

Results suggested that on criterion measures of "mechanical" and "problem" arithmetic tasks, children taught by discovery methods were significantly lower in performance than those taught by traditional or balanced methods. On a test of divergent thinking ability the discovery and balanced methods were superior to the traditional group.

Carlow's (1967) study suggested that students need consolidation opportunities to enhance retention and transfer of mathematical concepts learned through a guided discovery technique. There was also an indication that certain personality factors may influence ability to learn from guided discovery procedures. Sowder's (1974) study did not support Hendrix's (1947) hypothesis that verbalizing a generalization immediately after discovery may decrease its transfer power.

It seems that the classroom teacher must mix a great deal of common sense with the experimental findings in making decisions on the use of discovery learning in elementary school mathematics instruction. Jones (1970) places the matter in this perspective:

> The precise definition of discovery-teaching processes presents a difficulty in the design of experiments to test the value of discovery teaching. However, the most important question is not whether these processes should be called "discovery teaching," but whether these processes are "good teaching." . . . I believe . . . discovery teaching can be used in some form to teach practically every topic at practically every level of instruction, but that these procedures should, of course, be used as they are appropriate, with imagination, and in conjunction with other ways of teaching. Too often the impression is given that discovery teaching is a fine idea, but not feasible, and also that discovery teaching is going on only when there is some sort of induction or some sort of elaborate physical equipment and experimentation. I think the techniques for discovery teaching are multiple, varied, and broad, and that discovery should not be linked solely with induction or measurement, or field-work. Most of all the concern is for good mathematics in a classroom where both teachers and students are excited about learning and about pedagogy (p. 508).

How is mathematics learning motivated?

Skemp (1971) has pointed out that questions about motives are usually, in disguise, questions about needs. Mathematics is needed as a tool in science, technology, commerce, and for entry into various professions. These are often too remote to be applicable in the early school years. In the classroom, short-term motivations are likely to be effective, such as the desire to please the teacher, and the fear of displeasing her or him. However, these kinds of motivation are extrinsic to mathematics itself. From an intrinsic point of view Skemp points out the need for mental activity. Mathematics is a specialized form of intelligent activity.

The enjoyment from such activity serves the growth needs and is experienced as intrinsic in the activity itself.

Sears and Hilgard (1964) discuss three types of motives that may be considered: social motives, ego-integrative motives, and cognitive motives.

Social motives have to do with one's relationships with other people. Some teachers may be motivating forces for their students. Amidon and Flanders (1961) found that dependent-prone students learned more geometry in the classroom in which the teacher gave fewer directions, less criticism, less lecturing, more praise, and asked more questions than with the teacher using a highly direct, lecture method which did not allow for a great deal of participation. Wright, Muriel, and Proctor (1961) classified the content of what teachers of mathematics say to their pupils as promoting (a) ability to think, (b) appreciation of mathematics, and (c) curiosity and initiative. Peer-related motives may also play an important role. In a study cited within another context (Haskell, 1964), there appeared to be increased achievement when students were grouped according to their choice of peers in the group.

Ego-integrative motives can be exemplified by what McClelland (1953) termed "achievement motivation." The concept of achievement motivation refers to the need of an individual to perform according to a high standard of excellence. Atkinson (1965) hypothesized that ability grouping should enhance interest and performance when the achievement motive is strong and anxiety weak. But ability grouping should heighten the tendency to avoid failure when that motive (anxiety) is dominant in a person. The same treatment (ability grouping) should, in other words, have diametrically opposite motivational effects depending upon the personality of the students. He found that students who were strong in need achievement relative to test anxiety showed evidence of greater learning and stronger interest in ability-grouped classes than in control classes, irrespective of the level of intelligence. Students low in need achievement relative to test anxiety showed a decrement in interest and satisfaction but no significant change in scholastic performance. Lavin (1965) concluded from his survey of the research that achievement motivation, as a unitary factor, is not strikingly related to academic performance.

Cognitive motivation refers to motives residing in the task itself rather than external to it. Bruner (1960) suggested that "motives for learning must be kept from going passive in an age of spectatorship, they must be based as much as possible upon the arousal of interest in what there is to be learned, and they must be kept broad and diverse in expression" (p. 80). Bernstein (1964) wrote of two modes of arousal of interest in mathematics when he pointed out that the student who is intrigued by number structure and the student who is intrigued by the use of mathematics in the study of the stock market are experiencing two different kinds of motivational patterns. While it is true that the same individual may experience both of these, it is possible that one student's meat may be another student's poison in this type of situation.

Holton (1964) investigated the relative effectiveness of four types of instructional motivational vehicles on the achievement of a mathematical task using general mathematics students. The task was couched in four motivational vehicles: (a) automobile, (b) farming, (c) social utility, and (d) intellectual curiosity. Kuder preference tests were given to ascertain interests of the subjects. Significant differences were found between subjects whose program was related to their indicated interest preference and those whose program was not so related, with the former being more effective in regard to achievement and retention.

Slavina's (1957) work in the Soviet Union points up the effectiveness of cognitive motivation, but also the restrictions on effectiveness of any type of motivational approach. In his work with seven- and eight-year-olds he found many who exhibited "intellectual passivity." Didactic games involving number calculations were introduced with the object of transforming the subjects' motivation. In the description he writes:

When problems that could not be correctly solved by ordinary means were solved in play, the subject's negative emotions toward mental work began to be replaced by positive emotions and a lively cognitive activity. Initially, however, this new intellectual activity, and the resultant successful solution of the arithmetical problems, were confined to the particular play situation and not transferred to school tasks. But by the fifth and sixth day a significant improvement in this direction was noted, indicating that the new cognitive, problem-solving activity, stimulated at first by play, quickly became permanent and was engendered in other than play situations. Nevertheless when an attempt was made to encourage the subjects to use only the more abstract methods of calculation, calling for greater intellectual activity, this was not successful. It was found the subjects lacked the number skills essential to an understanding of addition and subtraction (p. 205).

The classroom teacher can be quite sure that the unique needs of individual students have an important impact on motivation to learn mathematics. Accordingly, such factors as the teacher, the teacher's methods, peer influences, and the nature of the mathematics itself will affect motivation to learn. The teacher should also be aware of the requisite skills necessary for a particular new learning, for without these it would appear that even the highly motivated student will be frustrated.

What are some considerations in choosing physical (concrete) models in elementary mathematics instruction?

Suzzallo (1911) commented that the use of objects in giving a concrete basis for abstract arithmetic concepts and for memoriter manipulations seems to have gained its initial hold on the schools through the introduction of Pestalozzian methods of teaching about the beginning of the 19th century. One hundred seventy-five years later, as Reys (1971) points out, "Classroom teachers of mathematics are witnessing an unprecedented period of proliferation in manipulative materials" (p. 551).

Although use of objects in teaching arithmetic predated the emergence of the discipline of psychology, the modern psychological movement has given the procedure a scientific sanction and some insight into their effective uses. Reys (1971) suggested that the following statements, subscribed to by most learning psychologists, form the basic foundation underlying the rationale for using manipulative materials in learning mathematics.

1. Concept formation is the essence of learning mathematics.

2. Learning is based on experience.

3. Sensory learning is the foundation of all experience and thus the heart of learning.

4. Learning is a growth process and is developmental in nature.

5. Learning is characterized by distinct, developmental stages.

6. Learning is enhanced by motivation.

7. Learning proceeds from the concrete to the abstract.

8. Learning requires active participation by the learner.

9. Formulation of a mathematical abstraction is a long process.

Williams (1963) has examined some of the issues involved with use of concrete analogies in school mathematics. One issue involves the "structural" vs. "environmental" position. The "environmentalist" suggests that arithmetic should be taught in a "real life" context, using shopping situations and other models that are used in everyday activities. The "structuralist" argues that math materials should be specially devised to precisely model the mathematical system being studied.

Another issue of concern to teachers is whether to use more than one model. Dienes (1970b) has spoken out in favor of multiple embodiments for purposes of abstracting a mathematical understanding. He has hypothesized that in mathematical learning, abstraction will be more likely to take place if a multiple embodiment of a mathematical idea is provided, rather than a single embodiment such as Cuisenaire rods by themselves. On the other hand, as Williams (1963) points out, when different parts of the mathematical system are represented by different kinds of devices, there is a danger that the child will not interrelate these parts. Also, the generality of what is to be learned first should be weighed against the possible disadvantages of increasing the complexity of the information to be absorbed.

The issue of *when* real models should be used has also been a concern to teachers. There is general agreement on the need for objective models in the primary grades. The general pedagogical tendency seems to be toward less use of concrete models as students increase in age. Stage theories of conceptual development (such as Piaget discussed in an earlier section) generally suggest early dominance of intuitive, sense-influenced learning; then lessening of such influences with increasing internal cognitive and more reflective processes. At the turn of the present century, Suzzallo (1911) pointed out that current practice does not proceed far beyond the application of the simple, and somewhat crude, psychological statement that the youngest children must have much objective teaching, the older less, the oldest least of all. He said at the time that lack of a more refined analysis of the worth of object teaching necessarily leads to some neglect and waste. By the latter he meant that often primary teachers may spend a great deal of time with objects after students have already conceptualized an idea and thereby perhaps waste time; at later stages objects that may in fact facilitate learning are neglected because the assumption is made that older students no longer need the concrete displays.

In regard to the latter point, Skemp (1971) writes,

But it may well be the case that we all have to go, perhaps more rapidly than the growing child, through similar stages in each new topic which we encounter—that the mode of thinking available is partly a function of the degree to which the concepts have been developed in the primary system. One can hardly be expected to reflect on concepts which have not yet been formed, however well-developed one's reflective system. So the "intuitive-before-reflective" order may be partially true for each new field of mathematical study (p. 66).

In choosing and using physical models in math, the concerned teacher should be aware of the issues in their use. It may be that "structural" materials are most appropriately used in the development of concepts; "environmental" materials may work with applications of those concepts. Some children may increase their depth and breadth of understanding through multiple embodiments in the teaching process; other children may be confused by such procedures and learn more effectively through a linear application of a single model. Teachers must also take care in not using models just for the sake of using models at the

Author[1]	Grade level	Test used	Significant difference in favor of Cuisenaire or traditional materials	Mathematical content
Aurich (1963)	First	Standardized achievement	Cuisenaire treatment	Total range of first-grade work
Hollis (1964)	First	Standardized achievement	Cuisenaire treatment	Total range of first-grade work
Crowder (1965)	First	Standardized achievement	Cuisenaire treatment	Total range of first-grade work
Nasca (1966)	Second	Standardized achievement	Neither treatment	Total range of second-grade work
		Cuisenaire achievement	Cuisenaire treatment	
Passy (1963)	Third	Standardized achievement	Traditional treatment	Computation and arithmetic reasoning
Haynes (1963)	Third	Author constructed	Neither treatment	Multiplication
		Standardized achievement	Neither treatment	
Lucow (1963)	Third	Author constructed	Neither treatment	Multiplication and division

[1] Omitted from this group of studies is Brownell's study (1966). It does not fit the paradigm of the other studies, and the results were ambiguous.

The Arithmetic Teacher, December 1972; p. 637.

Figure 2. Summary of Some Studies Comparing the Effectiveness of Cuisenaire and Traditional Materials

Author	Grade level	Concrete model	Test used	Significant difference in favor of:	Mathematical content
Lucas (1966)	First	Dienes Attribute Blocks	Standardized achievement and author constructed	Dienes treatment for conservation of number and conceptualization of mathematical principles; traditional for computation and solving of verbal problems	Identified in Piagetian terms: multiplication of relations and addition-subtraction relations

Study	Grade	Materials	Test	Results	Content
Ekman (1966)	Third	Counters	Author constructed	Neither treatment at end of instructional period; concrete-model group on a retention test	Addition and subtraction algorithms
Dawson & Ruddell ([b]1955)	Fourth	Many diverse models	Author constructed	Concrete-model group	Division of whole numbers
Norman (1955)	Third	Concrete and semiconcrete models (number lines, drawings, and counters)	Author constructed	Neither treatment at the end of instruction; concrete and semi-concrete-model group at the end of two weeks	Division of whole numbers
Howard (1950)	Fifth & Sixth	Concrete and semiconcrete models	No information available	Neither treatment at the end of instruction; concrete-model group three months later	No information available
Mott (1959)	Fifth & Sixth	Many multi-sensory aids	Standardized achievement	Neither treatment	Measurement
Spross (1962)	Fifth & Sixth	Concrete aids that had cultural significance	Standardized achievement	Neither treatment	Total range of fifth- & sixth-grade work
Price (1950)	Fifth & Sixth	Multisensory aids	No information available	Neither treatment	Division of fractions
Anderson (1957)	Eighth	Various visual-tactual devices	Author constructed	Neither treatment	Area, volume, & Pythagorean theorem

The Arithmetic Teacher, December 1972; p. 638.

Figure 3. Summary of Studies Comparing Effectiveness of Learning Mathematical Ideas Facilitated by Concrete or Symbolic Models

primary level or, on the other hand, denying older students an opportunity to gain an intuitive grasp of a mathematical idea by the non-use of models at upper grade levels.

What has research suggested about the effectiveness of physical (concrete) models in facilitating math learning?

Fennema (1972a) has examined and presented in concise tabled form a summary of some studies that have been carried out on effectiveness of concrete models in elementary math instruction. Figure 2 summarizes some studies that compared Cuisenaire material with more traditional materials. Figure 3 summarizes some studies that compared other kinds of concrete materials with more symbolic procedures.

It can be noted that the research findings are not consistent or unequivocal. Many of the studies also have serious limitations inasmuch as the "traditional" methods were left undefined. Also, the interest and enthusiasm of the teacher(s) for the various treatments were generally unknown. Brownell (1966) found that it was not the math materials, Cuisenaire rods, that affected achievement but the interest and enthusiasm of the teachers using the new (to them) materials that seemed to make a difference. Consistent with Brownell's observations was Reys' (1972) statement, after examining some of the reviews of research on this issue, that "the one common thread among these studies is that learning mathematics depends more on the teacher than on the embodiment used" (p. 490).

Fennema's (1972b) recent report of her research with second grade children on the relative effectiveness of symbolic and concrete (Cuisenaire) models in teaching multiplication as union of equivalent disjoint sets suggested that each method was effective in achieving immediate learning results. The symbolic representation seemed to be more effective, however, when the criteria included transfer or extension of the principle. Part of her summary and citations may serve as a useful caution for teachers when considering the use of manipulatives in mathematics:

This study does not refute the necessity of action experiences provided by use of concrete models in learning mathematical principles. It does indicate that concrete models are not always necessary or more effective than symbolic models. More empirical data must be collected to determine in which situations concrete models contribute most to the learning of mathematical ideas. However, until these data are available for formation of an "adequate theory for manipulative activity in mathematics instruction" (Kieren, 1971, p. 228), care must be taken that use of such models does not become an end in itself or a "seductive shibboleth" (Weaver, 1971a) (p. 238).

What part does teacher-student verbal interaction play in classroom instruction?

From the work of Flanders (1965) and others, it has been estimated that in the typical classroom talking is taking place two-thirds of the time. It has been further estimated that two-thirds of that talking is done by the teacher. Thus there is talk going on a majority of the time in the classroom and the teacher is the major contributor.

Teacher talk has been classified as exerting direct or indirect influence. Direct influence can be seen in such activities as lecturing and giving information, giving directions, and criticizing or justifying the authority of the teacher or institution. Indirect influences are those that encourage student involvement and participation, as in such verbal activities as praising and encouraging, accepting student ideas and feelings, and asking questions. Clayton (1965) and Flanders (1970) reported that teachers of higher achieving classes use five to six times as much acceptance of student ideas and encouragement of student ideas as teachers of lower achieving classes. They also use five to six times less direction and criticism of student behavior.

Using time-sampling observations of teacher verbal sanctioning patterns during mathematics and language arts classes in beginning primary and middle primary grades in open (informal) classrooms, Perez (1973) found a positive sanctioning pattern. Sanctions were found to be more frequent in language arts than in mathematics. There was generally no difference in verbal sanctioning of girls and boys in the open (informal) classrooms observed. This was in marked contrast with sanctioning patterns reported in studies of conventional classrooms, where it was found (Meyer and Thompson, 1956) that the boys received reliably more disapproval from their teachers than did girls. The suggestion was made that the difference in sanctioning for boys in an open classroom situation may be from the freedom of movement, the choice of activities, and the diversity of resources and procedures which may allow them to channel their energy, aggressiveness, and independence into learning experiences.

Aiken (1971) cited the results of a few studies (Fey, 1969; Lamanna, 1969) of teacher-student verbal interaction during mathematics classes in summarizing research on verbal factors involved in mathematics learning. He observed, "the analysis of teacher-student verbal interactions is still in its infancy, but this type of research adds another dimension to our understanding of the effects of classroom social climate on performance" (p. 311). In summarizing research on teacher-pupil interaction over the past decade, Soar (1972) indicates that growth-producing classrooms have a number of characteristics. They are low in criticism of pupils; pupil ideas are praised, accepted, and used by the teacher; there is a minimum of restrictive direction and control by the teacher. He also presents some qualifications of these characteristics, and concern for extremism by teachers in withdrawing control.

What is the effect of homework?

Gray and Allison (1971) have reviewed much of the research and writing on the topic of homework. The findings of the few research reports tend to be somewhat conflicting. Intuitively many teachers and parents seem to feel there is benefit to be derived from assigning homework; empirically the evidence for such benefits is far from persuasive.

Although some studies (Goldstein, 1960; Koch, 1965) suggest that if the objective of the homework is immediate increase in computational skill, then regularly assigned homework in the middle and upper grades may be of some benefit, this is not a consistent finding. Gray and Allison (1971) found no difference on computational skill with fractions between sixth graders receiving three 20-minute homework assignments per week (for eight weeks) and those receiving no homework assignments. This generally is in agreement with the results of Maertens and Johnston (1972).

Using a semantic-differential technique for studying attitude of third grade pupils, Maertens (1968) concluded that the administration of arithmetic homework does not seem to affect pupils' attitudes toward school, teacher, homework, spelling, arithmetic, or reading.

Depending on one's orientation toward homework, the empirical evidence seems to allow either a "partly sunny" or "partly cloudy" forecast. On the one hand, there is little unequivocal evidence to demonstrate a positive effect for homework on learning. It seems reasonable to say that indifferent, routinized homework assignments, imposed by the teacher and opposed by the pupil, bring about little or no growth in desirable mathematical learning. On the other hand, it would seem that meaningful assignments given to the student for homework will not negatively affect either achievement or attitude.

What emphasis on computational proficiency?

It is generally agreed that the computational proficiency of children and youth suffered during the revolutionary years of the new math, at least as evidenced by scores on standardized achievement tests. We are now witnessing a substantial amount of activity to change this situation—even including in some instances the attention of legislative bodies, local and state.

Publishers of new math programs are actively promoting some of their materials as being specifically targeted at this problem. The goal of maintaining a proper balance between the developmental (meaning) and consolidation (drill or practice) phases of the math programs is neither new nor readily achieved. The present problem of lack of computational proficiency was discussed by Brownell (1956) twenty years ago to aid school personnel to comprehend his distinction between meaning and skill—and the need for maintaining a balance.

It is this same problem we now face in the post new math revolutionary years. In the opinion of the writers, no mathematical psychologist has answered it any better, so we quote Brownell:

To sum up, the balance between meaning and skill has been upset, if indeed it ever was properly established. . . . The remedy I propose is as follows:

1. Accord to competence in computation its rightful place among the outcomes to be achieved through arithmetic

2. Continue to teach essential arithmetic meanings, but make sure that these meanings are just that and that they contribute as they should to greater computational skill

3. Base instruction on as complete data as are reasonably possible concerning the status of children as they progress toward meaningful habituation

4. Hold repetitive practice to a minimum until this ultimate stage has been achieved; then provide it in sufficient amount to assure real mastery of skills, real competence in computing accurately, quickly, and confidently (p. 136).

What is the place of the hand-held calculator in the elementary, middle, and junior high school?

The answer to this question can be found more in the realm of rational inquiry than in the area of scientific research.

After much deliberation, the Board of Directors of the National Council of Teachers of Mathematics recently adopted the following position statement (*Bulletin for Leaders*, 1974):

With the decrease in cost of the mini-calculator, its accessibility to students at all levels is increasing rapidly. Mathematics teachers should recognize the potential contribution of this calculator as a valuable instructional aid. In the classroom, the mini-calculator should be used in imaginative ways to *reinforce* learning [italics ours] and to motivate the learner as he becomes proficient in mathematics.

The writers added emphasis to the word "reinforce" to assist the reader in distinguishing between *learning* as the process by which cognition (associations, concepts, meanings, and problem solving) is acquired, and *reinforcement* as the process by which previously acquired cognition is consolidated. The hand-held calculator will not help the student know when to use subtraction to solve a problem nor help him understand the processing of the numerals in, say, $403 - 127 = n$.

What is the place of practice (drill) in the contemporary mathematics program?

Contemporary programs in elementary school mathematics provide for the attainment of a variety of cognitive skills, abilities, concepts, and understandings as well as for the maintenance of these cognitive learnings. Practice is of the essence in accomplishing the latter objective (maintenance) and is a necessary part of the former (attainment).

Practice has two essential phases, according to Burton (1952):

. . . (a) the integrative phase in which perception of the meaning is developed; and (b) the repetitive, or refining, or facilitating phase in which precision is developed.

The integrative phase . . . in which meaning is developed demands varied practice which means many functional contracts and exploratory activities. The refining phase in which precision is developed demands repetitive practice. Varied practice by itself yields efficiency but not meaning. Competent varied practice in early states will reduce greatly the amount of repetitive practice needed later.

An illustration of these two types of practice might occur in the learning of the addition combinations. During the initial stages of the learning, the teacher and children should make extensive use of many and varied manipulative and pictorial materials for the purpose of building the meanings of and relationships among the facts. This would be the integrative phase. Out of this practice would come the systematic arrangement of the addition tables; and further varied practice would result in the development of meanings. Following this careful development would come the repetitive phase of practice with the facts arranged in random order. The purpose of this phase would be the fixing of the facts for efficient recall.

From research studies such as that by Brownell and Chazal (1935) has come a major guiding principle in the use of repetitive practice: it must be preceded by a thorough teaching program aimed at the building of *meanings or understandings*; or, stated otherwise, practice must follow understanding. Weber (1965) has indicated that there still is a general misconception by teachers that drill is a way of learning, rather than a process for consolidating learning that has been attained during the developmental or integrative stages of learning.

Another section of this monograph (Part Three) deals with the ratio of class time spent on developmental activities compared to practice activities.

Aside from the appropriate positioning of repetitive practice in the instructional process, another consideration focuses on appropriateness of cognitive learnings to which repetitive practice is applied. The basic addition, subtraction, multiplication, and division combinations are examples of learning products of the elementary school mathematics program in which a high level of facility with these products is desirable. Therefore, practice in both the attainment and maintenance of these skills is important.

Many contemporary programs in mathematics encourage creative problem-solving activities in an attempt to develop certain process outcomes or objectives. The routinizing of such "process" objectives by drill or practice is quite inappropriate. Luchins' (1964) classical experiments point out the rigidity or *Einstellung* effect that is fostered when practice-type activities are applied to creative problem-solving tasks. This result is an antilogy (a contradiction in terms) with the desired outcome of flexible cognitive functioning.

Practice designed to maintain a desired level of functioning for a particular skill is an important consideration in the elementary school mathematics program. Because of the sequential development of a sound mathematics education program, much of the practice on previously learned skills can be "built in" to subsequently learned materials. This allows the child to use (and therefore practice) skills previously learned, in the development of new learnings. An illustration is pointed out by Capps (1962), who found that two groups of students, one group using a common-denominator approach to division of fractions and the other an inversion method, were significantly different at the end of the experimental period in their skill in multiplication of fractions.

One logical explanation that suggests itself would be that since the inversion method of division of fractions requires multiplication as part of the computational procedure, the skills in multiplication of fractions were reinforced. Consequently there was a maintenance of the skill in multiplication of fractions. The common-denominator method does not involve multiplication of fractions to derive the answer. Thus, there was no opportunity to maintain the skills in multiplication of fractions, and computational skill decreased.

Practice exercises are a place in the teaching/learning sequence where individualization of instruction can be carried out by the classroom teacher. Gay (1972) has indicated that a traditional method of mathematics instruction whereby all students receive the same amount of practice was not conducive to promoting immediate, or delayed, retention. Conditions for practice on learning a mathematics concept where a "retention index" was determined for each student, or where individual students could choose the number of practice exercises, were superior to a fixed number of practice exercises for each student.

The teacher can feel quite confident that practice is a necessary part of the elementary school mathematics program. Wise and discriminating use of practice is important, and this involves its use at the appropriate point, or stage, in the instructional process; its use with appropriate learning objectives of the program; and also differential application to individual children. Some children may need only a small amount of practice to consolidate and maintain high-level functioning, while other children may need a greater amount of practice.

How do we diagnose learning problems in elementary school mathematics?

Early work in diagnosis in arithmetic was largely limited to compilations of frequency of errors on computational tests. As the goals of school mathematics became more comprehensive, the concern for identifying difficulties in learning also grew. Diagnostic procedures have come to be concerned with the process used by students in their work in mathematics as well as the more comprehensive product outcomes of the program.

The etiology of learning problems in elementary school mathematics is a complex field of study. Reisman (1972) indicates that the reasons some children have difficulty learning arithmetic may include a gap in their mathematical foundation, lack of readiness for learning, emotional problems, deprived environment, or poor teaching. Glennon and Wilson (1972) presented a model for diagnosis and prescription which was restricted to cognitive considerations. Its three dimensions, composed of content, types of learning, and behavioral indicators, suggest the complexity of the field of diagnosis in mathematics. As part of the general area of communication activities, the work of Kirk and Kirk (1971) may give additional insight into mathematical learning difficulties. At the representational level they focus on learning difficulties associated with the receptive process, organizing process, and the expressive process.

Any of the aforementioned factors may interrelate to form a complex network of difficulties leading to learning difficulties in mathematics.

Untangling such a network through diagnostic procedures is a very complex process. Scattered studies (Ross, 1964; Bernstein, 1959) have suggested that arithmetic underachievement appeared as a complex and multiple-factored disability. The idiosyncratic nature of underachievement in mathematics was alluded to by Wilson (1967) when he suggested that in working with individual children it becomes increasingly apparent that underachievement in mathematics is far from being of one kind; of several children with the same degree of general underachievement in mathematics, each has unique symptomatic patterns of that underachievement.

With the realization of the complexity of the nature of underachievement, methods of diagnosis must also undergo change. Brueckner (1935) suggested four general methods that could be used to analyze errors and faulty methods of work: (a) observation of the pupil at work, (b) analysis of written work, (c) analysis of oral responses, and (d) interviews. The techniques of greatest use in a sound diagnostic program will be those that lean away from the more mechanical types and lean toward the more clinical procedures.

The day-by-day observations by the classroom teacher are probably the best source of data on the learning problems of children in mathematics. Additional insight into the problems may be gained through analysis of a student's written work. Procedures such as that used by Roberts (1968) may prove useful in pinpointing problems in computation. Ashlock (1972) has identified and compiled some common computational error patterns and presented some ways of correcting such errors.

The oral interview technique has been advocated by many (Brownell, 1935; Burge, 1934; Buswell, 1926; Weaver, 1955) over the years as a procedure for gaining insight into students' maturity of thinking in mathematics. Lankford (1974) used the interview to study computational strategies of 176 seventh grade pupils. Analysis of the interviews provided some interesting and useful information about differences in the computational practices of good and poor computers. Teachers may also find the guides for interviewing children very useful. Grouws (1974) used the interview in studying strategies used by children in solving verbal problems. Using the technique he was able to identify a wide range of methods that students use in solving simple addition and subtraction open sentences.

R. F. Smith (1973) used a task-analysis procedure in developing a diagnostic test of place-value concepts. Among other findings it was observed that low achievers indicated a lack of mastery of five of the 12 prerequisite skills identified as being fundamental in building an understanding of place-value in the base ten numeration system. Callahan and Robinson (1973) found the task-analysis procedure, when combined with meaningful mastery learning, an effective procedure for learning mathematical tasks. With open-ended time regulations in effect, there appeared to be no difference between achievers and underachievers in learning the criterion task. It was observed that the latter group tended to take more time in mastering the subordinate tasks, however.

Competencies needed by teachers for diagnosing children's learning difficulties in mathematics were suggested by Brueckner (1935). He suggested that teachers must have a clear conception of the functions and objectives of arithmetic instruction, must be thoroughly acquainted with the scientific studies of the factors that contribute to success in arithmetic, must know the symptoms and causes of various unsatisfactory conditions, must be able to use effective techniques for bringing to the surface facts concerning the nature of the pupil's disability and his thought processes that would ordinarily be unanalyzed, and must be able to interpret the facts revealed by his study of the pupil and to suggest steps to correct the condition.

How should we evaluate learning in elementary school mathematics?

A continuous concern in the instructional process is that of evaluation of learning. Brownell (1941a) suggested the chief purposes of evaluation are (a) to diagnose class and individual difficulty, (b) to inventory knowledge and abilities, (c) to determine the extent of learning over a limited period, (d) to measure learning over a relatively long period, and (e) to obtain rough measures for comparative purposes.

The first three purposes are very closely related to the teacher's daily, ongoing instruction program. The informational feedback that is received aids in adapting procedures, determining specific outcomes and emphasis, and deciding on areas for reteaching. The last two purposes are concerned with judging more general outcomes of the instructional program.

These two general categories of evaluation have come to be labeled "formative" and "summative" evaluation. Bloom (1971) states that the purpose of formative observations is to determine the degree of mastery of a given learning task and to pinpoint the part of the task not mastered. On the other hand, summative evaluation is directed toward a much more general assessment of the degree to which the larger outcomes have been attained over the entire course, or some substantial part of it.

Weaver (1970) points out that the school administrator is concerned more directly with summative evaluation in mathematics. The teacher, on the other hand, is concerned very directly with formative evaluation and its role in facilitating effective instruction. Formative and summative evaluation procedures are not mutually exclusive categories; teachers may gather insight into needed instructional adjustments from summative results, and formative procedures can give some insight on comparative program outcomes.

Within the general category of formative evaluation, the concept of learning for mastery has been receiving renewed emphasis. Drawing from the work of Carroll (1963) and others, Bloom (1971) presents the following distinction between the use of mastery on criterion-referenced tests and use of norm-referenced procedures.

> . . . if the students are normally distributed with respect to *aptitude* for some subject (mathematics, for example) and all the students are provided with exactly the *same instruction* (same in terms of amount and quality of instruction and time available for learning), the end result will be a normal distribution on an appropriate measure of achievement. Furthermore, the relation between aptitude and achievement will be fairly high. Conversely, if the students are normally distributed with respect to aptitude but the kind and quality of instruction and the amount of time available for learning are made appropriate to the characteristics and needs of *each* student, the majority of students may be expected to achieve mastery of the subject. And the relation between aptitude and achievement should approach zero (p. 45).

Ebel (1971) indicates that the arguments for mastery are compelling when applied to basic intellectual skills that everyone needs to exercise almost flawlessly in order to live effectively in modern society. But these basic skills make up only a small fraction of what the schools teach and of what various people are interested in learning. He cites the major limitations of criterion-referenced measurements as (a) not telling us all we need to know about achievement, (b) difficulty in obtaining any sound basis for the criterion, and (c) total mastery is only necessary for a small fraction of important educational achievements.

A complete evaluation program in mathematics will also measure growth in ability to make judgments in quantitative situations, ability to do mental arithmetic, attitudes toward mathematics, and appreciation of the uses and cultural contributions of mathematics. A comprehensive repertoire of techniques and instruments will be needed to evaluate such goals. Traditionally, teacher-made paper and pencil tests, standardized achievement tests, and interview and observational techniques have been valuable means of judging children's mathematical learning. Discussions of the use of some of these procedures may be found in Buswell (1949), Carry (1974), Clark (1954), Dutton (1964), Epstein (1968), Gray (1966), and others.

With the trend toward more informal classroom organization there is increased interest in less formal means of evaluation. The teacher in the informal classroom will make use of real and contrived problem situation tests, dramatizations, anecdotal records, growth charts, and other means for evaluating the mathematical progress of the student. Wilkinson (1974) has suggested some means for teacher-directed evaluation in the mathematics laboratories. Biggs and MacLean (1969) have cited the need for improving evaluation techniques in the informal classroom.

The teacher of mathematics is a teacher of the whole child; he is not a teacher of one "slice" of the child—the mathematics' slice. This means that the teacher must sensitively and systematically use a broad spectrum of evaluation procedures in making both immediate and longer-range judgments on children's mathematical development.

What are meaningful approaches to instruction in the primary mathematics program?

There is little "hard" research evidence that would indicate the existence of *one* best approach to meaningful learning at the primary level. In this section the objective will be to analyze the problem into various methods that have been advocated as effective ways of developing meaningfulness in the elementary school mathematics program at the primary level.

It may be of value to look at the nature of the learnings to be achieved in the primary program. Brownell's insightful analysis helps clarify the nature of some of these desired learnings. He writes (Brownell and Hendrikson, 1950):

. . . it is helpful to think of particular facts, concepts, and generalizations as occupying points on a continuum of meaningfulness.

(Zero) . . . _____ . . . N (Maximum)

At the left end of the scale, near the 0-point, are the ideational learning tasks with a minimum of meaningfulness. . . . At the upper end of the scale, near N, are ideational learning tasks which are heavily freighted with meaning. . . . "Two" is an idea which, properly learned, belongs well to the right on the scale of meaningfulness. How much more, then, does "2 + 2 = 4" belong near N, involving as it does, not only the idea "two" but the idea "four," an understanding of the equivalence (shown by "=") of "2 + 2" on the one hand and of "4" on the other (p. 94).

The numbers 2, 5, ½, etc., are concepts to be meaningfully acquired. Concepts are abstractions. As Clark (1954) points out, to learn the concept of four, or any other number, the learner proceeds from the concrete to the abstract, from things to symbols. Effective learning presupposes that the teacher provides the learner with wisely selected and properly related experiences, and constantly encourages the pupil to generalize, to abstract, to symbolize his responses to them.

What is the most efficient route to travel from things to symbols? What are wisely selected and properly related experiences?

Lovell (1962) identified and discussed three general methods of mathematical concept development. As in many attempts at classification of complex behaviors, there tends to be overlap, and seldom does one find in practice a "pure" case of a particular method. For purposes of analysis, however, Lovell's scheme is useful. He cites three general methods: (a) verbal methods, (b) methods based mainly on visual perception and imagery, (c) activity methods.

Verbal methods imply that mathematical concepts build up mainly on spoken and written symbols, in the sense that the child, by manipulating these symbols, comes to comprehend the ideas underlying them. Overzealous application of this approach by proponents of Connectionist Psychology during the early part of the 20th century led to some disillusionment and disfavor with the method. Some contemporary learning psychologists have warned against overgeneralizing the ineffectiveness of verbal methods, however. Ausubel (1968) suggests that *both* expository *and* problem solving techniques can be either rote or meaningful depending on the conditions under which learning occurs. In both instances meaningful learning tasks can be related in non-arbitrary, substantive fashion to what the learner already knows, and if the learner adopts a corresponding learning set to do so.

Gagné (1970) also points out the efficiency of verbal methods which allow for the "short-circuiting" of more time-consuming inductive techniques, given the necessary antecedent learnings. Since the primary school child may not have a large and varied arsenal of background knowledge with which to cope with verbal methods meaningfully, this method may be less appropriate at this stage than at later stages in the student's cognitive development.

Bereiter and Engelmann (1966) indicated some success with a direct verbal method in teaching culturally disadvantaged four- and five-year-old students. One observer (Pines, 1967) described a class in the following manner:

. . . the children started to roar, "eight plus zero equal eight, eight plus one equal nine, eight plus two equal ten, eight plus three equal eleven!" (p. 57).

Methods of concept development which are based mainly on visual perception and imagery seek to develop an intuitive cognition by presenting visual perceptual structures. A correspondence is then supposed to arise between the perceptual and physical structures and the mental structures involved. Some of Stern's (1949) writings may aid in illustrating some of this thinking. She indicates that in some semi-concrete approaches to numbers, the domino patterns are used in teaching addition.

Figure 4.

The sum is found by counting the single dots. With these patterns, a child may not see the equalness of (for example) $4 + 4 = 8$. Rather, it is suggested that even when separate cubes are used, the relation of the parts to the whole be shown. From his first experiments on, the child constructs the 8-pattern from the subgroups 4 plus 4.

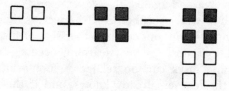

Figure 5.

This shows at a glance how the two addends build up the sum. The structure of the patterns is less forgettable, so that the child can see the subgroups in his mind whenever he reconstructs the picture of 8 and 9, etc.

Riess (1965) questioned the use of pictures of sets to establish the concept of number in kindergarten and first grade. Such use is based on the untested assumption that the child gains his concepts of number through a process of abstraction from groups or collections of objects presented to him.

The action method of number concept formation was popularized by McLellan and Dewey (1908). Dewey rejects visual perception and imagery as bases of number concepts. Rather, the child's ideas of number are built up by using each number in many different situations that involve him in action. However, Dewey sheds little light on the way in which physical activity is transformed into mental activity.

Galperin (1957) in his work at the University of Moscow has developed a theoretical model for the transference of knowledge from physical action to that of a purely mental action. To Galperin, the learning of every mental action passes through five basic states:

1. Creating a preliminary conception of the task
2. Mastering the action, using objects
3. Mastering the action on the plane of audible speech
4. Transferring the action to the mental plane
5. Consolidating the mental action (p. 217).

The process of teaching a mental action, to Galperin, then:

. . . begins with the task of learning something, a task usually set by other people; on the basis of demonstration and explanation, the child builds up a preliminary concept of the action as seen in the external action of another person. He then makes himself familiar with the action in its external material content, and gets to know it in practice, in its application to things. The first independent form of such activity in the child is, thus, inevitably the external material action.

Next, the action is separated from things and transferred to the plane of audible speech (Slavina, p. 205, describes an approach to this transition using imagery as a necessary intermediate step), where its material foundation is fundamentally changed: from being objective, it becomes linguistic verbal. But the crux of this change is that, from being an action with things, it becomes an action with concepts, i.e., a genuinely theoretical action.

Finally the action is transferred to the mental plane (pp. 222-23).

Piaget's work, which suggests qualitative changes in concept formation at various stages of cognitive development, has been cited elsewhere. Other approaches that tend to combine perceptual structures with active manipulation in the process of concept development such as that by Dienes (1960), Cuisenaire (1954), and Montessori (1964) should be examined by the teacher interested in the process of abstraction.

Much research must be carried out before one can suggest a particular route that is most efficient and effective on the way to the development of an abstraction in elementary school mathematics. It may be the case that there is not *one* most appropriate route for all children. The teacher must be able to recognize the characteristics of pupils' concepts at various ages and stages to be able to understand them adequately and contribute to their growth. It is to be hoped that future research in this area will then aid the teacher in his choice of a method that will facilitate the richness of association, accuracy, and precision which mark the qualitative changes in the emergence of a mathematical concept.

Should children be allowed to count when finding answers to number facts?

No two children in any grade are at the same level of development in their control over all aspects of number work. Where one child may be able to give a mature, automatic response to a number fact, another child is able to give a response to the same fact only on any one of several less mature levels. When two children seemingly give equally mature responses, further probing may give evidence of a more complete understanding by one child than by the other. Also, any child may give a mature response to one number fact and an immature response to another number fact.

Brownell (1928) identified four levels of development from immature to mature in responding to number facts: (a) counting, (b) partial counting, (c) grouping, and (d) meaningful habituation. Whether a child should be allowed to find answers by counting depends on his level of development. In the early stages of learning the facts, he should be allowed, even directed, to find answers by counting and grouping. As he matures, he should approach and attain the level of meaningful habituation.

Beckwith and Restle (1966), in their experimentation dealing with the process of enumeration, suggest that there may be differences between children's and college students' use of spatial arrangement in counting. Fairly young children, 7 to 10 years of age, seem to show sensitivity to the organization of the visual field. That is, even when a child is enumerating one by one, he may work rapidly within one group, then pause and consolidate his result in some way, and then attack the next group. The pausing, and the ability to divide the task into suitable parts, is a generally important part of a long serial task. College students seem to make special use of the rectangular array, presumably by using multiplication. For both young children and college students, the rectangular array may facilitate the process of enumeration to a greater degree than a linear, circular, or scrambled presentation of the objects.

We should not expect a child to begin with a mature level of response. Brownell and Chazal (1935) concluded that children do not come rapidly to mature thought processes and hence to true mastery of the facts. They move through levels of development from immature to mature.

The teacher can feel confident that counting is acceptable behavior for the child in the early stages of learning; he must also accept the fact that his guidance includes helping the child grow from less mature to more mature behavior.

What meaning(s), algorism(s), and sequence(s) for the operation of subtraction?

Three meanings for the operation of subtraction are generally developed: the "take-away" idea, the "additive" idea, and the "comparison" idea. Gibb (1965) reported the thought processes used by second grade children when solving problems involving subtraction situations, additive situations, and comparative situations. Crumley's (1956) study indicated that children tended to see the subtraction process as a "take-away" process regardless of the teaching method used. Schell and Burns (1962) found that:

1. Children's arithmetic textbooks that they examined for both grades 2 and 3 indicated considerably greater opportunity for work with "take-away" subtraction situations than for other types.

2. Pupils in the study performed best of all on "take-away" subtraction situations and least well on "comparison" situations.

3. The pupils themselves felt that the "take-away" situations were the easiest to work.

4. The pupils' drawings of their thinking of the solutions showed evidence of lack of understanding that the three situations, from the standpoint of visual manipulation, are different.

It would seem that thorough teaching of subtraction requires a systematic effort on the part of the teacher to build concepts for the three situational uses of the subtraction concept.

The subtraction algorism has been an object of investigation for many years. Two algorisms, equal additions and decomposition, have received the lion's share of attention.

In the equal-additions method (A) 10 ones are added to the 3 ones making 13 ones; 7 ones can be taken from the 13 ones leaving 6 ones. To compensate for the 10 ones added to the 3 ones in the minuend, 1 ten is added to the 2 tens making 3 tens in the subtrahend. Then, 3 tens from 4 tens is 1 ten.

In the decomposition method (B) 1 ten of the 4 tens is changed to 10 ones and added to the 3 ones; 7 ones can be taken from the 13 ones leaving 6 ones; 2 tens from the remaining 3 tens is 1 ten.

$$(A) \quad 4^{\,1}3 \qquad\qquad (B) \quad {}^{3}4^{\,1}3$$
$$\quad\;\; -{}^{3}\!\!\not{2}\,7 \qquad\qquad\qquad\;\; -\,2\,7$$

Early research studies (see summaries by Ruch and Mead, 1930; Johnson, 1938; Brownell and Moser, 1949) show that neither of the two methods was markedly more efficient than the other, but when both were taught in a mechanical fashion pupils who use the equal-additions method had a slight advantage in rate and accuracy.

In a study termed by Cronbach (1965) "one of the best-executed of all educational experiments," Brownell and Moser (1949) compared the effectiveness of the decomposition and equal-additions methods when each was taught two ways—meaningfully and mechanically. The success of the methods was judged not only on the basis of rate of work and accuracy of work, but also on the basis of smoothness of performance, degree of transfer of training, and the values inherent in the use of a crutch in the early stages of learning. Using a variety of data, the researchers found that: (a) the decomposition method when taught meaningfully was the most successful method; (b) the equal-additions method was difficult to rationalize; (c) the use of the crutch facilitated the teaching and learning of the decomposition method; (d) children discarded the crutch when encouraged to do so by the teachers.

Hutchings (1975) has recently reported the development of "low-stress" algorisms for the operations of addition, subtraction, multiplication, and division of whole numbers. These algorisms are characterized by (a) their use of concise, definable, easily read, supplementary notation used to record every step, and (b) the opportunity they afford learners to complete any intermediate step of a distinct kind rather than alternate between different kinds of intermediate steps. He argues that these characteristics allow students to do computational work with a minimum of stress and also facilitate identification of specific errors and the analysis of error patterns by teachers.

Wiles, Romberg, and Moser (1973) compared the relative effectiveness of two instructional sequences designed to teach addition and subtraction algorisms for two-digit whole numbers. One sequence integrated instruction on the addition and subtraction algorisms. All daily activities placed approximately equal emphasis on the two operations. The mechanics and mathematics of carrying and borrowing were treated as a separate entity, regrouping.

The other instructional sequence segregated instruction of the addition and subtraction algorisms. All the addition activities were completed before the subtraction activities were begun. In work with two classes of second grade children it was found that comparisons of group means favored the separation of instruction for teaching the addition and subtraction algorisms, at least for two-digit number situations.

The past few decades have seen less attention given to speed and accuracy in paper-and-pencil computation and more concern for meaning, understanding, and ability to apply operations to appropriate social situations. Algorisms and sequences of instruction that contribute to meaning and understanding will continue to be emphasized in the future. As societies more and more depend on electronic processing procedures to give speed and accuracy, the question of which paper-and-pencil procedure is more proficient becomes less of a concern. The more important concern is for the student to understand the nature of the operation and when, and under what conditions, to apply it.

What about the use of open addition and subtraction sentences in primary arithmetic?

Weaver (1971b, 1972a, 1973b) has examined certain variables that may affect the performance of first, second, and third grade pupils in solving open addition and subtraction sentences. Examples of open addition and subtraction sentences are: $7 + 2 = \square$, and $10 - 7 = \square$. The unknown quantity, $\square$, could be located in any one of the three positions in the equation. The symmetric property of the equality relationship allows previous examples to be written as $\square = 7 + 2$, and $\square = 10 - 7$. Task items used in the study allowed examination of the effect of the operation $(+, -)$, placement of the variable in the mathematics sentence, and symmetric form of the sentence on performance.

Results from the data led Weaver (1973b) to the following conjectures:

1. It is likely that performance is *NOT* independent of open-sentence form as determined by the symmetric property of the equality relation. (Performance tended to be better on sentences of the form $7 + 3 = \square$ and $12 - 5 = \square$ than $\square = 7 + 3$.)

2. It is likely that performance also is related to one or more of the following factors:

   a. Grade level (second graders performed better than first, third graders better than second)

   b. The operation used in the statement of an open sentence (at each grade level the subjects performed better on addition sentences than subtraction sentences)

   c. The position of the placeholder in an open sentence (there was a tendency for open sentences with the placeholder in the initial position to be more difficult, e.g., $\square - 3 = 5$ or $5 = \square - 3$).

3. It is likely that some interaction (between and among the above factors) exists . . . (p. 55).

Teachers should be aware that many specific factors incorporated in a simple addition or subtraction open sentence may affect performance of their students. Also, age and intellectual stage of development (Howlett,

1973) would seem to be related to performance on the sentences. Weaver suggested that it seemed desirable, even necessary, to provide a balance of experiences with the variety of forms of addition and subtraction open sentences.

What algorism should be used in dividing by a fraction?

Bidwell (1968, 1971) found three main types of meaningful approaches to teaching division with fractions. They were the "common denominator" method, the "complex fraction" method, and the "inverse operation" method. Research carried out to determine the superiority of any one of these procedures is inconclusive.

Some studies (Brooke, 1954; Stephens, 1960) have compared the performance of students using a "common denominator" procedure with others using an "inversion" procedure. The general conclusion to be drawn was that there was little difference between the two procedures in division skill attained, or retained.

With the increasing concern for meaningful learning, the mathematical rationale for the "inversion" method has received some empirical scrutiny. Bidwell (1971) analyzed the aforementioned three meaningful approaches in terms of Gagné's hierarchy of dependent tasks, and Ausubel's "advanced organizer" concept. He found that using an appropriate conceptual hierarchy and the idea of "inverse operation" as an advanced organizer seemed to produce beneficial learning of division with fractions.

Ingersoll (1971) compared a "complex fraction" algorism and an "associative" algorism in rationalizing the inversion procedure with division of fractions. He also used a random treatment composed of tasks from the "complex fraction" and "associative" treatments. Overall results favored the "complex fraction" approach. This seemed particularly true when the pre-experimental level of learning was low. When the pre-experimental level of learning was high, the random procedure seemed most beneficial. Sluser's (1962) study tended to point up the differential effect of attempting to rationalize the inversion procedure. Those students with higher intellectual aptitude seemed to be able to comprehend the mathematical principle underlying the inversion procedure, and instruction tended to improve performance. Students with lower intellectual aptitude seemed not to comprehend the rationalization, and instruction seemed to result in some confusion.

Capps' (1962) study pointed out the differential effect of the "common denominator" and "inverse" methods of dividing by fractions on skill in multiplying fractions.

As previously stated, the empirical data on comparisons of algorisms for division of fractions are far from conclusive. The "inversion" procedure, when appropriately conceptualized, may have more carry-over value in mathematics than the "common denominator" procedure. The techniques used in rationalizing the "inversion" procedure may have a very individualized impact on students. It would seem advisable for teachers to have a variety of procedures available for their classroom instruction. A procedure meaningful to some may be quite meaningless to others; thus the need for teachers with confidence in a variety of procedures.

What method of division should be used with whole numbers?

Two kinds of division situations were generally identified, measurement and partitive. Given a set of elements that is to be separated into equivalent subsets, measurement problems are those requiring that the number of subsets be found, and partitive problems are those requiring that the numbers of elements in each subset be found.

Gunderson's (1953) study suggested that problems based on partitive-type division situations were more difficult for second grade children than problems based on measurement division situations. Hill's (1952) study with upper grade children suggested that these children prefer measurement problems, but their performance on the two types was not significantly different.

Zweng (1964) introduced a further analysis of division situations by discriminating between "basic" measurement situations and "rate" measurement situations, as well as "basic" partitive situations and "rate" partitive situations. Examples of the four situations follow:

1. *"Basic" measurement:* If I have 8 balloons and separate them into bunches of 2 balloons, how many bunches will I obtain?

2. *"Rate" measurement:* If I have 8 balloons and put the balloons into sacks, placing 2 balloons in each sack, how many sacks will be used?

3. *"Basic" partitive:* If I have 8 balloons and separate them into 4 bunches, with the same number of balloons in each bunch, how many balloons will there be in a bunch?

4. *"Rate" partitive:* If I have 8 balloons and put them into 4 sacks with the same number of balloons in each sack, how many balloons will there be in each sack?

Another aspect of this study dealt with the effect of different methods of presenting the problems to the children. All "basic" problems were illustrated with just one set of objects, the set of objects given in the problem. For "rate" problems, which describe two sets of objects, some were illustrated with both sets of objects and some were illustrated with only one.

Some of the findings would suggest that:

1. Partitive division problems are more difficult for second grade pupils than measurement problems.

2. Partitive "basic" problems are considerably more difficult for second grade children than partitive rate problems.

3. Overall, division problems presented with one set of objects are more difficult for second grade children than problems presented with two groups of objects.

4. Most of the difficulty that the children had with problems using one set of objects could be accounted for by the partitive situations where only one group of objects was used. The differences between partitive situations, using two groups of objects, and measurement problems were in no instance significant.

Another interesting observational outcome of this study concerned the manner in which partitive problem situations were solved by children. Two methods of solving these partitive situations were identified: (a) sharing, where the child assigned the same number of elements to each of the required subsets but did not use all elements on the first assignment; (b) grouping, where the child assigned all the elements on the first processing. The children in the study solved the majority of the problems by means of grouping procedures. Children who used a sharing technique seldom used one-by-one sharing, but would choose as their first assignment to each group a number of elements that was over 50 percent of the number of elements required in the group.

Algorisms used in processing division situations generally fall into two main categories: one can be referred to as a subtractive (or Greenwood) algorism, the other the standard (or distributive) algorism. These two algorisms are illustrated in Figure 6 in their most mature form. Each can be carried out in many less mature ways during developmental stages of learning.

Van Engen and Gibb (1956) compared the effect of the two algorisms. Generally their study seemed to suggest that the subtractive algorism had some beneficial effects on performance in division. This seemed especially true where understanding of the idea of division and transfer to unfamiliar situations was the criterion. Children of low intellectual ability seemed to have less difficulty understanding the process of division; high intellectual ability groups indicated little difference in performance between the two methods.

Subsequent to the Van Engen and Gibb study many elementary school mathematics programs employed the subtractive algorism, espe-

Subtractive Algorism   Standard Algorism

```
                                              604
16 ) 9679                           16 ) 9679
     6400  400  (Subtracting 400 sixteens)    96    (6 hundreds × 16)
     3279                                      79
     3200  200  (Subtracting 200 sixteens)     64  (4        × 16)
       79                                      15
       64    4  (Subtracting    4 sixteens)
       15  604  (Adding the partial quotients)
```

Figure 6.

cially for initially introducing the process. Many programs would then, at a later point, move the students to the use of the standard algorism. Little data are available on the difficulties students experienced in the transition from the one algorism to the other.

More recent research seemed to favor the standard approach over the subtractive approach. Kratzer and Willoughby (1973) studied the effect of the two procedures with fourth graders. They summarized their results as follows:

1. There was a significant difference in achievement between the partitioning and subtractive approaches of teaching long division on the total set of computational problems. The direction of the difference favored the partitioning approach. This situation existed for the immediate test, the four-week retention test, and the delayed retention test.

2. There was no significant difference in achievement between the partitioning and subtractive approaches of teaching long division on problems similar to those problems studied in the sequence; . . .

3. There was a significant difference in achievement between the partitioning and the subtractive approaches of teaching long division on problems not involved in the instructional sequence, that is, on unfamiliar problems. The direction of the difference of the means was in favor of the partitioning group. . . .

4. There was no significant difference in achievement between the partitioning and subtractive approaches of teaching long division on an immediate test of verbal problems. . . . On the four-week retention test, there existed a significant difference in favor of the partitioning instructional approach. This was true for both familiar and unfamiliar verbal problems . . . (p. 203).

Other studies have suggested that when the procedures are taught meaningfully, there may not be a great deal of difference in student performance. Dilley (1970) found little difference in performance of fourth graders in the two treatments. He found no interaction between socioeconomic level or ability level and the two treatments. Scott (1963) suggested the possible benefit that may be derived from learning both algorisms.

The teacher can be quite sure that young children initially introduced to division situations will generally find measurement-type problem situations more understandable than partitive situations. However,
the superiority of any one algorism for division under all conditions has
not been demonstrated.

With electronic means assuming much of the routine processing,
teachers should be familiar with the various algorisms for division so that
they can bring into instruction those procedures that seem to contribute
meaning and understanding in applying the operation of division to
appropriate quantitative situations.

What effect does the teaching of non-decimal numeration systems have on learning of topics in elementary school mathematics?

With the increased emphasis on structure, the basic concepts of a
body of knowledge around which it is organized, it has been suggested
that the basic properties of the Hindu-Arabic system of numeration come
into focus more clearly for students when systems with bases other than
ten are taught.

The Dienes (1960) Mathematical Variability Principle urges teachers to expose children to the numeration systems with bases other than
ten. Children should learn several place-value systems.

Diedrich and Glennon (1970) studied the comparative effects of
having different groups of fourth-grade children study base 10 only,
three different bases (3, 5, and 10), five different bases (3, 5, 6, 10,
and 12), and a control group. They concluded that if one wishes to foster
understanding of the decimal system, the evidence suggests that only the
decimal system need be taught.

Various other studies (Higgins, 1972; Hollis, 1964b; Jackson, 1965;
Lerch, 1963; Schlinsog, 1968) have been carried out at the intermediate
and upper elementary grades to study the impact of non-decimal instruction. The findings generally do not support a commitment of vast
amounts of time to such study. After reviewing some of the studies on
the topics, Cruickshank and Arnold (1969) concluded that the research
reported did not convincingly support the allotment of what could
become a disproportionate amount of time to the study of other number
systems.

Critics of teaching other base systems of numeration in the elementary school, such as Fehr (1966), state that all over the world, in every
nation, bar none, and in every type of communication—social, business,
scientific, professional, etc.—the one system that is used is the decimal
system. This is the only system that most of the population will ever use

the rest of their lives, and they will probably use it every day of their lives.

The hypothesis that the study of other base systems will enhance understanding of our own decimal system would seem to be a reasonable justification for its inclusion as a topic for study in the elementary grades. Evidence is not conclusive, however, that this is the only or best way of accomplishing this objective.

The evidence would suggest that the teacher can feel quite confident at this point that some supplementary work in other base systems of numeration can be done with no evidence of a decrement in learning in other areas of arithmetic which are judged to be of value. Whether there is any advantage in supplementing instruction with other base numeration instruction over supplementary work with base ten material is yet unclear.

How can we improve ability to solve verbal problems?

One of the important objectives of the elementary school mathematics program is the development of the ability to solve verbal problems. It is through the provision of large and well-ordered amounts of experience with verbal problems within a sound textbook program that the child develops ability to solve arithmetic problems and transfers this ability to solving similar problems occurring in out-of-school, real life situations.

Buswell and Kersh (1956) used tests and recordings to get at the thought processes of a group of high school and university students as they attempted to solve six sets of problems. From the evidence gathered in these studies, it would appear that the following factors contribute to success in verbal problem solving:

1. General reading skill, including a knowledge of word meanings and of words used singly, in phrases, and in sentences

    2. Problem-solving reading skills, including:
      a. Comprehension of statements in problems
      b. Selection of relevant details in problems
      c. Selection of procedure to solve problems

3. An arithmetic factor, which includes computational skills in which the pupil understands *when* to use a process as well as *how* to use it, and also a mathematical understanding whereby the pupil has meaningful concepts of quantity, of the number system, and of important arithmetic relationships

4. A spatial factor, which involves an ability to visualize and think about objects and symbols in more than one dimension and the use of mental

imagery to help clarify word meanings when making comparisons and judgments.

Loftus and Suppes (1972) studied the structural variables that determined problem-solving difficulty of sixth graders using a computer-assisted instruction mode. The results of their analysis implied that a word problem would be difficult to solve if it differs from the problem type that preceded it, if its solution required a large number of words, or if it requires a conversion of units. Earlier studies (Emm, 1959; Engelhard, 1955; Hansen, 1944; Kliebhan, 1955) of verbal problem-solving ability attempted to isolate other factors that contributed to success in verbal problem solving in arithmetic.

In a series of reports Jerman (1972, 1973, 1974) examined variables contributing to problem-solving ability. In the most recent report, 73 linguistic variables and six computational variables were examined for their contribution to problem-solving ability. Results for the grades 4-6 analysis would suggest that certain computational variables played the dominant role in performance on the tasks. Results of the grades 7-9 analysis indicated that linguistic variables began to assume a more important role at this level. The trend toward importance of the linguistic variables continued at the college level. The investigators concluded that linguistic variables may not be as robust for students in grades 4-6 as those in grades 7-9.

Various studies (Hansen, 1944; Johnson, 1949; Treacy, 1944; Martin, 1963) have suggested that the study of mathematical vocabulary should be an important part of instruction in the area of verbal problem solving in arithmetic. Vanderlinde's (1964) study indicated that individuals in classes in which direct study of vocabulary was used achieved significantly higher on a test of arithmetic problem solving than did individuals in classes in which no special attention was devoted to the study of quantitative vocabulary. The direct study of quantitative vocabulary was significantly more effective with pupils who had above-average and average intelligence than with pupils who had below-average intelligence. Smith (1971) examined the reading level of sixth-grade problems in popular arithmetic textbook series and the reading level of problems found in standardized achievement tests. The level of vocabulary found led to the conclusion that the readability level may not be the primary reason for low scores on the problem-solving portions of achievement tests.

The work of Steffe and Johnson (1971) and others (LeBlanc, 1968; Steffe, 1966) has begun to examine the impact of problem structural type and problem conditions on younger children at early stages of intellectual functioning.

Pace (1961) attempted to determine the effect of understanding of the four operations—addition, subtraction, multiplication, and division—upon problem-solving ability of fourth-grade students. During periods of systematic instruction, children in the experimental group were asked to read the problems, tell how they were to be solved, and then defend their choice of process. Emphasis was upon *how* the problem was to be solved, and *why* a given process was appropriate. The control group in the study merely solved the sets of problems, identical to Group I, but there was no discussion of the work. Standardized instruments as well as interviews were used in evaluating results.

It was found that both groups showed improvement on "conventional" type problems; however, the experimental group showed greater improvement than did the control group. The interview evaluation indicated that both groups showed an increase in number of correct solutions to "conventional" problems based upon mature and immature understanding; however, the experimental group showed a greater increase than did the controls. With problems on the measurement instruments which contained "distorted cues," both groups showed improvement in number of correct processes and procedures; however, the experimental group showed greater improvement than did the controls.

Results of the study would suggest that children show gains in problem-solving ability if they are merely presented with many problems to solve, but they show even greater gains if systematic instruction for the purpose of developing understanding of the four processes is provided by the teacher.

Irish's (1964) study would also suggest that where students are given opportunities to develop systematically their ability to generalize the meaning of the number operations and the relationships among these operations and to develop ability in formulating original statements to express these generalizations, the result will be increased ability in solving verbal problems in arithmetic.

Wilson (1964), using fourth-grade subjects and one-step addition and subtraction problem situations as a vehicle, compared two specific problem-solving approaches. Program A attempted to create a mental "set" in the subjects which called for a focusing on the sequence of the actions and events in the verbal problem situation. Essentially, Program A involved training the subjects to:

1. "See" or recognize the real or imagined action-sequence structure of a problem

2. Express the action-sequence in an equation

3. Compute using the operations indicated by a direct equation.

Program B attempted to create a mental "set" in the subjects which called for a focusing on the "wanted-given" relationship in a problem. Essentially, Program B involved training the subjects to:

1. Recognize the wanted-given relationship embedded in a problem
2. Express the wanted-given relationship in an equation
3. Compute using the operation directly indicated by the equation.

Under Program A, when a child is faced with a verbal problem he presumably "sees" the action-sequence structure of that problem. His choice of operation would be based on his recognition of the commonality of that structure's attributes with those action-sequence attributes of one of the operations. Under Program B, when a child is faced with a verbal problem he presumably "sees" the wanted-given structure of that problem. His choice of operation would be based on his recognition of the commonality of that structure's wanted-given attributes with those wanted-given attributes of one of the operations.

Of main concern in the study was the ability of the groups to choose the correct operation to use in solving the types of problems tested. Of lesser interest was the ability to obtain the correct answer and speed in obtaining correct answers. A summary of the results indicated that for all types of problems combined, and for all mental age levels involved (low, medium, high), the "wanted-given" treatment group was found to be superior on all dependent variables measured, that is, choice of operation, correct answers, and speed. Whether these findings would hold for other types of one-step verbal problems, for two- and three-step problems, and for a wider range of age-grade level children is, of course, not known.

Burns and Yonally (1964) attempted to study the effect of varying the order of presentation of numerical data on achievement in two- and three-step verbal arithmetic problems. In other words, if problems are stated with numerical data not given in the order in which they are needed to solve the problem, will pupils solve as many of them successfully as problems stated with numerical data given in the order in which they will be used to solve the problem? They also found that arithmetic reasoning ability, as measured by a standardized test, is positively related to ability to do problems which present the numerical data in mixed order.

What is the effect of unfamiliarity of setting on verbal problem ability? Brownell and Stretch (1931) reported that, for 65 percent to 80 percent of the children, unfamiliar situations have little effect, but that for 20 percent to 35 percent, unfamiliar settings introduce a new source of difficulty.

Scott and Lighthall (1967) explored the possible relationship between high need (that is, love and belongingness) and low need (that is, food and shelter) contents of arithmetic problems and advantaged background of students. No statistically significant relationship was found between need content in arithmetic problem solving and degree of disadvantage.

Lyda and Church (1964) found that the probability of working verbal problems in arithmetic satisfactorily when there has not been direct, practical experience with that particular arithmetic situation is considerably greater for the above average group of children than the below average and average; and greater for the average than the below average.

The teacher of elementary school mathematics can feel quite sure that just giving many verbal problems of appropriate difficulty to students will effect some increment in ability to solve problems. The ubiquitous factor, "opportunity to learn," is important. However, as the studies cited suggest, there are specific procedures and techniques that can be utilized that appear to facilitate achievement in verbal problem solving. Riedesel (1969) has summarized many of these suggestions. In many cases the typical textbook program will have to be supplemented by these suggested experiences and techniques, and others.

What about CAI (Computer Assisted Instruction) in elementary school mathematics instruction?

Each successive generation of computers advances in sophistication and potential. Few aspects of human existence on earth, and fewer in space, are unaffected by the incredible advances in computer technology. The computer impact on instruction in elementary education, however, has been minimal. There are probably many reasons for this, but economic and philosophical factors have probably weighed heavily. Direct costs of equipment tend to be high; also, education has traditionally committed few funds for research and development. There tends to be an ambivalence toward commitment to technology in the instructional process. Proponents often wax enthusiastic about technology's potential for individualizing instruction; opponents often react strongly to its potential for depersonalizing, or dehumanizing, education.

Suppes (1968) refers to three different systems of instruction in discussing computer technology in education. At the simplest level, there are the drill and practice systems. These are generally meant to supplement the regular curriculum taught by the teacher. At the second level there are the tutorial systems which take over the main responsibility both for presenting a concept and for developing skill in its use. At the third level there are dialogue systems aimed at permitting the student to conduct a genuine dialogue with the computer.

In elementary school mathematics the most widely used system of instruction has been the simplest level drill and practice. Suppes, Jerman, and Groen (1966) have described the procedure at the intermediate grade level.

Vinsonhaler and Bass (1972) have summarized 10 major studies on CAI drill and practice. Criteria for inclusion were: (a) that they were designed to assist a learner in the maintenance and improvement of a skill, (b) the evaluation criterion was a standardized test in mathematics, and (c) a basic experimental/control group design was used. Generally, the experimental group received traditional instruction augmented by five to fifteen minutes of drill and practice per day. The control groups received traditional instruction without any special assistance.

Based on the reports of five studies in arithmetic, and others in language arts, they concluded that in the field of elementary education, there appears to be little reason to doubt that CAI plus traditional classroom instruction is usually more effective than traditional instruction alone in developing skills—at least during the first year or two. What remains in doubt is the advantage of CAI over other, less expensive methods of augmenting traditional instruction and the long-term effect of CAI on both cognitive and affective goals.

Travers (1971) has discussed some of the implications of computers for instruction, learning, and the curriculum in mathematics. One point in regard to curriculum seems especially important, and that has to do with computation. The point is made that computers might be used primarily as a device for reducing the burden and barrier of computation. There are many points in teaching in which, if computation is a hangup, then assistance should be provided so the role of computing is minimized and the concept at hand is given proper importance. Riedesel and Suydam (1967) have discussed the implications of CAI for teacher education.

The elementary school teacher should be aware of the potential of the computer in education. Electronic processing of data has assumed a significant role in routine day-to-day activities. The challenge ahead for the teacher will be the delegation of appropriate routines to technology, while freeing the teacher for the work of education . . . which is a human enterprise.

References

Adler, I. "Mental Growth and the Art of Teaching." *The Arithmetic Teacher* 13: 576-84; 1966.

Aiken, L. R. "Affective Factors in Mathematics Learning: Comments on a Paper by Neale and a Plan for Research." *Journal for Research in Mathematics Education* 1: 251-55; 1970a.

Aiken, L. R. "Attitudes Toward Mathematics." *Review of Educational Research* 40: 551-96; 1970b.

Aiken, L. R. "Nonintellective Variables and Mathematics Achievement: Directions for Research." *Journal of School Psychology* 8: 28-36; 1970c.

Aiken, L. R. "Verbal Factors and Mathematics Learning: A Review of Research." *Journal for Research in Mathematics Education* 2: 304-13; 1971.

Aiken, L. R. "Research on Attitudes Toward Mathematics." *The Arithmetic Teacher* 19: 229-34; 1972.

Aiken, L. R., and R. M. Dreger. "The Effect of Attitudes on Performance in Mathematics." *Journal of Educational Psychology* 52: 19-24; 1961.

Allendoerfer, C. B. "The Utility of Behavioral Objectives: A Valuable Aid to Teaching." *The Mathematics Teacher* 64: 686, 738-42; 1971.

Almy, M. *Young Children's Thinking.* New York: Teachers College Press, 1966.

Alpert, R., G. Stellwagon, and D. Becker. "Psychological Factors in Mathematics Education." Report summary in: *Newsletter No. 15.* Stanford, California: School Mathematics Study Group, Stanford University, 1963.

Amidon, E., and N. Flanders. "The Effects of Direct and Indirect Teacher Influence on Dependent-Prone Students Learning Geometry." *Journal of Educational Psychology* 52: 286-91; 1961.

Anderson, G. L. "What the Psychology of Learning Has To Contribute to the Education of Teachers." *Journal of Educational Psychology* 41: 362-65; 1957a.

Anderson, G. "Visual-Tactual Devices and Their Efficacy: An Experiment in Grade Eight." *The Arithmetic Teacher* 4: 196-203; 1957b.

Anttonen, R. G. "A Longitudinal Study in Mathematics Attitude." *Journal of Educational Research* 62: 467-71; 1969.

Armstrong, J., and K. Senzig. "Instructional Materials Used and Preferred by Wisconsin Teachers of the Mentally Retarded." *Education and Training of the Mentally Retarded* 5: 73-86; 1970.

Ashlock, R. B. *Error Patterns in Computation.* Columbus, Ohio: Charles E. Merrill Publishing Company, 1972.

Astin, H. S. "Sex Differences in Mathematical and Scientific Precocity." In: J. Stanley, D. Keating, and L. Fox, editors. *Mathematical Talent.* Baltimore: Johns Hopkins University Press, 1974.

Atkin, J. M. "Behavioral Objectives in Curriculum Design: A Cautionary Note." *Science Teacher* 35: 27-30; 1968.

Atkinson, J. "Mainsprings of Achievement-Oriented Activity." In: J. Krumboltz, editor. *Learning and the Educational Process.* Chicago: Rand McNally & Company, 1965.

Aurich, Sister M. R. "A Comparative Study To Determine the Effectiveness of the Cuisenaire Method of Arithmetic Instruction with Children of the First Grade Level." Unpublished master's thesis, The Catholic University of America, 1963.

Austin, G., B. Rogers, and H. Walbesser, Jr. "The Effectiveness of Summer Compensatory Education: A Review of Research." *Review of Educational Research* 42: 171-81; 1972.

Ausubel, D. *The Psychology of Meaningful Verbal Learning.* Second edition. New York: Grune and Stratton, 1963.

Ausubel, D. P. "How Reversible Are the Cognitive and Motivational Effects of Cultural Deprivation? Implications for Teaching the Culturally Deprived Child." *Urban Education* 1: 16-38; 1964.

Ausubel, D. "Facilitating Meaningful Verbal Learning in the Classroom." *The Arithmetic Teacher* 15: 126-32; 1968.

Baer, C. J. "The School Progress and Adjustment of Underage and Average Students." *Journal of Educational Psychology* 49: 17-19; 1958.

Bailey, S. K. "Teachers' Centers: A British First." *Phi Delta Kappan* 53: 146-49; 1971.

Baker, N., and E. Sullivan. "The Influence of Some Task Variables and of Socioeconomic Class on the Manifestation of Conservation of Number." *Journal of Genetic Psychology* 116: 21-30; 1970.

Barth, R. S. "So You Want To Change to an Open Classroom." *Phi Delta Kappan* 53: 97-99; 1971.

Barth, R. S. "Should We Forget About Open Education?" *Saturday Review World* 1: 58-59; November 1973.

Bassham, H. "Teacher Understanding and Pupil Efficiency in Mathematics—A Study of Relationship." *The Arithmetic Teacher* 9: 383-87; 1962.

Bassler, O., W. Hill, J. Ingle, and B. Sparks. "Comparison of Two Levels of Guidance in Teaching Elementary School Mathematics." *School Science and Mathematics* 71: 303-12; 1971.

Baumann, R. R. "Children's Understanding of Selected Mathematical Concepts in Grades Two and Four." *Dissertation Abstracts* 26: 5219; March 1966.

Bean, J. E. "Arithmetic Understanding of Elementary School Teachers." *Elementary School Journal* 59: 447-50; 1959.

Beckwith, M., and F. Restle. "Process of Enumeration." *Psychological Review* 73: 437-44; 1966.

Beers, C. *The Mind That Found Itself.* New York: Doubleday, Doran & Co., 1939. First edition, 1908.

Begle, E., and J. Wilson, editors. "Evaluation of Mathematics Programs." In: *Mathematics Education.* Sixty-ninth Yearbook of the National Society for the Study of Education (Part I). Chicago: University of Chicago Press, 1970.

Beilin, H. "The Training and Acquisition of Logical Operations." In: M. Rosskopf, L. Steffe, and S. Taback, editors. *Piagetian Cognitive-Development Research and Mathematical Education.* Washington, D.C.: National Council of Teachers of Mathematics, 1971.

Bereiter, C., and S. Engelmann. "Observations on the Use of Direct Instruction with Young Disadvantaged Children." *Journal of School Psychology* 4: 55-62; 1966.

Bernard, R. T. "The Historical Development of the Laboratory Approach to Elementary School Mathematics." Unpublished doctoral dissertation, Indiana University, 1972.

Bernstein, A. "Library Research—A Study in Remedial Arithmetic." *School Science and Mathematics* 59: 185-95; 1959.

Bernstein, A. "Motivation in Mathematics." *School Science and Mathematics* 64: 749-54; 1964.

Bidwell, J. K. "A Comparative Study of the Learning Structures of Three Algorisms for the Division of Fractional Numbers." Unpublished doctoral dissertation, University of Michigan, 1968.

Bidwell, J. K. "Some Consequences of Learning Theory Applied to Division of Fractions." *School Science and Mathematics* 71: 426-34; 1971.

Biggs, E., and J. MacLean. *Freedom To Learn.* Don Mills, Ontario: Addison-Wesley (Canada) Ltd., 1969.

Biggs, J. B. "The Psychopathology of Arithmetic." In: F. N. Land, editor. *New Approaches to Mathematics Teaching.* New York: St. Martin's Press, 1965.

Bjonerod, C. E. "Arithmetic Concepts Possessed by the Pre-School Child." *The Arithmetic Teacher* 7: 347-50; 1960.

Bloom, B., editor. *Taxonomy of Educational Objectives: Cognitive Domain.* New York: David McKay Company, 1956.

Bloom, B., J. Hastings, and G. Madaus. *Handbook on Formative and Summative Evaluation of Student Learning.* New York: McGraw-Hill Book Co., 1971.

Bodwin, R. F. "The Relationship Between Immature Self-Concept and Certain Educational Disabilities." Unpublished doctoral dissertation, Michigan State University, 1957.

Bogatz, G. A., and S. Ball. "The Second Year of Sesame Street: A Continuing Evaluation—Volume 1." Princeton, New Jersey: Educational Testing Service, 1971.

Bogut, T. L. "Comparison of Achievement in Arithmetic in England, California, and St. Paul." *The Arithmetic Teacher* 6: 87-94; 1959.

Brace, A., and D. L. Nelson. "The Pre-School Child's Concept of Number." *The Arithmetic Teacher* 12: 126-33; 1965.

Bradley, B., and M. Hundziak. "TMI-Grolier Time Telling Program for the Mentally Retarded." *Exceptional Children* 32: 17-20; 1965.

Braunfeld, P., B. Kaufman, and V. Haag. "Mathematics Education: A Humanist Viewpoint." *Educational Technology* 13: 43-48; 1973.

Brooke, G. M. "The Common Denominator Method in the Division of Fractions." Unpublished doctoral dissertation, State University of Iowa, 1954.

Brothers, R. J. "Arithmetic Computation by the Blind: A Look at Current Achievement." *Education of the Visually Handicapped* 4: 1-8; 1972.

Brothers, R. J. "Arithmetic Computation Achievement of Visually Handicapped Students in Public Schools." *Exceptional Children* 39: 575-76; 1973.

Brown, P. G. "Tests of Development in Children's Understanding of the Laws of Natural Numbers." Unpublished master's thesis, University of Manchester, 1969.

Brown, S. I. "Mathematics and Humanistic Themes: Sum Consideration." *Educational Theory* 23: 191-214; 1973.

Brownell, W. A. "The Development of Children's Number Ideas in the Primary Grades." Supplementary Educational Monographs, No. 35. Chicago: University of Chicago Press, 1928.

Brownell, W. A. "Psychological Considerations in the Learning and Teaching of Arithmetic." *The Teaching of Arithmetic.* Tenth Yearbook, National Council of Teachers of Mathematics. Washington, D.C.: the Council, 1935.

Brownell, W. A. "The Evaluation of Learning in Arithmetic." In: *Arithmetic and General Education.* Sixteenth Yearbook of the National Council of Teachers of Mathematics. Washington, D.C.: the Council, 1941a.

Brownell, W. A. *Arithmetic in Grades I and II: A Critical Summary of New and Previously Reported Research.* Duke University Research Studies in Education. Durham, North Carolina: Duke University Press, 1941b.

Brownell, W. A. "Problem Solving." In: *The Psychology of Learning.* Forty-first Yearbook of the National Society for the Study of Education, Part II. Chicago: the Society, 1942.

Brownell, W. A. "Arithmetic Readiness as a Practical Classroom Concept." *Elementary School Journal* 52: 15-22; 1951.

Brownell, W. A. "Meaning and Skill—Maintaining the Balance." *The Arithmetic Teacher* 3: 129-36; 1956. © 1956 by the National Council of Teachers of Mathematics.

Brownell, W. A. "Arithmetic Abstractions—Progress Toward Maturity of Concepts Under Differing Programs of Instruction." *The Arithmetic Teacher* 10: 329; 1963.

Brownell, W. A. "The Evaluation of Learning Under Dissimilar Systems of Instruction." *The Arithmetic Teacher* 13: 267-74; 1966.

Brownell, W. A. *Arithmetic Abstractions: The Movement Toward Conceptual Maturity Under Differing Systems of Instruction.* Berkeley: University of California Press, 1967.

Brownell, W. A. "Conceptual Maturity in Arithmetic Under Differing Systems of Instruction." *Elementary School Journal* 69: 151-63; 1968.

Brownell, W. A., and C. Chazal. "The Effects of Premature Drill in Third-Grade Arithmetic." *Journal of Educational Research* 29: 17-28; 1935.

Brownell, W. A., and G. Hendrikson. "How Children Learn Information, Concepts, and Generalizations." In: *Learning and Instruction.* Forty-ninth Yearbook, National Society for the Study of Education, Part I. Chicago: University of Chicago Press, 1950. pp. 92-128.

Brownell, W. A., and H. Moser. *Meaningful vs. Mechanical Learning: A Study in Grade III Subtraction.* Duke University Research Studies in Education No. 8. Durham, North Carolina: Duke University Press, 1949.

Brownell, W. A., and L. B. Stretch. *The Effects of Unfamiliar Settings on Problem Solving.* Duke University Research Studies in Education. Durham, North Carolina: Duke University Press, 1931.

Brueckner, L. J. "Diagnosis in Arithmetic." In: *Educational Diagnosis.* Thirty-fourth Yearbook, National Society for the Study of Education. Bloomington, Illinois: Public School Publishing Company, 1935.

Brumbaugh, D. K. "Isolation of Factors That Influence the Ability of Young Children To Associate a Solid with a Representation of That Solid." *The Arithmetic Teacher* 18: 49-52; 1971.

Bruner, J. *The Process of Education.* Cambridge, Massachusetts: Harvard University Press, 1960.

Bruner, J. "The Act of Discovery." *Harvard Educational Review* 31: 21-32; 1961.

Brydegaard, M., and J. E. Inskeep, Jr., editors. *Readings in Geometry.* Washington, D.C.: National Council of Teachers of Mathematics, 1970.

Burge, L. W. "Interview Technique as a Means of Diagnosing." *Journal of Educational Research* 27: 422-29; 1934.

Burns, P. C. "Arithmetic Fundamentals for the Educable Mentally Retarded." *American Journal of Mental Deficiency* 66: 57-61; 1962.

Burns, P. C., and J. L. Yonally. "Does the Order of Presentation of Numerical Data in Multi-Step Arithmetic Problems Affect Their Difficulty?" *School Science and Mathematics* 64: 267-70; 1964.

Burton, W. H. *The Guidance of Learning Activities: A Summary of the Principles of Teaching Based upon the Growth of the Learner.* New York: Appleton-Century-Crofts, 1952. Reprinted by permission of Prentice-Hall, Inc., Englewood Cliffs, New Jersey.

Buswell, G. T. *Diagnostic Studies in Arithmetic.* Chicago: The University of Chicago, 1926.

Buswell, G. T. "Methods of Studying Pupils' Thinking in Arithmetic." *Arithmetic, 1949.* Supplementary Educational Monographs, No. 70. Chicago: University of Chicago Press, 1949.

Buswell, G. T. "A Comparison of Achievement in Arithmetic in England and Central California." *The Arithmetic Teacher* 5: 1-9; 1958.

Buswell, G. T., and L. John. *Vocabulary of Arithmetic.* Chicago: University of Chicago, 1931.

Buswell, G. T., and B. Y. Kersh. *Patterns of Thinking in Solving Problems.* University of California Publications in Education, Vol. 12, No. 2. Berkeley: University of California Press, 1956.

Callahan, L. G. "Remedial Work with Under-Achieving Children." *The Arithmetic Teacher* 9: 138-40; 1962.

Callahan, L. G. "A Study of Knowledge Possessed by Elementary School Teachers In-Service and In-Training, of the Cultural, Psychological, and

Mathematical Foundations of the Elementary School Mathematics Program." Unpublished doctoral dissertation, Syracuse University, 1966.

Callahan, L. G., and S. L. Passi. "The Relationship Between the Ability To Conserve Length and Conceptual Tempo." *Journal for Research in Mathematics Education* 2: 36-43; 1971.

Callahan, L. G., and M. Robinson. "Task-Analysis Procedures in Mathematics Instruction of Achievers and Underachievers." *School Science and Mathematics* 73: 578-84; 1973.

Callahan, W. J. "Adolescent Attitudes Toward Mathematics." *The Mathematics Teacher* 64: 751-55; 1971.

Capps, L. R. "Division of Fractions." *The Arithmetic Teacher* 9: 10-16; 1962.

Carlow, C. "A Study of Variables Within the Method of Individually Guided Discovery in Secondary School Mathematics." Unpublished doctoral dissertation, Syracuse University, 1967.

Carroll, J. B. "A Model of School Learning." *Teachers College Record* 64: 723-33; 1963.

Carroll, J. B. "On Learning from Being Told." *Educational Psychologist*, Vol. 5, No. 2; 1968.

Carroll, M. L. "Academic Achievement and Adjustment of Underage and Average Third Graders." *Journal of Educational Research* 56: 415-519; 1963.

Carry, L. R. "A Critical Assessment of Published Tests for Elementary School Mathematics." *The Arithmetic Teacher* 21: 14-18; 1974.

Carry, L. R., and J. F. Weaver. "Patterns of Mathematics Achievement in Grades 4, 5, and 6: X-Population." Report No. 10. In: J. W. Wilson, L. S. Cohen, and E. G. Begle, editors. *NLSMA Reports.* Stanford, California: School Mathematics Study Group, 1969.

Carter, L. "The Effect of Early School Entrance on the Scholastic Achievement of Elementary School Children in the Austin Public Schools." *Journal of Educational Research* 50: 91-103; 1956.

Cathcart, W. G., and W. Liedtke. "Reflectiveness/Impulsiveness and Mathematics Achievement." *The Arithmetic Teacher* 16: 563-67; 1969.

Cawley, J. F. "Teaching Arithmetic to Handicapped Children." *Focus on Exceptional Children* 2: 1-12; 1970.

Cawley, J., and J. Goodman. "Interrelationships Among Mental Abilities, Reading, Language Arts, and Arithmetic with the Mentally Handicapped." *The Arithmetic Teacher* 15: 631-36; 1968.

Cawley, J., and J. Goodman. "Arithmetic Problem Solving: A Demonstration with the Mentally Handicapped." *Exceptional Children* 36: 83-88; 1969.

Cawley, J., and S. Vitello. "Model for Arithmetical Programming for Handicapped Children." *Exceptional Children* 39: 101-10; 1972.

Central Advisory Council on Education. *Children and Their Primary Schools.* Volume I, *The Report;* Volume II, *Research and Surveys.* London: Her Majesty's Stationery Office, 1967.

Chalfant, J., and M. Scheffelin. *Central Processing Disfunctions in Children: A Review of Research.* NIMDS Monograph No. 9. Bethesda, Maryland: U.S. Department of Health, Education, and Welfare, 1969.

Clark, J. R., editor. "The Evaluation of Mathematical Learning." In: *Emerging Practices in Mathematics Education.* Twenty-second Yearbook, National Council of Teachers of Mathematics. Washington, D.C.: the Council, 1954.

Clark, J., and L. Eads. *Guiding Arithmetic Learning.* New York: Harcourt, Brace & World, 1954.

Clayton, T. E. *Teaching and Learning: A Psychological Perspective.* Englewood Cliffs, New Jersey: Prentice-Hall, Inc., 1965.

Cohn, R. "Dyscalculia." *Archives of Neurology* 4: 301-307; 1961.

Cohn, R. "Arithmetic and Learning Disabilities." In: H. R. Myklebust, editor. *Progress in Learning Disabilities.* New York: Grune and Stratton, 1971.

Coleman, J. S., and others. *Equality of Educational Opportunity.* Washington, D.C.: Superintendent of Documents, U.S. Government Printing Office, 1966.

Collins, J. F. "The Making of a Teaching Center." *Journal of Teacher Education* 25: 13-20; 1974.

Committee on the Metric System. *The Metric System of Weights and Measures.* Twentieth Yearbook of the National Council of Teachers of Mathematics. New York: Bureau of Publications, Columbia University, 1948.

Conant, E. H. "What Do Teachers Do All Day?" *Saturday Review World* 1: 55; June 1, 1974.

Connally, A. "Research in Mathematics Education and the Mentally Retarded." *The Arithmetic Teacher* 20: 491-97; 1973.

Crawford, D. "An Investigation of Age-Grade Trends in Understanding the Field Axioms." Unpublished doctoral dissertation, Syracuse University, Syracuse, New York, 1964.

Cristantiello, P. D. "Attitude Toward Mathematics and the Predictive Validity of a Measure of Quantitative Aptitude." *Journal of Educational Research* 55: 184-86; 1962.

Critchley, M. "The Dyslexic Child." London: William Heinemann Medical Books Limited, 1970.

Cronbach, L. "Issues Current in Educational Psychology." *Monographs of the Society for Research in Child Development,* Vol. 30, No. 1; 1965.

Cronbach, L. "The Logic of Experiments on Discovery." In: L. S. Shulman and E. R. Keislar, editors. *Learning by Discovery: A Critical Appraisal.* Chicago: Rand McNally & Company, 1966.

Crowder, A. "A Comparative Study of Two Methods of Teaching Arithmetic in the First Grade." Unpublished doctoral dissertation, North Texas State University, 1965.

Cruickshank, D., and W. Arnold. "Non-Decimal Instruction Revisited." *Elementary School Journal* 70: 108-11; 1969.

Cruickshank, W. M. "A Comparative Study of Psychological Factors Involved in the Response of Mentally Retarded and Normal Boys to Problems in Arithmetic." Unpublished doctoral dissertation, University of Michigan, 1946.

Cruickshank, W., F. Bentzen, F. Ratzeburg, and M. Tannhauser. *A Teaching Method for Brain-Injured and Hyperactive Children*. Syracuse, New York: Syracuse University Press, 1961.

Crumley, R. "A Comparison of Different Methods of Teaching Subtraction in the Third Grade." Unpublished doctoral dissertation, University of Chicago, 1956.

Cuisenaire, G., and C. Gattegno. *Numbers in Colour*. London: William Heinemann, 1954.

Dale, E. "How Do We Provide Access to Excellence?" *Apropos*, Summer 1974. Columbus: National Center on Educational Media and Materials for the Handicapped, The Ohio State University.

Dawson, D., and A. Ruddell. "An Experimental Approach to the Division Idea." *The Arithmetic Teacher* 2: 6-9; 1955.

DeSimone, D. V. *A Metric America: A Decision Whose Time Has Come*. U.S. Metric Study. Washington, D.C.: Superintendent of Documents, U.S. Government Printing Office, 1971.

Deutsch, M. "The Role of Social Class in Language Development and Cognition." *American Journal of Orthopsychiatry* 35: 78-87; 1965.

Dewey, J. *Democracy and Education*. New York: The Free Press, 1930. p. 6.

Dickenson, D., and J. D. Larson. "The Effects of Chronological Age in Months on School Achievement." *Journal of Educational Research* 56: 492-93; 1963.

Diedrich, R., and V. J. Glennon. "The Effects of Studying Decimal and Non-Decimal Numeration Systems on Mathematical Understanding, Retention, and Transfer." *Journal for Research in Mathematics Education* 1: 162-72; 1970.

Dienes, Z. P. *Building Up Mathematics*. London: Hutchinson Publishing Group, 1960.

Dienes, Z. P. "Comments on Some Problems of Teacher Education in Mathematics." *The Arithmetic Teacher* 17: 268; 1970a.

Dienes, Z. P. "Some Basic Processes Involved in Mathematics Learning." In: R. Ashlock and W. L. Herman, Jr. *Current Research in Elementary School Mathematics*. New York: The Macmillan Co., 1970b.

Dilley, C. "A Comparison of Two Methods of Teaching Long Division." Unpublished doctoral dissertation, University of Illinois, 1970.

D'Mello, S., and E. Willemsen. "The Development of the Number Concept: A Scalogram Analysis." *Child Development* 40: 681-88; 1969.

Dominy, M. M. "A Comparison: Textbooks, Domestic and Foreign." *The Arithmetic Teacher* 10: 428-34; 1963.

Dreger, R. M., and L. R. Aiken. "The Identification of Number Anxiety in College Populations." *Journal of Educational Psychology* 48: 344-51; 1957.

Duckworth, E. "The Having of Wonderful Ideas." *Harvard Educational Review* 42: 217-31; 1972.

Dunkley, M. E. "Some Number Concepts of Disadvantaged Children." *The Arithmetic Teacher* 12: 359-61; 1965.

Dunkley, M. E. "Mathematics and the Disadvantaged Child." *The Elementary School Journal* 73: 44-49; 1972.

Dutton, W. H. "Attitudes of Junior High School Pupils Toward Arithmetic." *School Review* 64: 18-22; 1956.

Dutton, W. H. "Growth in Number Readiness in Kindergarten Children." *The Arithmetic Teacher* 10: 251-55; 1963.

Dutton, W. H. *Evaluating Pupils' Understanding of Arithmetic.* Englewood Cliffs, New Jersey: Prentice-Hall, Inc., 1964.

Ebel, R. L. "Criterion-Referenced Measurements: Limitations." *School Review* 79: 282-88; 1971.

Eddy, W. P. "How Successful Are the British Teachers' Centers?" *Educational Leadership* 31: 509-11; 1974.

Eisner, E. W. "Educational Objectives: Help or Hindrance?" *School Review* 75: 250-61; 1967.

Ekman, L. "A Comparison of the Effectiveness of Different Approaches to the Teaching of Addition and Subtraction Algorithms in the Third Grade." Unpublished doctoral dissertation, University of Minnesota, 1966.

Emm, Sister M. E. *A Factorial Study of the Problem Solving Ability of Fifth Grade Boys.* Washington, D.C.: The Catholic University of America Press, 1959.

Engelhard, Sister M. D. *An Experimental Study of Arithmetic Problem Solving Ability of Sixth Grade Girls.* Washington, D.C.: The Catholic University of America Press, 1955.

Epstein, M. G. "Testing in Mathematics: Why? What? How?" *The Arithmetic Teacher* 15: 311-19; 1968.

Erlwanger, S. H. "Benny's Conception of Rules and Answers in IPI Mathematics." *Journal of Children's Mathematical Behavior* 1: 7-27; 1973.

Evaluating Instructional Systems. From *EPIE Report: Number 58.* © 1974 by EPIE Institute. Reprinted with permission.

Faust, C. E. "A Study of the Relationship Between Attitude and Achievement in Selected Elementary School Subjects." Unpublished doctoral dissertation, State University of Iowa, 1962.

Featherstone, J. "The Primary School Revolution in Britain: I." *New Republic* 157: 17-21; 1967a.

Featherstone, J. "Schools for Children: II." *New Republic* 157: 17-21; 1967b.

Featherstone, J. "How Children Learn: III." *New Republic* 157: 17-21; 1967c.

Featherstone, J. "Measuring What Schools Achieve." *Phi Delta Kappan* 55: 448-50; 1974. Originally published as: "Learning and Testing." *New Republic* 169: 19-21; 1973.

Fedon, P. "The Role of Attitude in Learning Arithmetic." *The Arithmetic Teacher* 5: 304-10; 1958.

Fehr, H. "Sense and Nonsense in a Modern School Mathematics Program." *The Arithmetic Teacher* 13: 83-91; 1966.

Feldhusen, J. M. "Anxiety, Divergent Thinking, and Achievement." *Journal of Educational Psychology* 56: 40-45; 1965.

Feldhusen, J., J. Thurston, and J. Benning. "Aggressive Classroom Behavior and School Achievement." *Journal of Special Education* 4: 431-39; 1970.

Fennema, E. "Models and Mathematics." *The Arithmetic Teacher* 19: 635-40; 1972a.

Fennema, E. "The Relative Effectiveness of a Symbolic and a Concrete Model in Learning a Selected Mathematical Principle." *Journal for Research in Mathematics Education* 3: 233-38; 1972b.

Fennema, E. "Mathematics Learning and the Sexes: A Review." *Journal for Research in Mathematics Education* 5: 126-39; 1974.

Fey, J. T. "Patterns of Verbal Communication in Mathematics Classes." Unpublished doctoral dissertation, Columbia University, 1969.

Fink, M. "Self-Concept as It Relates to Academic Underachievement." *California Journal of Educational Research* 13: 57-61; 1962.

Fisher, J. "Extent of Implementation of CUPM Level I Recommendations." *The Arithmetic Teacher* 14: 194-97; 1967.

Flanders, N. A. "Teacher Influence, Pupil Attitudes, and Achievement." Washington, D.C.: Superintendent of Documents, U.S. Government Printing Office, 1965.

Flanders, N. A. *Analyzing Teacher Behavior.* Reading, Massachusetts: Addison-Wesley Publishing Co., 1970.

Flavell, J. *The Developmental Psychology of Jean Piaget.* Princeton, New Jersey: D. Van Nostrand Company, 1963.

Forbes, J. E. "The Utility of Behavioral Objectives: A Source of Dangers and Difficulties." *The Mathematics Teacher* 69: 687, 744-47; 1971.

Foshay, A. W. "From the Association." In: *Balance in the Curriculum.* Yearbook of the Association for Supervision and Curriculum Development. Washington, D.C.: the Association, 1961.

Foster, K. R. "The Implementation of the CUPM Recommendations for Elementary School Mathematics Teachers into the Curricula of Certain NCATE-Approved and Non-NCATE Approved Institutions in the United States." Unpublished doctoral dissertation, University of Tennessee, 1970.

Fox, L. H. "Facilitating Educational Development of Mathematically Precocious Youth." In: J. Stanley, D. Keating, and L. Fox, editors. *Mathematical Talent.* Baltimore: Johns Hopkins University Press, 1974.

Frayer, D. A. "Effects of Number of Instances and Emphasis of Relevant Attribute Values on Mastery of Geometric Concepts by Fourth- and Sixth-Grade Children." Unpublished doctoral dissertation, University of Wisconsin, 1969.

Freudenthal, H. "Initiation into Geometry." *Mathematics Student* 24: 82-97; 1956.

Friedlander, B. "A Psychologist's Second Thought on Concepts, Curiosity, and Discovery in Teaching and Learning." *Harvard Educational Review* 35: 18-38; 1965.

Friedlander, B. "Psychology and the Third R in Special Education." *Education and Training of the Mentally Retarded* 3: 80-89; 1968.

Frost, B. P. "Anxiety and Educational Achievement." *British Journal of Educational Psychology* 38: 293-301; 1968.

Frostig, M., and P. Maslow. *Learning Problems in the Classroom.* New York: Grune and Stratton, 1973.

Gagné, R. M. *The Conditions of Learning.* New York: Holt, Rinehart and Winston, Inc., 1970.

Gagné, R. M., J. R. Mayor, H. L. Garstens, and N. E. Paradise. "Factors in Acquiring Knowledge of a Mathematical Task." *Psychological Monographs,* Vol. 76; 1962.

Gallagher, J. J. "Analysis of Research on the Education of Gifted Children." Springfield: State of Illinois, Office of the Superintendent of Public Instruction, 1960.

Galperin, P. "An Experimental Study in the Formation of Mental Actions." In: B. Simon, editor. *Psychology in the Soviet Union.* Palo Alto, California: Stanford University Press, 1957. pp. 217, 222-23.

Garai, J. E., and A. Scheinfell. "Sex Differences in Mental and Behavioral Traits." *Genetic Psychology Monographs* 77: 169-299; 1968.

Gay, J., and M. Cole. *The New Mathematics and an Old Culture.* New York: Holt, Rinehart & Winston, Inc., 1967.

Gay, L. R. "Use of a Retention Index for Mathematics Instruction." *Journal of Educational Psychology* 63: 466-72; 1972.

Gibb, E. G. "Children's Thinking in the Process of Subtraction." *Journal of Experimental Education* 25: 71-80; 1965.

Gibney, T., J. Ginther, and F. Pigge. "The Mathematical Understandings of Pre-Service and In-Service Teachers." *The Arithmetic Teacher* 17: 155-62; 1970a.

Gibney, T., J. Ginther, and F. Pigge. "What Influences the Mathematical Understanding of Elementary School Teachers?" *Elementary School Journal* 70: 367-73; 1970b.

Glavin, J. "Followup Behavioral Research in Resource Rooms." *Exceptional Children* 40: 211-13; 1973.

Glavin, J., and F. Annesley. "Reading and Arithmetic Correlates of Conduct—Problem and Withdrawn Children." *Journal of Special Education* 5: 213-19; 1971.

Glavin, J., H. Quay, and J. Werry. "Behavioral and Academic Gains of Conduct Problem Children in Different Classroom Settings." *Exceptional Children* 37: 441-46; 1971.

Glennon, V. J. "A Study in Needed Redirection in the Preparation of Teachers of Arithmetic." *The Mathematics Teacher* 42: 389-96; 1949.

Glennon, V. J. "Some Perspectives in Education." In: *Enrichment Mathematics for the Grades.* Twenty-seventh Yearbook, National Council of Teachers of Mathematics. Washington, D.C.: the Council, 1963.

Glennon, V. J. ". . . And Now Synthesis: A Theoretical Model for Mathematics Education." *The Arithmetic Teacher* 12: 134-41; 1965. © 1965 by the National Council of Teachers of Mathematics.

Glennon, V. J. "The 3 R's Are Alive and Well." *The Instructor* 83: 45; 1974.

Glennon, V. J., and J. W. Wilson. "Diagnostic Prescriptive Teaching." In: W. C. Lowry, editor. *The Slow Learner in Mathematics.* Thirty-fifth

Yearbook of the National Council of Teachers of Mathematics. Washington, D.C.: the Council, 1972.

Goals for Mathematical Education of Elementary School Teachers. A report of the Cambridge Conference on Teacher Training. Boston: Educational Development Center, Inc., and Houghton Mifflin Company, 1967.

Goals for School Mathematics. The Report of the Cambridge Conference on School Mathematics. Published for Educational Services Incorporated. Boston: Houghton Mifflin Company, 1963.

Goldberg, M. L., A. H. Passow, and J. Justman. *The Effect of Ability Grouping.* New York: Teachers College Press, 1966.

Goldstein, A. "Does Homework Help? A Review of Research." *The Elementary School Journal* 60: 213-24; 1960.

Goodstein, H., H. Bessant, G. Thibodeau, S. Vitello, and I. Vlahakos. "The Effect of Three Variables on the Verbal Problem Solving of Educable Mentally Handicapped Children." *American Journal of Mental Deficiency* 76: 703-709; 1972.

Gordon, E. W. "Characteristics of Socially Disadvantaged Children: Summary and Outlook." *Review of Educational Research* 35: 384-85; 1965.

Gott, M. "The Effect of Age Differences at Kindergarten Entrance on Achievement and Adjustment in the Elementary School." Unpublished doctoral dissertation, University of Colorado, 1963.

Grafft, W. D., and A. K. Ruddell. "Cognitive Outcomes of the SMSG Mathematics Program in Grades 4, 5, and 6." *The Arithmetic Teacher* 15: 161-65; 1968.

Graubard, P. "Extent of Academic Retardation in a Residential Treatment Center." *Journal of Educational Research* 58: 78-80; 1964.

Gray, R. F. "An Experiment in the Teaching of Introductory Multiplication." *The Arithmetic Teacher* 12: 199-203; 1965.

Gray, R. F. "An Approach to Evaluating Arithmetic Understandings." *The Arithmetic Teacher* 13: 187-91; 1966.

Gray, R., and D. Allison. "An Experimental Study of the Relationship of Homework to Pupil Success in Computation with Fractions." *School Science and Mathematics* 71: 339-46; 1971.

Greabell, L. "The Effect of Three Different Methods of Implementation of Mathematics Programs on Children's Achievement in Mathematics." *The Arithmetic Teacher* 16: 288-92; 1969. © 1969 by the National Council of Teachers of Mathematics.

Greenfield, P. M. "On Culture and Conservation." In: J. S. Bruner, R. Olver, and P. M. Greenfield, editors. *Studies in Cognitive Growth.* New York: John Wiley & Sons, Inc., 1966.

Grossnickle, F. E. "The Arithmetic Program." In: L. A. Fliegler, editor. *Curriculum Planning for the Gifted.* Englewood Cliffs, New Jersey: Prentice-Hall, Inc., 1961.

Grouws, D. A. "Solution Methods Used in Solving Addition and Subtraction." *The Arithmetic Teacher* 21: 255-61; 1974.

Guidelines for the Preparation of Teachers of Mathematics. Reston, Virginia: National Council of Teachers of Mathematics, 1973a.

"Guidelines for the Preparation of Teachers of Mathematics." *The Arithmetic Teacher* 20: 705-707; 1973b.

Gunderson, A. "Thought Patterns of Young Children in Learning Multiplication and Division." *Elementary School Journal* 55: 453-61; 1953.

Gustafson, R., and T. Owens. "Children's Perceptions of Themselves and Their Teacher's Feelings Toward Them Related to Actual Teacher Perceptions and School Achievement." Paper presented at the fifty-first annual meeting of the Western Psychological Association, San Francisco, California, 1971.

Haddon, F. A., and H. Lytton. "Primary Education and Divergent Thinking Abilities—Four Years On." *British Journal of Educational Psychology* 42: 136-47; 1971.

Haggard, E. A. "Specialization, Personality, and Academic Achievement in Gifted Children." *School Review* 65: 388-414; 1957.

Hallerberg, A. E. "The Metric System: Past, Present, Future?" *The Arithmetic Teacher* 20: 247-55; 1973.

Hand, E. F. "Evaluation of a Large-Scale Mathematics In-Service Institute for Elementary Teachers." Unpublished doctoral dissertation, University of Georgia, 1967.

Hansen, C. "Factors Associated with Successful Achievement in Problem Solving in Sixth Grade Arithmetic." *Journal of Educational Research* 38: 15; 1944.

Hargis, C. H. "The Grammar of the Noun Phrase and Arithmetic Instruction for Deaf Children." *American Annals of the Deaf* 114: 766-69; 1969.

Haskell, S. "Some Observations on the Effects of Class Size Upon Pupil Achievement in Geometric Drawing." *Journal of Educational Research* 58: 27-30; 1964.

Hawkins, D. "Learning the Unteachable." In: L. S. Shulman and E. R. Keislar, editors. *Learning by Discovery: A Critical Appraisal.* Chicago: Rand McNally & Company, 1966.

Haynes, J. "Cuisenaire Rods and the Teaching of Multiplication to Third Grade Children." Unpublished doctoral dissertation, Florida State University, 1963.

Heard, I. M. "Mathematical Concepts and Abilities Possessed by Kindergarten Entrants." *The Arithmetic Teacher* 17: 340-41; 1970.

Hebron, M. E. "A Factorial Study of Learning a New Number System and Its Relation to Attainment, Intelligence, and Temperament." *British Journal of Educational Psychology* 32: 38-45; 1962.

Heddons, J., and K. Smith. "The Readability of Elementary Mathematics Books." *The Arithmetic Teacher* 11: 466-68; 1964.

Henderson, G. L. "Individualized Instruction: Sweet in Theory, Sour in Practice." *The Arithmetic Teacher* 19: 17-22; 1972. © 1972 by the National Council of Teachers of Mathematics.

Hendrix, G. "A New Clue to Transfer of Training." *Elementary School Journal* 48: 197-208; 1947.

Hendrix, G. "Learning by Discovery." *The Mathematics Teacher* 54: 290-99; 1961.

Hess, E. H. "Attitude and Pupil Size." *Scientific American* 212: 46-54; 1965.

Hicks, R. C. "Elementary Series and Texts of Teachers—How Well Do They Agree?" *The Arithmetic Teacher* 15: 266-70; 1968.

Higgins, C. "Mathematics for the Handicapped: Programming Concepts." *Focus on Exceptional Children* 2: 12-14; 1970.

Higgins, J. E. "An Investigation of the Effects of Non-Decimal Numeration Instruction on Mathematical Understanding." *School Science and Mathematics* 72: 293-97; 1972.

Higgins, J. L. "Attitude Changes in a Mathematics Laboratory Utilizing a Mathematics Through Science Approach." *Journal for Research in Mathematics Education* 1: 43-56; 1970.

Hilgard, E., and G. Bowers. *Theories of Learning*. New York: Appleton-Century-Crofts, 1966.

Hilgren, F. J. "Schools Are Going Metric." *The Arithmetic Teacher* 20: 265-76; 1973. © 1973 by the National Council of Teachers of Mathematics.

Hill, E. "A Study of Preference and Performance on Partition and Measurement Division Problems." Unpublished doctoral dissertation, State University of Iowa, 1952.

Hill, J. P. "Similarity and Accordance Between Parents and Sons in Attitudes Toward Mathematics." *Child Development* 30: 777-91; 1967.

Hill, S. A. "A Study of Logical Abilities of Children." Unpublished doctoral dissertation, Stanford University, 1960.

Hlavaty, J. H. *Mathematics for the Academically Talented Student in the Secondary School*. Washington, D.C.: National Council of Teachers of Mathematics, 1959.

Hollis, L. "A Study To Compare the Effects of Teaching First Grade Mathematics by the Cuisenaire-Gattegno Method with the Traditional Method." Unpublished doctoral dissertation, Texas Technical College, 1964a.

Hollis, L. "Why Teach Numeration?" *The Arithmetic Teacher* 11: 94-97; 1964b.

Holton, B. "Motivation and General Mathematics Students." *The Mathematics Teacher* 57: 20; 1964.

Houston, R. W., and M. V. DeVault. "Mathematics In-Service Education: Teacher Growth Increases Pupil Growth." *The Arithmetic Teacher* 10: 243-47; 1963. © 1963 by the National Council of Teachers of Mathematics.

Howard, C. "Three Methods of Teaching Arithmetic." *California Journal of Educational Research* 1: 25-29; 1950.

Howlett, K. D. "A Study of the Relationship Between Piagetian Class Inclusion Tasks and the Ability of First Grade Children To Do Missing Addend Computation and Verbal Problems." Unpublished doctoral dissertation, State University of New York at Buffalo, 1973.

Howson, A. G., editor. *Developments in Mathematical Education*. Proceedings of the Second International Congress on Mathematical Education. London: Cambridge University Press, 1973.

Hungerman, A. D. "Achievement and Attitude of Sixth-Grade Pupils in Conventional and Contemporary Mathematics Programs." *The Arithmetic Teacher* 14: 30-39; 1967.

Hunkler, R. "A New Look at the Implementation of the CUPM Level I Recommendations." *School Science and Mathematics* 71: 423-25; 1971a.

Hunkler, R. "An Evaluation of a Short-Term In-Service Mathematics Program for Elementary School Teachers." *School Science and Mathematics* 71: 650-54; 1971b.

Husén, T., editor. *International Study of Achievement in Mathematics: A Comparison of Twelve Countries.* Volume I and Volume II. New York: John Wiley & Sons, 1967.

Hutchings, B. "Low-Stress Subtraction." *The Arithmetic Teacher* 22: 226-32; 1975.

Hynes, M. E., M. Hynes, M. Kysilka, and D. Brumbaugh. "Mathematics Laboratories: What Does Research Say?" *Educational Leadership* 31: 271-74; 1973.

Ilg, F., and L. Ames. *School Readiness.* New York: Harper and Row, Publishers, 1964.

Ilika, J. "Age of Entrance into the First Grade as Related to Scholastic Achievement." Unpublished doctoral dissertation, University of Michigan, 1963.

Ingersoll, G. M. "An Experimental Study of Two Methods of Presenting the Inversion Algorism in Division of Fractions." *California Journal of Educational Research* 22: 17-25; 1971.

Inhelder, B., and J. Piaget. *The Growth of Logical Thinking from Childhood to Adolescence.* London: Routledge and Kegan Paul, 1958.

Inskeep, J. E., Jr. "Building a Case for the Application of Piaget's Theory and Research in the Classroom." *The Arithmetic Teacher* 19: 255-62; 1972.

Irish, E. H. "Improving Problem Solving by Improving Verbal Generalization." *The Arithmetic Teacher* 11: 196; 1964.

Jackson, R. L. "Numeration Systems: An Experimental Study of Achievement on Selected Objectives of Mathematics Education Resulting from the Study of Different Numeration Systems." Unpublished doctoral dissertation, University of Minnesota, 1965.

Jacobs, J., A. Beery, and J. Lernwohl. "Evaluation of an Accelerated Arithmetic Program." *The Arithmetic Teacher* 12: 113-19; 1965.

Jarvis, O. T. "Boy-Girl Ability Differences in Elementary School Arithmetic." *School Science and Mathematics* 64: 657-59; 1964.

Jerman, M. "Problem Length as a Structural Variable in Verbal Arithmetic Problems." *Educational Studies in Mathematics* 5: 109; 1973.

Jerman, M., and R. Rees. "Predicting the Relative Difficulty of Verbal Arithmetic Problems." *Educational Studies in Mathematics* 4: 306; 1972.

Jerman, M., and M. Sanford. "Linguistic and Computational Variables in Problem Solving in Elementary Mathematics." *Educational Studies in Mathematics* 5: 317-62; 1974.

Johnson, D. A. "Behavioral Objectives for Mathematics." *School Science and Mathematics* 71: 109-15; 1971.

Johnson, D., and H. Myklebust. *Learning Disabilities, Educational Principles, and Practices.* New York: Grune and Stratton, 1967.

Johnson, J. "Relative Merits of Three Methods of Subtraction." Contributions to Education No. 738. New York: Bureau of Publications, Teachers College, Columbia University, 1938.

Johnson, J. T. "On the Nature of Problem-Solving in Arithmetic." *Journal of Educational Research* 43: 110-15; 1949.

Johnson, R. L., and J. Moser. "Effects of Varying Concrete Activities on Achievement of Objectives in Perimeter, Area, and Volume by Students of Grades Four, Five, and Six." Research report read at the annual meeting of the American Educational Research Association, 1971.

Johonnot, J. *Principles and Practice of Teaching.* New York: D. Appleton and Company, 1883. By permission of Prentice-Hall, Inc., Englewood Cliffs, New Jersey.

Jones, P. "Discovery Teaching: From Socrates to Modernity." *The Mathematics Teacher* 63: 501-508; 1970.

Jonsson, H. A. "Interaction of Test Anxiety and Test Difficulty in Mathematics Problem Solving Performance." Unpublished doctoral dissertation, University of California, Berkeley, 1966.

Josephina, Sister M. "A Study of Attitudes in the Elementary Grades." *Journal of Educational Sociology* 37: 56; 1959.

Joyce, B. R., and M. Weil. *Concepts of Teacher Centers.* Washington, D.C.: ERIC Clearinghouse on Teacher Education, 1973.

Junge, C. W. "Gifted Children and Arithmetic." *The Arithmetic Teacher* 4: 141-46; 1957.

Kagan, J. "Impulsive and Reflective Children: Significance of Conceptual Tempo." In: J. D. Krumboltz. *Learning and the Educational Process.* Chicago: Rand McNally & Company, 1965.

Kagan, J. *Understanding Children.* New York: Harcourt Brace Jovanovich, Inc., 1971.

Kaliski, L. "Arithmetic and the Brain-Injured Child." In: E. Frierson and W. E. Barbe. *Educating Children with Learning Disabilities.* New York: Appleton-Century-Crofts, 1967.

Keating, D. P. "The Study of Mathematically Precocious Youth." In: J. Stanley, D. Keating, and L. Fox, editors. *Mathematical Talent.* Baltimore: Johns Hopkins University Press, 1974.

Kemp, C. G. "Effect of Dogmatism on Critical Thinking." *School Science and Mathematics* 60: 314-19; 1960.

Kenney, R. A. "Mathematical Understandings of Elementary School Teachers." *The Arithmetic Teacher* 12: 431-42; 1965.

Kersh, R. "Learning by Discovery: What Is Learned?" *The Arithmetic Teacher* 11: 226-31; 1964.

Kidd, K., S. Myers, and D. Cilley. *The Laboratory Approach to Mathematics.* Chicago: Science Research Associates, 1970. Reprinted by permission of the publisher.

Kieren, T. "Manipulative Activity in Mathematics Learning." *Journal for Research in Mathematics Education* 2: 228-34; 1971.

King, W. L. "Learning and Utilization of Conjunctive and Disjunctive Classification Rules: A Developmental Study." *Journal of Experimental Child Psychology* 4: 217-31; 1966.

Kirk, S., and O. Johnson. *Educating the Retarded Child.* Boston: Houghton Mifflin Co., 1951.

Kirk, S. A., and W. D. Kirk. *Psycholinguistic Learning Disabilities: Diagnosis and Remediation.* Urbana: University of Illinois Press, 1971.

Kliebhan, Sister M. C. *An Experimental Study of Arithmetic Problem Solving Ability of Sixth Grade Boys.* Washington, D.C.: The Catholic University of America Press, 1955.

Kline, M. "Intellectuals and the Schools: A Case History." *Harvard Educational Review* 36: 505-11; 1966.

Kline, M. *Why Johnny Can't Add.* New York: St. Martin's Press, 1973.

Koch, E. "Homework in Arithmetic." *The Arithmetic Teacher* 12: 9-13; 1965.

Koeckeritz, W. A. "An Analysis of Mathematical and Professional Knowledge of Present and Future Elementary Teachers." Unpublished doctoral dissertation, Utah State University, 1970.

Kramer, K. "Comparison of Objectives, Methods, and Achievement in the United States and in the Netherlands." Unpublished doctoral dissertation, University of Iowa, 1957.

Krathwohl, D., B. Bloom, and B. Masia. *Taxonomy of Educational Objectives, Handbook II: Affective Domain.* New York: David McKay Company, 1956.

Kratzer, R., and S. Willoughby. "A Comparison of Initially Teaching Division Employing the Distributive and Greenwood Algorithms with the Aid of a Manipulative Material." *Journal for Research in Mathematics Education* 4: 197-204; 1973.

Lamanna, J. B. "The Effect of Teacher Verbal Behavior on Pupil Achievement in Problem Solving in Sixth Grade Mathematics." Unpublished doctoral dissertation, St. Johns University, 1969.

Lankford, F. G., Jr. "What Can a Teacher Learn About a Pupil's Thinking Through Oral Interviews?" *The Arithmetic Teacher* 21: 26-32; 1974.

Laurendeau, M., and A. Pinard. *The Development of the Concept of Space in the Child.* New York: International Universities Press, Inc., 1970.

Lavin, D. *The Prediction of Academic Performance.* New York: Russell Sage Foundation, 1965.

Lazarus, M. "EDC's New Program in Mathematics: Purposes and Goals." Special Projects EDC/7. Newton, Massachusetts: Education Development Center, Inc. From the *EDC News,* No. 3; Winter 1974.

LeBlanc, J. F. "The Performances of First-Grade Children in Four Levels of Conservation of Numerousness and Three I.Q. Groups When Solving Arithmetic Subtraction Problems." Unpublished doctoral dissertation, University of Wisconsin, 1968.

LeBlanc, J. F. "Pedagogy in Elementary Mathematics Education—Time for Change." *The Arithmetic Teacher* 17: 605; 1970.

Lerch, H. H. "Fourth-Grade Pupils Study a Number System with Base 5." *Journal of Educational Research* 57: 59-63; 1963.

Levine, G. "Attitudes of Elementary School Pupils and Their Parents Toward Mathematics and Other School Instruction." *Journal for Research in Mathematics Education* 3: 51-58; 1972.

Levy, D. M. *Maternal Over-Protection.* New York: Columbia University Press, 1943.

Lewis, M. "Teaching Arithmetic Computation Skills." *Education of the Visually Handicapped* 2: 66-72; 1970.

Lipson, J. I. "IPI Math—An Example of What's Right and Wrong with Individualized Modular Programs." Reprinted by special permission of *Learning*, The Magazine for Creative Teaching, March 1974. © 1974 by Education Today Company, Inc., 530 University Avenue, Palo Alto, California 94301.

Lister, C. M. "The Development of a Concept of Volume Conservation in ESN Children." *British Journal of Educational Psychology* 40: 55-64; 1970.

Lloyd, B. B. "Studies of Conservation with Yoruba Children of Differing Ages and Experience." *Child Development* 42: 415-28; 1971.

Loftus, E. F., and P. Suppes. "Structural Variables That Determine Problem-Solving Difficulty in Computer-Assisted Instruction." *Journal of Educational Psychology* 63: 521-42; 1972.

Lovell, K. *The Growth of Basic Mathematical and Scientific Concepts in Children.* London: University of London Press, 1962.

Lovell, K. "The Development of the Concept of Mathematical Proof in Abler Pupils." In: M. Rosskopf, L. Steffe, and S. Taback, editors. *Piagetian Cognitive-Development Research and Mathematical Education.* Washington, D.C.: National Council of Teachers of Mathematics, 1971a.

Lovell, K. "The Development of Some Mathematical Ideas in Elementary School Pupils." In: M. Rosskopf, L. Steffe, and S. Taback, editors. *Piagetian Cognitive-Development Research and Mathematical Education.* Washington, D.C.: National Council of Teachers of Mathematics, 1971b.

Lovell, K. *The Growth of Understanding in Mathematics: Kindergarten Through Grade Three.* Early Childhood Education Series. New York: Holt, Rinehart and Winston, Inc., 1971c.

Lovell, K. "Intellectual Growth and Understanding Mathematics." Reprinted with permission from the *Journal for Research in Mathematics Education*, May 1972 (Vol. 3, pp. 164-82). © by the National Council of Teachers of Mathematics.

Lovell, K., and J. Shields. "Some Aspects of a Study of the Gifted Child." *British Journal of Educational Psychology* 37: 201-207; 1967.

Lucas, J. "The Effect of Attribute-Block Training on Children's Development of Arithmetic." Unpublished doctoral dissertation, University of California, Berkeley, 1966.

Luchins, A. S. "Classroom Experiments on Mental Set." *American Journal of Psychology* 59: 295-98; 1964.

Lucow, W. "Testing the Cuisenaire Method." *The Arithmetic Teacher* 10: 435-38; 1963.

Lyda, W. J., and R. S. Church. "Direct, Practical Arithmetical Experiences and Success in Solving Realistic Verbal Reasoning Problems in Arithmetic." *Journal of Educational Research* 57: 530-33; 1964.

McCandless, B. R., and A. Casteneda. "Anxiety in Children, School Achievement, and Intelligence." *Child Development* 27: 379-82; 1956.

McClelland, D. *The Achievement Motive.* New York: Appleton-Century-Crofts, 1953.

McGowan, E. "Anxiety, Reality of Aspiration, and the Academic Achievement of Fourth Grade Children." Unpublished doctoral dissertation, New York University, 1960.

McLellan, J., and J. Dewey. *The Psychology of Number.* New York: D. Appleton, 1908.

McManis, D. "Conservation of Identity and Equivalence of Quantity by Retardates." *Journal of Genetic Psychology* 115: 63-69; 1969a.

McManis, D. "Conservation of Mass, Weight, and Volume by Normal and Retarded Children." *American Journal of Mental Deficiency* 73: 762-67; 1969b.

McManis, D. "Conservation and Transitivity of Weight and Length by Normals and Retardates." *Developmental Psychology* 1: 373-82; 1969c.

McManis, D. "Conservation, Seriation, and Transitivity Performance by Retarded and Average Individuals." *American Journal of Mental Deficiency* 74: 784-91; 1970.

Maertens, N. "Effects of Arithmetic Homework upon the Attitudes of Third Grade Pupils Toward Certain School-Related Structures." *School Science and Mathematics* 68: 657-62; 1968.

Maertens, N., and J. Johnston. "Effects of Arithmetic Homework upon the Attitudes and Achievement of Fourth, Fifth, and Sixth Grade Pupils." *School Science and Mathematics* 72: 117-26; 1972.

Martin, M. D. "Reading Comprehension, Abstract Verbal Reasoning, and Computation as Factors in Arithmetic Problem Solving." Unpublished doctoral dissertation, State University of Iowa, 1963.

Maslow, A. "Some Educational Implications of the Humanistic Psychologies." *Harvard Educational Review* 38: 685-95; 1968.

Melton, A. W. "The Science of Learning and the Technology of Educational Method." *Harvard Educational Review* 29: 96-106; 1959.

Menniti, D. J. "A Study of the Relationship Between Class Size and Pupil Achievement in the Catholic Elementary School." Unpublished doctoral dissertation, The Catholic University of America, 1964.

Meserve, B. E. "Geometry Is a Gateway to Mathematics." In: A. G. Howson, editor. *Developments in Mathematical Education.* London: Cambridge University Press, 1973.

Meyer, W., and G. Thompson. "Sex Differences in the Distribution of Teacher Approval and Disapproval Among Sixth-Grade Children." *Journal of Educational Psychology* 47: 385-95; 1956.

Milgram, J. "Time Utilization in Arithmetic Teaching." *The Arithmetic Teacher* 16: 213-15; 1969. © 1969 by the National Council of Teachers of Mathematics.

Milliken, R. L. "Mathematical-Verbal Ability Differentials of Situational Anxiety as Measured by Blood Pressure Change." *Journal of Experimental Education* 32: 309-11; 1964.

Montague, D. "Arithmetic Concepts of Kindergarten Children in Contrasting Socio-Economic Areas." *The Elementary School Journal* 64: 393-97; 1964.

Montessori, M. *The Montessori Method.* New York: Schocken Books, 1964.

Moody, W. B., R. B. Bausell, and J. R. Jenkins. "The Effect of Class Size on the Learning of Mathematics: A Parametric Study with Fourth-Grade Students." *Journal of Research in Mathematics Education* 4: 170-76; 1973.

Mott, E. "An Experimental Study Testing the Value of Using Multisensory Experiences in the Teaching of Measurement Units on the Fifth- and Sixth-Grade Level." Unpublished doctoral dissertation, Pennsylvania State University, 1959.

Mullins, W. H. "An Arithmetic Program for the Superior Student." Unpublished doctoral dissertation, University of Iowa, 1958.

Myen, E., and A. Hieronymus. "The Age Placement of Academic Skills in Curriculum for the EMR." *Exceptional Children* 36: 333-39; 1970.

Myers, K. R. *The Self Concept of Students in Individually Prescribed Instruction.* Bloomington, Indiana: Center for Innovation in Teaching the Handicapped, 1972.

Nasca, D. "Comparative Merits of a Manipulative Approach to Second-Grade Arithmetic." *The Arithmetic Teacher* 13: 221-26; 1966.

National Assessment of Educational Progress. *Math Fundamentals.* Mathematics Report, No. 04-MA-01. Washington, D.C.: Superintendent of Documents, U.S. Government Printing Office, January 1975.

National Council of Teachers of Mathematics. *An Analysis of New Mathematics Programs.* Washington, D.C.: the Council, 1963.

National Council of Teachers of Mathematics. *Bulletin for Leaders.* Reston, Virginia: the Council, November 1974.

Natkin, G. L. "The Treatment of Mathematical Anxiety Through Mediated Transfer of Attitude Toward Mathematics." Unpublished doctoral dissertation, Indiana University, 1967.

Neale, D. C. "The Role of Attitudes in Learning Mathematics." *The Arithmetic Teacher* 16: 631-40; 1969.

Neale, D. C., N. Gill, and W. Tismer. "Relationship Between Attitudes Toward School Subjects and School Achievement." *Journal of Educational Research* 63: 232-37; 1970.

Neale, D. C., and J. M. Proshek. "School Related Attitudes of Culturally Disadvantaged Elementary School Children." *Journal of Educational Psychology* 58: 238-44; 1967.

Neatrour, C. R. "Geometric Content in the Mathematics Curriculum of the Middle School." Unpublished doctoral dissertation, Indiana University, 1968.

Neill, A. S. *Summerhill: A Radical Approach to Child Rearing*. New York: Hart Publishing Company, 1960.

Newsom, C. V. "The Image of the Mathematician." *American Mathematical Monthly* 79: 878-82; 1972.

Nichols, E. D. "Are Behavioral Objectives the Answer?" *The Arithmetic Teacher* 19: 419, 474-76; 1972.

Noffsinger, T., and V. Dobbs. "Teaching Arithmetic to Educable Mentally Retarded Children." *Journal of Educational Research* 64: 177-84; 1970.

Nolan, C. Y. "Achievement in Arithmetic Computation: Analysis of School Differences and Identification of Areas of Low Achievement." *International Journal for the Education of the Blind* 8: 125-28; 1959.

Nolan, C. Y. "Research in Education of the Blind." In: M. Goldberg and J. Swinton, editors. *Blindness Research: The Expanding Frontiers*. University Park: Pennsylvania State University Press, 1969.

Nolan, C. Y., and S. C. Ashcroft. "The Stanford Achievement Arithmetic Computation Test: A Study of an Experimental Adaption for Braille Administration." *International Journal for the Education of the Blind* 8: 89-92; 1959.

Norman, M. "Three Methods of Teaching Basic Division Facts." Unpublished doctoral dissertation, State University of Iowa, 1955.

Ogletree, E. "Intellectual Growth in Children and the Theory of Bioplasmic Forces." *Phi Delta Kappan* 55: 407-12; 1974.

Olander, H., and H. Robertson. "The Effectiveness of Discovery and Expository Methods in the Teaching of Fourth-Grade Mathematics." *Journal for Research in Mathematics Education* 4: 33-44; 1973.

Overholt, E. D. "A Piagetian Conservation Concept." *The Arithmetic Teacher* 12: 317-25; 1965.

Pace, A. "Understanding and the Ability To Solve Problems." *The Arithmetic Teacher* 8: 226-32; 1961.

Pace, A. "Understanding of Basic Concepts of Arithmetic: A Comparative Study." *Journal of Educational Research* 60: 107-20; 1966.

Parsley, K. M. "Further Investigation of Sex Differences in Achievement of Under-Average and Over-Achieving Students Within Five I.Q. Groups in Grades Four Through Eight." *Journal of Educational Research* 57: 268-70; 1964.

Passy, R. "The Effects of Cuisenaire Materials on Reasoning and Computation." *The Arithmetic Teacher* 10: 439-40; 1963.

Passy, R. "Socio-Economic Status and Mathematics Achievement." *The Arithmetic Teacher* 11: 469-70; 1964.

Penner, W. J. "Effects of Cue Word Form Class on the Solving of Arithmetic Word Problems by the Mentally Handicapped." Unpublished doctoral dissertation, University of Connecticut, 1972.

Peper, J. B., and N. Chansky. "'Self Esteem and Achievement in Arithmetic." *The Elementary School Journal* 70: 284-88; 1970.

Perez, G. S. "The Verbal Sanctioning Behavior of Teachers in an Open Classroom Environment." Unpublished doctoral dissertation, State University of New York at Buffalo, 1973.

Peskin, A. S. "Teacher Understanding and Attitudes and Student Achievement and Attitude in Seventh Grade Mathematics." Unpublished doctoral dissertation, New York University, 1966.

Phillips, B. N. "Sex, Social Class, and Anxiety as Sources of Variation in School Achievement." *Journal of Educational Psychology* 53: 316-22; 1962.

Phillips, J. "Basic Laws for Young Children." *The Arithmetic Teacher* 12: 525-32; 1965.

Phillips, R. B. "Teacher Attitude as Related to Student Attitude and Achievement in Elementary School Mathematics." *School Science and Mathematics* 73: 501-507; 1973.

Piaget, J. "Comments on Mathematical Education." In: A. G. Howson, editor. *Developments in Mathematical Education.* Proceedings of the Second International Congress on Mathematical Education. London: Cambridge University Press, 1973.

Piaget, J., and B. Inhelder. *The Child's Conception of Space.* London: Routledge and Kegan Paul, 1956.

Piaget, J., B. Inhelder, and A. Szeminska. *The Child's Conception of Geometry.* London: Routledge and Kegan Paul, 1960.

Piaget, J., and A. Szeminska. *The Child's Conception of Number.* London: Routledge and Kegan Paul, 1952.

Pilcher, P. S. "Teacher Centers: Can They Work Here?" *Phi Delta Kappan* 54: 340-43; 1973.

Pines, M. A. "A Pressure Cooker for Four-Year-Old Minds." *Harper's* 234: 55-61; 1967.

Plank, E. N. "Observations on Attitudes of Young Children Toward Mathematics." *The Mathematics Teacher* 43: 252-63; 1950.

Poffenberger, T., and D. Norton. "Factors Determining Attitudes Toward Arithmetic and Mathematics." *The Arithmetic Teacher* 3: 113-16; 1956.

Poffenberger, T., and D. Norton. "Factors in the Formation of Attitudes Toward Mathematics." *Journal of Educational Research* 52: 171-76; 1959.

Poliakoff, L. "Opening Up the View." *Journal of Teacher Education* 25: 52-58; 1974.

Postlethwaite, T. N. "International Association for the Evaluation of Educational Achievement—the Mathematics Study." *Journal for Research in Mathematics Education* 2: 69-103; 1971.

Potter, M. C., and E. I. Levy. "Spatial Enumeration Without Counting." *Child Development* 39: 265-72; 1968.

Prehm, H. J. "Concept Learning in Culturally Disadvantaged Children as a Function of Verbal Pretraining." *Exceptional Children* 32: 599-604; 1966.

Price, J. "Automated Teaching Programs with Mentally Retarded Students." *American Journal of Mental Deficiency* 68: 69-72; 1963.

Price, R. "An Experimental Evaluation of the Relative Effectiveness of the Use of Certain Multi-Sensory Aids in Instruction in the Division of Fractions." Unpublished doctoral dissertation, University of Minnesota, 1950.

Rainey, D., and F. Kelly. "An Evaluation of a Programmed Textbook with Educable Mentally Retarded Children." *Exceptional Children* 34: 169-74; 1967.

Rea, R., and R. Reys. "Mathematical Competencies of Entering Kindergarteners." *The Arithmetic Teacher* 17: 65-74; 1970. © 1970 by the National Council of Teachers of Mathematics.

Rea, R., and R. Reys. "Competencies of Entering Kindergarteners in Geometry, Number, Money, and Measurement." *School Science and Mathematics* 71: 389-402; 1971.

Recommendations on Course Content for the Training of Teachers of Mathematics. Berkeley, California: Committee on the Undergraduate Program in Mathematics of the Mathematical Association of America, 1971.

Reed, M. K. "Vocabulary Load of Certain State-Adopted Mathematics Textbooks, Grades 1-3." Unpublished doctoral dissertation, University of Southern California, 1965.

Reisman, F. K. *A Guide to the Diagnostic Teaching of Arithmetic.* Columbus, Ohio: Charles E. Merrill Publishing Company, 1972.

"Report to the Board of Education on the Class Size Experiment." San Diego, California: San Diego City Schools, Elementary Schools Division, 1965. Mimeo.

Repp, F. C. "The Vocabularies of Five Recent Third Grade Arithmetic Textbooks." *The Arithmetic Teacher* 7: 128-32; 1960.

Research for Better Schools, Inc. *Progress Report.* Philadelphia, June 1974.

Reys, R. E. "Considerations for Teachers Using Manipulative Materials." *The Arithmetic Teacher* 18: 551-58; 1971.

Reys, R. E. "Mathematics, Multiple Embodiment, and Elementary Teachers." *The Arithmetic Teacher* 19: 489-93; 1972. © 1972 by the National Council of Teachers of Mathematics.

Reys, R. E., and T. Post. *The Mathematics Laboratory: Theory to Practice.* Boston: Prindle, Weber and Schmidt, 1973.

Reys, R. E., and R. Rea. "The Comprehensive Mathematics Inventory: An Experimental Instrument for Assessing Youngsters Entering School." *Journal for Research in Mathematics Education* 1: 180-86; 1970.

Rice, J. "Educational Research: Causes of Success and Failure in Arithmetic." *The Forum* 34: 437-52; 1903.

Richards, P., and N. Bolton. "Type of Mathematics Teaching, Mathematical Ability, and Divergent Thinking in Junior School Children." *British Journal of Educational Psychology* 41: 32-37; 1971.

Riedesel, C. A. "Problem Solving: Some Suggestions from Research." *The Arithmetic Teacher* 16: 54-58; 1969.

Riedesel, C. A. "Research Suggestions: Use of Time in Teaching Elementary School Mathematics." *The Arithmetic Teacher* 18: 177-79; 1971. © 1971 by the National Council of Teachers of Mathematics.

Riedesel, C. A., and M. Suydam. "Computer-Assisted Instruction: Implication for Teacher Education." *The Arithmetic Teacher* 14: 24-29; 1967.

Riess, A. "The New Arithmetic and 'Abstraction': A Critical View." *School Science and Mathematics* 65: 409-15; 1965.

Rising, G. "Teacher Education and Teacher Training in Perspective." *Educational Technology* 13: 53-59; 1973.

Roberts, G. H. "The Failure Strategies of Third Grade Arithmetic Pupils." *The Arithmetic Teacher* 15: 442-46; 1968.

Robinson, A. E. *The Professional Education of Elementary Teachers in the Field of Arithmetic.* New York: Bureau of Publications, Teachers College, Columbia University, 1936.

Robinson, M. L. "An Investigation of Problem Solving Behavior and Cognitive and Affective Characteristics of Good and Poor Problem Solvers in Sixth Grade Mathematics." Unpublished doctoral dissertation, State University of New York at Buffalo, 1973.

Rogers, C. *Freedom To Learn.* Columbus, Ohio: Charles E. Merrill Publishing Co., 1969.

Rogers, V. "Open Schools on the British Model." *Educational Leadership* 29: 401-404; 1972.

Rose, A., and H. Rose. "Intelligence, Sibling Position, and Sociocultural Background as Factors in Arithmetic Performance." *The Arithmetic Teacher* 8: 50-56; 1961.

Rosner, B. *The Power of Competency-Based Teacher Education: A Report.* Boston: Allyn and Bacon, Inc., 1972.

Ross, R. "A Description of Twenty Arithmetic Underachievers." *The Arithmetic Teacher* 11: 235-41; 1964.

Rosskopf, M., L. Steffe, and S. Taback, editors. *Piagetian Cognitive-Development Research and Mathematical Education.* Proceedings of a conference conducted at Columbia University. Washington, D.C.: National Council of Teachers of Mathematics, 1971.

Rowland, N., and J. Inskeep. "Subject Preferences of Upper Elementary School Children in Cajon Valley Union School Districts." *California Journal of Educational Research* 14: 189; 1963.

Ruch, G., and C. Mead. "A Review of Experiments on Subtraction." *Report of the Society's Committee on Arithmetic.* Twenty-ninth Yearbook of the National Society for the Study of Education. Bloomington, Illinois: Public School Publishing Co., 1930.

Ruddell, A. K., and G. W. Brown. "In-Service Education in Arithmetic: Three Approaches." *Elementary School Journal* 64: 377-82; 1964.

Ryan, J. J. "Effects of Modern and Conventional Mathematics Curricula on Pupil Attitudes, Interests, and Perception of Proficiency." Washington, D.C.: U.S. Office of Education, Bureau of Research, 1968.

Sarason, E. K., and S. Sarason. "Some Observations on the Introduction and Teaching of the New Math." In: F. Kaplan and S. Sarason, editors. *The Psycho-Educational Clinic: Papers and Research Studies.* Springfield: Department of Mental Health, The Commonwealth of Massachusetts, 1969. (Available from Dr. Seymour B. Sarason, 70 Sachem Street, New Haven, Connecticut 06520.)

Sarason, S., *et al. Anxiety in Elementary School Children.* New York: John Wiley & Sons, Inc., 1960.

Sarason, S., K. Hill, and P. Zimbardo. "A Longitudinal Study of the Relation of Test Anxiety to Performance on Intelligence and Achievement Tests." *Monograph Society for Research in Child Development,* Vol. 29, No. 7; 1964.

Sarnoff, I. "Test Anxiety and the 'Eleven Plus' Examinations." *British Journal of Educational Psychology* 40: 42-46; 1970.

Sato, R. "Commentary on the International Study of Achievement in Mathematics." *The Arithmetic Teacher* 15: 103-107; 1968.

Sawada, D. "Piaget and Pedagogy: Fundamental Relationships." *The Arithmetic Teacher* 19: 293-98; 1972.

Schell, L. M. "Learning the Distributive Property by Third Graders." *School Science and Mathematics* 68: 28-32; 1968.

Schell, L. M., and P. Burns. "Pupil Performance with Three Types of Subtraction Situations." *School Science and Mathematics* 62: 208-14; 1962.

Schlinsog, G. W. "The Effects of Supplementing Sixth-Grade Instruction with a Study of Non-Decimal Numbers." *The Arithmetic Teacher* 15: 254-60; 1968.

Schmieder, A. A., and S. Yarger. "Teacher/Teaching Centering in America." *Journal of Teacher Education* 25: 5-12; 1974. Published by permission of the American Association of Colleges for Teacher Education and the *Journal of Teacher Education.*

Schnur, J. O., and L. G. Callahan. "Knowledge of Certain Geometric Concepts Possessed by Students on Leaving Elementary School." *School Science and Mathematics* 73: 471-78; 1973.

School Mathematics Study Group. *Final Report of the SMSG Panel on Research.* Newsletter No. 39; August 1972.

Schroeder, L. "Study of the Relationship Between Five Descriptive Categories of Emotional Disturbance and Reading and Arithmetic Achievement." *Exceptional Children* 32: 111-12; 1965.

Schwartz, A. N. "Assessment of Math Concepts of Five-Year-Old Children." *Journal of Experimental Education* 37: 67-74; 1969.

Schwebel, A. I., and C. R. Schwebel. "The Relationship Between Performance on Piagetian Tasks and Impulsive Responding." *Journal for Research in Mathematics Education* 5: 98-104; 1974.

Scott, J., A. Frayer, and H. Klausmeier. "The Effects on Short- and Long-Term Retention and on Transfer of Two Methods of Presenting Selected Geometry Concepts." Research report read at the annual meeting of the American Educational Research Association, 1971.

Scott, L. "A Study of Teaching Division Through the Use of Two Algorisms." *School Science and Mathematics* 63: 739-52; 1963.

Scott, R., and F. Lighthall. "Relationship Between Content, Sex, Grade, and Degree of Disadvantage in Arithmetic Problem Solving." *Journal of School Psychology* 6: 61-67; 1967.

The Scottish Council for Research in Education: Its Aims and Activities. A publication of the Scottish Council for Research in Education. Number 24. Revised edition. London: University of London Press, 1953.

Sears, P., and E. Hilgard, editors. *Theories of Learning and Instruction.* Sixty-third Yearbook of the National Society for the Study of Education, Part I. Chicago: University of Chicago Press, 1964.

Sears, P., L. Katz, and L. Soderstrum. "Psychological Development of Children Participating in a Vertically Accelerated Mathematics Program." *Psychology in the Schools* 4: 307-18; 1966.

Shah, S. A. "Selected Geometric Concepts Taught to Children Ages Seven to Eleven." *The Arithmetic Teacher* 16: 119-28; 1969.

Shah, S. A. "The Relationship Between 'Age of Entrance' and Achievement of 13-Year-Olds." *Journal for Research in Mathematics Education* 2: 121-23; 1971.

Shane, H. G. "Grouping Practices Seem To Favor Composite Plan." *Nation's Schools* 49: 72-73; 1952.

Shapiro, B., and T. O'Brien. "Logical Thinking in Children Ages Six Through Thirteen." *Child Development* 41: 823-29; 1970.

Sherrill, J. "In-Service Mathematics Education as Viewed by Elementary School Teachers." *School Science and Mathematics* 71: 615-18; 1971.

Shipp, D. E., and G. Deer. "The Use of Class Time in Arithmetic." *The Arithmetic Teacher* 7: 117-21; 1960.

Shuster, A. H., and F. Pigge. "Retention Efficiency of Meaningful Teaching." *The Arithmetic Teacher* 12: 24-31; 1965.

Silberman, C. E. *Crisis in the Classroom.* New York: Random House, Inc., 1970.

Sime, M. "Implications of the Work of Piaget in the Training of Students To Teach Primary Mathematics." In: A. G. Howson, editor. *Developments in Mathematical Education.* London: Cambridge University Press, 1973.

Sinclair, H. "Piaget's Theory of Development: The Main Stages." In: M. Rosskopf, L. Steffe, and S. Taback, editors. *Piagetian Cognitive-Development Research and Mathematical Education.* Washington, D.C.: National Council of Teachers of Mathematics, 1971.

Skemp, R. R. *The Psychology of Learning Mathematics.* Baltimore: Penguin Books, 1971.

Slavina, L. "Specific Features on the Intellectual Work of Unsuccessful Pupils." In: B. Simon, editor. *Psychology in the Soviet Union.* Palo Alto, California: Stanford University Press, 1957. p. 205.

Sluser, T. "A Comparative Study of Division of Fractions in Which an Explanation of the Reciprocal Principle Is the Experimental Factor." Unpublished doctoral dissertation, University of Pittsburgh, 1962.

Smith, E. P. "A Look at Mathematics Education Today." *The Arithmetic Teacher* 20: 503-508; 1973. © 1973 by the National Council of Teachers of Mathematics.

Smith, E. P. "The Metric System: Effects on Teaching Mathematics." National Council of Teachers of Mathematics *Newsletter,* March 1974.

Smith, E., and J. Quackenbush. "Devereux Teaching Aids Employed in Presenting Elementary Mathematics in a Special Education Setting." *Psychological Reports* 7: 333-36; 1960.

Smith, F. "The Readability of Junior High School Mathematics Textbooks." *The Mathematics Teacher* 62: 289-91; 1969.

Smith, F. "The Readability of Sixth Grade Word Problems." *School Science and Mathematics* 71: 559-62; 1971.

Smith, G. "Commentary upon Suppes-Binford Report of Teaching Mathematical Logic to Fifth- and Sixth-Grade Pupils." *The Arithmetic Teacher* 13: 640-43; 1966.

Smith, R. F. "Diagnosis of Pupil Performance on Place-Value Tasks." *The Arithmetic Teacher* 20: 403-408; 1973.

Snow, C., and M. Rabinovitch. "Conjunctive and Disjunctive Thinking in Children." *Journal of Experimental Child Psychology* 7: 1-9; 1969.

Soar, R. S. "Teacher-Pupil Interaction." In: *A New Look at Progressive Education.* Yearbook of the Association for Supervision and Curriculum Development. Washington, D.C.: the Association, 1972.

Sowder, L. "The Influence of Verbalization of Discovered Numerical- or Sorting-Task Generalization on Short-Term Retention in Connection with the Hendrix Hypothesis." *Journal for Research in Mathematics Education* 5: 167-76; 1974.

Spross, P. "A Study of the Effect of a Tangible and Conceptualized Presentation of Arithmetic on Achievement in the Fifth and Sixth Grades." Unpublished doctoral dissertation, Michigan State University, 1962.

Stanley, J. C. "Intellectual Precocity." In: J. Stanley, D. Keating, and L. Fox, editors. *Mathematical Talent.* Baltimore: Johns Hopkins University Press, 1974.

Stanley, J., D. Keating, and L. Fox, editors. *Mathematical Talent.* Proceedings of the third annual Hyman Blumberg symposium on research in early childhood education. Baltimore: Johns Hopkins University Press, 1974.

Stauffer, R. G. "Vocabulary Study Comparing Reading, Arithmetic, Health, and Science Texts." *The Reading Teacher* 20: 141-47; 1966.

Steffe, L. P. "The Performance of First-Grade Children in Four Levels of Conservation of Numerousness and Three I.Q. Groups When Solving Arithmetic Addition Problems." *Technical Report No. 14.* Research and Development Center for Cognitive Learning. Madison: University of Wisconsin, 1966.

Steffe, L. P., and D. C. Johnson. "Problem-Solving Performances of First-Grade Children." *Journal for Research in Mathematics Education* 2: 50-64; 1971.

Stephens, B., E. Manhaney, and J. McLaughlin. "Mental Ages for Achievement of Piagetian Reasoning Assessments." *Education and Training of the Mentally Retarded* 7: 124-28; 1972.

Stephens, L. E. "Retention of the Skill of Division of Fractions." *The Arithmetic Teacher* 7: 28-31; 1960.

Stern, C. *Children Discover Arithmetic.* New York: Harper & Row, Publishers, 1949.

Stevenson, H. W., and R. D. Odom. "Relation of Anxiety to Children's Performance on Learning and Problem-Solving Tasks." *Child Development* 36: 1003-12; 1965.

Stodolsky, S., and G. Lesser. "Learning Patterns in the Disadvantaged." *Harvard Educational Review* 37: 546-93; 1967.

Stone, F., and V. Rowley. "Educational Disability in Emotionally Disturbed Children." *Exceptional Children* 30: 423-26; 1964.

Stone, M. "Remarks on the Teaching of Logic." In: W. E. Lamon, editor. *Learning and the Nature of Mathematics*. Chicago: Science Research Associates, 1972.

Suppes, P. "Accelerated Program in Elementary School Mathematics—The Second Year." *Psychology in the Schools* 3: 294-307; 1966.

Suppes, P. "A Reply to Gary R. Smith." *The Arithmetic Teacher* 14: 635; 1967a.

Suppes, P. *Sets and Numbers*. Teacher's edition. New York: L. W. Singer, 1967b.

Suppes, P. "Computer Technology and the Future of Education." *Phi Delta Kappan* 49: 420-23; 1968.

Suppes, P. "Computer Assisted Instruction for Deaf Students." *American Annals of the Deaf* 116: 500-508; 1971.

Suppes, P. "A Survey of Cognition in Handicapped Children." *Review of Educational Research* 44: 145-76; 1974.

Suppes, P., and F. Binford. "Experimental Thinking of Mathematical Logic in the Elementary School." *The Arithmetic Teacher* 12: 187-95; 1965. © 1965 by the National Council of Teachers of Mathematics.

Suppes, P., and H. Duncan. "Accelerated Program in Elementary School Mathematics—The First Year." *Psychology in the Schools* 2: 195-203; 1965.

Suppes, P., and C. Ihrke. "Accelerated Program in Elementary School Mathematics—The Third Year." *Psychology in the Schools* 4: 293-309; 1967.

Suppes, P., and C. Ihrke. "Accelerated Program in Elementary School Mathematics: The Fourth Year." *Psychology in the Schools* 7: 111-26; 1970.

Suppes, P., M. Jerman, and G. Groen. "Arithmetic Drills and Review on a Computer-Based Teletype." *The Arithmetic Teacher* 13: 303-309; 1966.

Sussman, D. "Number Readiness of Kindergarten Children." Unpublished doctoral dissertation, University of California at Los Angeles, 1962.

Suydam, M. N., and J. F. Weaver. *Individualizing Instruction*. Research Utilization Branch, U.S. Office of Education. Publication of the Interpretive Study of Research and Development in Elementary School Mathematics, 1970.

Suydam, M. N., and J. F. Weaver. *Bulletin, Set A, No. 2*. Project on Interpreting Mathematics Education Research. Sponsored by Bureau of Research, U.S. Office of Education. University Park: Pennsylvania State University (undated).

Suzzallo, H. *The Teaching of Primary Arithmetic*. Boston: Houghton Mifflin Co., 1911.

Swenson, E. J. "Arithmetic for Preschool and Primary-Grade Children." In: *The Teaching of Arithmetic*. Fiftieth Yearbook of the National Society for the Study of Education, Part II. Chicago: University of Chicago Press, 1951.

Symonds, P. M. "Education and Psychotherapy." *Journal of Educational Psychology* 40: 5-20; 1949.

Tamkin, A. "A Survey of Educational Disability in Emotionally Disturbed Children." *Journal of Educational Research* 53: 313-15; 1960.

Thomason, G. M., and A. F. Perrodin. "Comparison of Arithmetic Achievement in England, Central California, and Georgia." *The Arithmetic Teacher* 11: 181-85; 1964.

Thresher, J. "A Problem for Educators: Arithmetic Concept Formation in the Mentally Retarded Child." *American Journal of Mental Deficiency* 66: 766-73; 1962.

Tillman, M. H. "The Performance of Blind and Sighted Children: Interaction Effects." *Education of the Visually Handicapped* 1: 1-4; 1969.

Todd, R. "A Mathematics Course for Elementary Teachers: Does It Improve Understanding and Attitude?" *The Arithmetic Teacher* 13: 198-202; 1966.

Torrance, E. "Conditions of Creative Learning." *Childhood Education* 39: 367; 1963.

Torrance, E. P., and E. Parent. "Characteristics of Mathematics Teachers That Affect Students' Learning." Report No. CRP-1020, Contract No. OEC-SAE 8993, U.S. Office of Education; September 1966.

Tracey, N. H. "Comparison of Test Results—North Carolina, California, and England." *The Arithmetic Teacher* 6: 199-202; 1959.

Trafton, P. R. "Individualized Instruction: Developing Broadened Perspectives." *The Arithmetic Teacher* 19: 7-12; 1972.

"The Training of Elementary School Mathematics Teachers." An abridgement of the recommendations of the Mathematical Association of America for the training of teachers of mathematics. *The Arithmetic Teacher* 7: 421-25; 1960.

Travers, K. "Mathematics Education and the Computer Revolution." *School Science and Mathematics* 71: 24-34; 1971.

Treacy, J. P. "The Relationship of Reading Skills to the Ability To Solve Arithmetic Problems." *Journal of Educational Research* 38: 94; 1944.

Troutman, A. P. "Strategies for Teaching Elementary School Mathematics." *The Arithmetic Teacher* 20: 425-36; 1973.

Unkel, E. "A Study of the Interaction of Socio-Economic Groups and Sex Factors with the Discrepancy Between Anticipated Achievement and Actual Achievement in Elementary School Mathematics." *The Arithmetic Teacher* 13: 662-70; 1966.

Uprichard, A. E. "The Effect of Sequence in the Acquisition of Three Set Relations: An Experiment with Pre-Schoolers." *The Arithmetic Teacher* 17: 597-604; 1970.

Vance, J., and T. Kieren. "Laboratory Setting in Mathematics: What Does Research Say to the Teacher?" *The Arithmetic Teacher* 18: 585-89; 1971. © 1971 by the National Council of Teachers of Mathematics.

Vanderlinde, L. F. "Does the Study of Quantitative Vocabulary Improve Problem Solving?" *Elementary School Journal* 65: 143-52; 1964.

Van Engen, H. "Epistemology, Research, and Instruction." In: M. Rosskopf, L. Steffe, and S. Taback, editors. *Piagetian Cognitive-Development Research and Mathematical Education.* Washington, D.C.: National Council of Teachers of Mathematics, 1971.

Van Engen, H. "The Next Decade." *The Arithmetic Teacher* 19: 615-16; 1972. © 1972 by the National Council of Teachers of Mathematics.

Van Engen, H. "Geometry in the Elementary School." *The Arithmetic Teacher* 20: 423-24; 1973. © 1973 by the National Council of Teachers of Mathematics.

Van Engen, H., and E. Gibb. *General Mental Functions Associated with Division.* Educational Service Studies No. 2. Cedar Falls: Iowa State Teachers College, 1956.

Vinsonhaler, J. F., and R. Bass. "A Summary of Ten Major Studies in CAI Drill and Practice." *Educational Technology* 12: 29-32; 1972.

Walbesser, H. H. "Behavioral Objectives, a Cause Célèbre." *The Arithmetic Teacher* 19: 418, 436-40; 1972. © 1972 by the National Council of Teachers of Mathematics.

Wallach, M. "The Humble Things We Know—and Ignore—About Quality in Elementary Education." *Harvard Educational Review* 41: 542-49; 1971.

Walter, M. *Informal Geometry for Young Children.* Cambridge Conference on School Mathematics. Feasibility Study No. 346. Newton, Massachusetts: Education Development Center, 1969.

Wang, M., L. Resnick, and R. Boozer. "The Sequence of Development of Some Early Mathematical Behaviors." *Child Development* 42: 1767-78; 1971.

Washburne, C. W. "The Work of the Committee of Seven on Grade-Placement in Arithmetic." In: *Child Development and the Curriculum.* Thirty-eighth Yearbook of the National Society for the Study of Education, Part I. Bloomington, Illinois: Public School Publishing Company, 1939.

Weaver, J. F. "Big Dividends from Little Interviews." *The Arithmetic Teacher* 11: 40-47; 1955.

Weaver, J. F. "A Crucial Problem in the Preparation of Elementary School Teachers." *Elementary School Journal* 56: 255-61; 1956.

Weaver, J. F. "Levels of Geometric Understanding Among Pupils in Grades 4, 5, and 6." *The Arithmetic Teacher* 13: 686-90; 1966.

Weaver, J. F. "Evaluation and the Classroom Teacher." In: E. G. Begle and H. Richey, editors. *Mathematics Education.* Sixty-ninth Yearbook of the National Society for the Study of Education. Chicago: University of Chicago Press, 1970.

Weaver, J. F. "Seductive Shibboleths." *The Arithmetic Teacher* 18: 263-64; 1971a.

Weaver, J. F. "Some Factors Associated with Pupils' Performance Levels on Simple Open Addition and Subtraction Sentences." *The Arithmetic Teacher* 18: 513-19; 1971b.

Weaver, J. F. "The Ability of First, Second, and Third Grade Pupils To Identify Open Addition and Subtraction Sentences for Which No Solution Exists Within the Set of Whole Numbers." *School Science and Mathematics* 72: 679-91; 1972a.

Weaver, J. F. "Some Concerns About the Application of Piaget's Theory and

Research to Mathematical Learning and Instruction." *The Arithmetic Teacher* 19: 263-70; 1972b.

Weaver, J. F. "Pupil Performance on Examples Involving Selected Variations of the Distributive Idea." *The Arithmetic Teacher* 20: 697-704; 1973a.

Weaver, J. F. "The Symmetric Property of the Equality Relation and Young Children's Ability To Solve Open Addition and Subtraction Sentences." *Journal for Research in Mathematics Education* 4: 45-56; 1973b.

Weaver, J. F., and C. F. Brawley. "Enriching the Elementary School Mathematics Program for More Capable Children." *Journal of Education* 142: 1-40; 1959. © by the Trustees of Boston University.

Weber, C. A. "Do Teachers Understand Learning Theory?" *Phi Delta Kappan* 46: 433-35; 1965.

Whitehead, A. N. *The Aims of Education.* New York: The Macmillan Company, 1929. p. 6. Reprinted by permission of The Macmillan Company, Inc. Copyright renewed 1957 by Evelyn Whitehead.

Whitney, H. "Are We Off the Track in Teaching Mathematical Concepts?" In: A. G. Howson, editor. *Developments in Mathematical Education.* London: Cambridge University Press, 1973.

Wiles, C., T. Romberg, and J. Moser. "The Relative Effectiveness of Two Different Instructional Sequences Designed To Teach the Addition and Subtraction Algorithms." *Journal for Research in Mathematics Education* 4: 251-61; 1973.

Wilkinson, J. D. "Teacher-Directed Evaluation of Mathematics Laboratories." *The Arithmetic Teacher* 21: 19-24; 1974.

Williams, A. H. "Mathematical Concepts, Skills, and Abilities of Kindergarten Entrants." *The Arithmetic Teacher* 12: 261-68; 1965.

Williams, J. D. "Teaching Arithmetic by Concrete Analogy." *Educational Research* 4: 120-31; 1963.

Williford, H. J. "A Study of Transformational Geometry Instruction in the Primary Grades." Unpublished doctoral dissertation, University of Georgia, 1970.

Williford, H. J. "What Does Research Say About Geometry in the Elementary School?" *The Arithmetic Teacher* 19: 97-104; 1972. © 1972 by the National Council of Teachers of Mathematics.

Wilson, G. M. *Teaching the New Arithmetic.* New York: McGraw-Hill Book Company, Inc., 1951.

Wilson, J. W. "The Role of Structure in Verbal Problem-Solving in Arithmetic: An Analytical and Experimental Comparison of Three Problem-Solving Programs." Unpublished doctoral dissertation, Syracuse University, 1964.

Wilson, J. W. "Diagnosis and Treatment in Mathematics: Its Progress, Problems, and Potential Role in Educating Emotionally Disturbed Children and Youth." In: P. Knoblock and J. J. Johnson, editors. *The Teaching-Learning Process in Educating Emotionally Disturbed Children.* New York: Syracuse University Press, 1967.

Wittrock, M. "The Learning by Discovery Hypothesis." In: L. S. Shulman and E. R. Keislar, editors. *Learning by Discovery: A Critical Appraisal.* Chicago: Rand McNally & Company, 1966.

Wohlwill, J. F. "A Study of the Development of the Number Concept by Scalogram Analysis." *Journal of Genetic Psychology* 87: 345-77; 1960.

Woolcock, C. W. *New Approaches to the Education of the Gifted.* Morristown, New Jersey: Silver Burdett Company, 1961.

Worthen, B. "Discovery and Expository Task Presentation in Elementary Mathematics." *Journal of Educational Psychology* 59: 1-13; 1968.

Worthen, B., and J. Collins. "Reanalysis of Data from Worthen's Study of Sequencing in Task Presentation." *Journal of Educational Psychology* 62: 15-16; 1971.

Wright, E., J. Muriel, and V. Proctor. "Systematic Observation of Verbal Interaction as a Method of Comparing Mathematics Lessons." U.S. Office of Education Cooperative Research Project No. 816. St. Louis: Washington University, 1961.

Zahn, K. G. "Use of Class Time in Eighth-Grade Arithmetic." *The Arithmetic Teacher* 13: 113-20; 1966.

Zweibelson, I., and F. Lodato. "Relationship of Pupil Anxiety and Attitude to Arithmetic Readiness and Achievement." *Psychology in the Schools* 2: 140-42; 1965.

Zweng, M. "Division Problems and the Concept of Rate." *The Arithmetic Teacher* 8: 547-56; 1964.

Index

Ability grouping, 94; motivation and, 116; narrow range, 95

Ability to conserve, 29

Achievement: attitude and, 79-80; class size and, 97; comparison of, among countries, 48-49; computational, 15; in mathematics, 16, 46-48, 48-49, 66-67, 67-69, 69-70, 79-81, 105; international, 46-48; motivation, 115; of teachers, 105; social environment and, 99

Achievement tests: ethnic groups and, 99-100; standardized, 76, 83; traditional, 14

Accuracy: of response, 27; of work, 138

Addition and subtraction, open sentences in, 139-40

Addition facts, 29

Affective factors in readiness to learn, 58

Age: of entry to first grade, 63-64; of kindergarten entrants, 83; number sentences and, 139, 140

Algorisms: for division of fractions, 140-41; for division of whole numbers, 142; for subtraction, 137-38; Greenwood (subtractive), 142, 143; standard (distributive), 142, 143

Anxiety in mathematical learning, 81-84; correlation with achievement, 82, 83; factors associated with, 83; indicators of, 82

Appreciation of mathematics, 116, 131

Arithmetic disability, 66-67

Arithmetic reasoning ability, 148

Arithmetic teaching, structural *vs.* environmental, 118

Arithmetic test scores: correlation with anxiety, 83; personality and, 85, 86

Associationist theory of learning, 22, 27

Associativity, 38

Attitude toward mathematics, 47, 77-81, 99, 131; and sociometric groupings, 81; correlation with ability level, 79, 81; correlation with achievement, 79-80; factors influencing, 80-81; "math lab" and, 93

Basic concepts, 39; attainment and use of, 38; for elementary school, 37-39
Behavioral objectives, 22-25, 45; claims for, 23, 24; concerns about, 24; taxonomies of, 23
Behaviorist theories, 27
Birth order in mathematical precocity, 73
Blind children's mathematics achievement, 67-68
British primary movement, 89

CAI: see Computer Assisted Instruction
Calculator (hand-held), 125-26
Cambridge Conference on School Mathematics, 7-10, 102
Cardinality, of number, 51, 56
Class size and mathematics achievement, 46, 97
Class time, effective use of, 95-96
"Closure," study on, 38
Cognitive development of the child, 25-26, 133
Cognitive processes, 13, 110, 119; conceptual tempo and, 85; disfunctions in, 65; type of, and anxiety, 84
Cognitive product, 110
Combinations of addition of whole numbers, 27
Commission on Preservice Education of Teachers of Mathematics, 107-108
Committee on the Undergraduate Program in Mathematics (CUPM), 101
Committee of Seven, 33
"Commutativity," study on, 38
Comparisons among different countries on mathematics achievement, 48-49
Competency-Based Teacher Education (CBTE), 107

Comprehensive Mathematics Inventory (CMI), 53-55
Computation, 16, 114; error patterns in, 129; of the educable mentally retarded, 69
Computational ability, 17, 69, 92, 124, 127
Computational processes, 100
Computational proficiency, 124-25
Computer Assisted Instruction (CAI), 68, 146, 149-50; dialogue systems in, 150; drill and practice systems in, 149, 150; tutorial systems in, 149
Conceptual tasks, 15, 91, 92
Concrete (manipulative) mode, 37, 72, 118-22
Concrete models: see Physical models
Connectionist psychology, 133
Conservation, 26, 32, 72; of liquids, 33-35; of number, 55, 56, 120; of numerousness, 30; test, 30
Consolidation (in learning), 60, 125, 135; reinforcement in, 126
Content of textbooks, comparison of among countries, 49
"Convergent" tasks, 91, 92
Counting, development of, 56; in learning disabled, 66; number facts and, 136; rational, 57
Counting behaviors, 55-57
Criterion-referenced tests, 131
Cuisenaire rods, 15, 118, 120, 122
Cultural deprivation, 59-60; and cognitive development, 59, 133
Cultural factors, 64
"Cumulative deficit phenomenon," 59
Curricular validity, 12
Curriculum: grades 3 to 6, 7-10; logical basis of, 4; "modern math," 104; Piaget's work and, 26-29; psychological basis of, 1; sociological basis of, 2; sources of, 1-6
Curriculum development, 107; projects, 13
Curriculum theory, 1; clinical-personality approach to, 2; cognitive-

developmental approach to, 2; logical basis for, 4; model of, 5; psychological basis for, 1; sociological basis for, 2

Dalrymple study of fractions used in business, 3

Deaf children's mathematics performance, 68-69

Development: of early number behaviors, 55-57; of the educable mentally retarded, 69; physical and neurological, 58; stages of, 25, 118, 119

Developmental activities, 95, 96, 127

Developmental (meaning) phase, 125

Developmental process, 56

Diagnostic procedures, 129

Diagnostic test, 129

Diagnosis: methods of, 129; of learning problems in mathematics, 128-30; prescription, model for, 128

Dienes attribute blocks, 120

Disadvantaged children, 18, 45, 149; learning of, 60; summer programs for, 44-46

Discovery learning, 113-15; programmed materials in, 114

Discovery teaching, 110, 112; attitudes toward, 114; effects of, 113-14; vs. expository teaching, 114

Distributivity, 38

Divergent thinking ability, 91, 92, 115

Division: "common denominator" method of, 140; "complex fraction" method of, 140; "inverse operation" method of, 140; measurement and partitive, 141; of fractions, 140-41; of whole numbers, 141-44

Drill: activities, 95, 96; for mastery, 3; in CAI, 149; in consolidation phase, 125; in teaching EMH children, 71; phases, 4; place of, in math program, 126-28; procedures, 87; theory of, 110

Educable mentally retarded: learning characteristics of, 69-70; mathematics teaching for, 70-72

Educational objectives, 22

Educational opportunity, 99

Emotional disturbance, 66, 128

English schools, 15

Enrichment for the mathematically gifted, 75-77

Enumeration behaviors, 55-57

Ethnic groups: achievement and, 100; patterns of mental abilities in, 60-63

Evaluation: formative and summative, 130-31; of instruction, 27; of mathematics learning, 130-32; purposes of, 130; resources, 13; teacher-directed, 132

Expository methods (didactics), 110, 133

Father's occupation, 53

Field axioms, 38, 39

"Formal" classroom setting, 91

Formative evaluation, 130-31

Fractions used in business situations, 3-4

Froebel, 4, 90

Gagné's hierarchy of tasks, 140

Geometry: dependent-prone students and, 116; Euclidean, 40; kindergarten children's knowledge of, 51; topological, 40; transformational, 40

Geometry program: elementary school, 39, 42-43; scope and sequence of, 39-41

Gestaltist theory of learning, 22

Goals for School Mathematics, 10, 102

Grade level, and anxiety, 84

Grouping numbers, 136

Grouping of children, 88, 94-95; for large-group instruction, 97; for small-group instruction, 97; heterogeneous, 94; homogeneous, 94

Guided discovery, 110, 111

"Guidelines for the Preparation of Teachers of Mathematics," 108

Homework: attitude of pupils toward, 124; effect of, 124

Hyperactive child, 65

"Identity," study on, 38

Incidental-learning theory, 110

Individualization, 21, 90

Individualized instruction, 24, 128, 149; in mathematics, 87-89

Individualizing learning, 87; "modified whole-group" approach to, 88; "self-selected activities" approach to, 88; "whole-group" approach to, 88

Individually Prescribed Instruction (IPI), 19-22; cost of, 22; effect of, 21; objectives of, 20

"Informal" classroom, 89-92; characteristics of, 90-91

In-service education, 104-106

Instructional materials (concrete), 118-22

Interest in mathematics, 117

International Study of Achievement in Mathematics, 46-48

IPI math program: see Individually Prescribed Instruction

Kindergarten: geometric concepts for, 43; mathematics program for, 36-37; studies on children entering, 50-53

Kindergarten entrants: mathematical performance of, 53-55; studies on, 50-55

Learning disabilities in mathematics, 65-67, 129

Learning environment: class size, 97; classroom, 87-89; math lab, 92-93

Learning problems, 128-30; deprived environment and, 128

Leicestershire Plan, 89

Liberia, number estimation in, 35

Logic, mathematical, 43-44

Logical structure, 6

Logical theory, 1, 4

Manipulative materials, 118, 126

Mastery: consolidation and, 60; learning for, 130, 131; of actions, 135; of addition combinations, 29; of computation skills, 125; of number tasks, 56; program, 2

Mathematical Association of America, 101

Mathematical concepts: development of, 133; teachers' understanding of, 104-105

Mathematical knowledge: ability to apply, 114; of children entering school, 50-53; of teachers, 100, 103, 105

Mathematical logic, learning of, 43-44

Mathematical performance of kindergarten entrants, 53-55

Mathematical structure, 11, 23

Mathematical Variability Principle (Dienes), 144

Mathematical vocabulary, 146

Mathematically gifted, the, 13, 72-77, 96; ability grouping and, 95; birth order in, 73; characteristics of, 72-75; enrichment program for, 75-77; longitudinal study of, 74; sex differences in, 74; socioeconomic class and, 75

Mathematics achievement: anxiety and, 82, 83; attitudes toward mathematics and, 79-81; class size and, 97; comparisons of among countries, 48-49; ethnic group and, 100; international study of, 46-48; national assessment of, 16; of the blind, 67-68; of the deaf, 68-69; of the educable mentally retarded, 69-70; of the emotionally disturbed, 66-67; self-concept and, 85

Mathematics laboratory ("math lab"), 92-93, 132; achievement in, 93; characteristics of, 93; effect on attitude, 93; origins of, 92

Mathematics teachers: professional knowledge of, 102-104; training of, 100-108; understanding of math concepts, 104-105

Maturity: of response, 27, 136; of thinking in mathematics, 129; physical and mental, 58

Meaning theory, 110

Meaningful habituation, 125, 136

Meaningful learning and instruction: approaches to, 132-35; division of fractions and, 140; vs. mechanical learning, 138

Meaningful teaching, 81; of subtraction, 143

Meaningful thinking, 44

Meaningfulness: continuum of, 132; development of, 126; in class activities, 95; in mastery learning, 130; in subtraction, 137; logico-mathematical, 27-28; of items, 56; of mathematics learning, 92

Measurement: kindergarten children's knowledge of, 51; of achievement, 131; of learning, 130-32

Mental age (MA), 19

Mental structures, 134

Mentally retarded, the: teaching mathematics to, 70-72; teachers of, 71

Metric system, implications for U.S. education, 41-42

Modern math programs, 15, 104

Modes of learning, 36-37

Money, kindergarten children's knowledge of, 51

Motivation: anxiety in mathematics learning and, 82; in mathematics learning, 115-17; intrinsic and extrinsic, 115

Multiple embodiment of a mathematical idea, 118

Multisensory aids, 121

National Assessment of Educational Progress (NAEP), 16

National Longitudinal Study of Mathematical Abilities (NLSMA), 14

"Needs of adult society" theory of curriculum, 1, 2-4

"Needs-of-the-child" theory of curriculum, 1-2

"New math," 37, 91, 110; curricula, 6-13; programs, 7, 11-12; teaching of, 110

Nigeria, conservation studies in, 35

Norm-referenced tests, 131

Number: anxiety, 83; behaviors in young children, 55-57; cardinality of, 56; concept formation in, 134; conservation tasks on, 85; estimation, 35; kindergarten children's ideas of, 51; ordinality of, 56; readiness, 32

Number facility, 60-63

Number facts, 136

Numeration system, 144-45; decimal, 145; Hindu-Arabic, 144

Numerical reasoning of EMH, 70

One-to-one correspondence ability, 57; in learning disabled, 66

Open Education, 89-92

Opportunity to learn, mathematics achievement and, 47

Ordinality of number, 51, 56

Parental education, 17, 53, 73

Patterns among mental abilities, 60-63

Personality: dogmatic, 86; effect on mathematics learning, 85; influence on guided discovery learning, 115; introvert-extrovert traits, 85, 86; motivation and, 116

Pestalozzi, 4, 90-91

Physical (concrete) models, 118-22, 134; effectiveness of, 120-21; in elementary math teaching, 118-22; rationale for using, 118; sensory learning and, 118

Piagetian tasks, 29-30, 120; preschool children's performance on, 52; reflective and impulsive behavior and, 84, 85; relation with arithmetic tasks, 30; relation with school mathematics, 29; the mentally handicapped and, 69

Piaget's theories: mathematics education and, 31-33; of cognitive development, 25-26; of logical processes, 26, 55; of logical thought, 25-26

Piaget's work, 25-33, 135; criticisms of, 32-33; implication for teaching, 30-31

Practice, 126-28, 149; integrative, 126; repetitive, 125, 126, 127

Preservice education, 101, 102

Previous education of kindergarten entrants, 53

Principles and Practice of Teaching (Johonnot), 90

Problem solving, 32, 117, 127; ability in, 27, 31, 146, 147; correlation with anxiety, 83; of EMH children, 70; performance of Dutch and American children in, 48; power in, 31; techniques of, 133; tests in, 30, 48, 146; verbal, 16, 120, 145-49

Problem-solving approaches, comparison of, 147-48

The Process of Education, 7

Professional knowledge, 102-104, 108

Programmed instruction for EMH children, 71-72

Project ONE, 12

Psychological theory, 1, 2

Psychotherapy, 111, 112

Quantitative situations, 73, 144; judgment in, 131

Quantitative thinking, 13, 73

Race, 17, 18

Readability of textbooks, 98

Readiness: affective factors and, 58; for mathematics learning, 58-59, 128

Rectangular array, 136

Representational (pictorial) mode, 37, 72

Retention, 27, 113, 115; index of, 128

Retentivity of school systems, 47

Rote learning, 133

School Mathematics Study Group (SMSG), 14

Schools: age of entry to, 46; age of entry to first grade in, 63; good vs. poor, 99-100

Scope and sequence of geometry program, 39-41

Scottish schools, 15

Second International Congress on Mathematical Education, 25

Self-concept, 22; correlation with verbal problem solving, 85; mathematics achievement and, 85

Semi-concrete models, 121, 134

Senegal, conservation studies in, 33-34

Sensory learning, 118

Sesame Street, 18

Set relations, 57

Sex differences: in international mathematics achievement, 47-48; in mathematics achievement, 64-65; in the mathematically gifted, 74; in the NAEP, 17

Sex of child: amount of learning and, 17; anxiety in mathematics learning and, 84; mathematics achievement and, 47, 64-65

Slow learners, 12, 13, 15, 95

Small classes, mathematics achievement and, 97

Social-class level, 63, 114

Social environment, 99

Social utility, 1, 10, 117

Socioeconomic factors, 18

Socioeconomic status (level), 18, 92, 143; impulsive responders and, 85; language development and, 59; mathematics achievement and, 59; the mathematically gifted and, 75

Socioeconomic variability, 47

Sociological theory of curriculum, 1, 2-4

Socrates, 109

Sources of curriculum, 1-6

Space: children's conceptualization of, 60-63; Euclidean characteristics of, 40; topological characteristics of, 40

Space conceptualization, 60-63

Spatial relations, kindergarten children's knowledge of, 52

Specialized schools, 46

Speed of response, 27; in computation, 138; mathematics achievement and, 84

Study of Mathematically and Scientifically Precocious Youth, 72

Subtraction: algorisms for, 137; decomposition method of, 137; equal-additions method of, 137; meanings for, 137; sequences for, 138; studies on, 137-39; use of crutch in, 138

Summative evaluation, 130-31

Summer Compensatory Education Program, 45

Summer programs for the disadvantaged, 44-46

Symbolic (abstract) mode, 37, 72, 122

Système International (S.I.), 41

Task-analysis procedure, in developing diagnostic tests, 129-30

Taxonomies: affective, 23; cognitive, 23

Teacher attitudes: toward mathematics, 80, 102; toward new materials, 122

Teacher certification, 107

Teacher-pupil ratio, 97

Teacher-student verbal interaction, 123-24

Teacher training, 100-108; adequacy of, 102-104; performance criteria in, 107-108; programs for, 108

"Teaching Centers," 106-107

Teaching methods: place of drill in, 126; motivation and, 115-18; sources of, 109-13; use of physical models in, 118-22

Test anxiety, 83, 116

Test of Basic Mathematical Understandings, 48

Test of Mathematical Principles and Relationships, 114

Tests: criterion-referenced, 131; interview, 131; norm-referenced (standardized), 131, 146, 148; observational, 131; paper and pencil, 131

Textbooks: for EMH children, 71; for teachers, 100; readability of, 98

Therapeutic methods in facilitating learning, 112

Title I program, 45

"Traditional" classroom, 91-92

Traditional instruction, 150

"Traditional" math programs, 6, 13, 14, 15, 16, 21

Training: correlation with mathematical knowledge, 100; of elementary school math teachers, 100-108

Transfer: ability to, 15; nonspecific, 37; of learning, 43, 73, 113; of mathematical concepts, 115; of training (in subtraction), 138; specific, 37; test, 14

Underachievement: anxiety and, 83; in arithmetic, 67, 129; in learning place-value concepts, 130

Unifying strands, 12

Utilitarian perspective, 27, 28

Validity: curricular, 12; of "new math" curricula, 6-13

Variables affecting mathematical performance, 53-55

Verbal problem solving, 145-49; computational skill and, 145; effect of setting on, 148; mental "set" in, 147, 148; reading skill and, 145; spatial visualization and, 145; structural variables in, 147, 148; vocabulary and, 146

Verbal problem-solving ability, 145, 146, 147; correlation with self-concept, 85; of EMH children, 71; strategies associated with, 129

Verbal sanctioning patterns, 122

Verbalization of mathematical concepts, 52, 53, 59

Visual perception, 133, 134; structures of, 134, 135

Visual-tactual devices, 121

Wisconsin Studies, 29

Yerkes-Dodson law, 82